California Real Property Sales Transactions

UPDATE
MAY 1992

Author
C. Darrell Sooy

Editor
John K. Chapin
CEB Attorney

CONTINUING EDUCATION OF THE BAR • BERKELEY, CALIFORNIA

Book Authors
Burch Fitzpatrick
Bruce W. Hyman
John P. Killeen
Robert D. Lynch
James A. Moewe
Richard P. Sims
C. Darrell Sooy
John F. Soukup
Edward S. Washburn

Book Editors
Gordon Graham, CEB Attorney
Craig H. Scott, CEB Attorney

Library of Congress Catalog Card No. 81–65233
© 1981, 1982, 1983, 1984, 1985, 1986, 1987, 1988, 1989, 1990, 1991, 1992
by The Regents of the University of California
Printed in the United States of America
ISBN 0-88124-501-1

RE–36612

CONTINUING EDUCATION OF THE BAR • CALIFORNIA

By agreement between the Board of Governors of the State Bar of California and The Regents of the University of California, Continuing Education of the Bar – California offers an educational program for the benefit of practicing lawyers. The program is administered by a Governing Committee through the University of California in cooperation with local bar associations and the Joint Advisory Committee made up of the State Bar Committee on Continuing Education of the Bar and the Deans of accredited law schools.

Practice books are published as part of the educational program. Authors are given full opportunity to express their individual legal interpretations and opinions, and these obviously are not intended to reflect any position of the State Bar of California or of the University of California. Chapters written by employees of state or federal agencies are not to be considered statements of governmental policies.

Continuing Education of the Bar – California publications and oral programs are intended to provide current and accurate information about the subject matter covered and are designed to help attorneys maintain their professional competence. Publications are distributed and oral programs presented with the understanding that CEB does not render any legal, accounting, or other professional service. Attorneys using CEB publications or orally conveyed information in dealing with a specific client's or their own legal matters should also research original sources of authority.

Governing Committee
Barbara K. Mizuno, San Francisco, Chairperson
Keith Sexton, Dean, University Extension Programs,
University of California (Oakland), Vice Chairperson
Edward E. Kallgren, San Francisco, Liaison Governor
Margaret Mary Morrow, Los Angeles, Liaison Governor
Professor Alison Grey Anderson, University of California,
School of Law (Los Angeles)
William A. Carroll, Director, Continuing Education of the Bar
Raymond J. (Jerry) Coughlan, Jr., San Diego
Paul F. Dauer, Sacramento
Professor Edward C. Halbach, Jr., University of California
School of Law (Berkeley)
Joseph A. Pastrone, University Controller, University of California (Oakland)
Barry A. Weiss, Irvine

Joint Advisory Committee

State Bar Committee Members
Marcia Haber Kamine, Los Angeles, Chairperson
Palmer Brown Madden, Walnut Creek, Vice Chairperson
Edward E. Kallgren, San Francisco, Liaison Governor
John F. (Fritz) Kraetzer, Oakland, Liaison Governor
Malvina E. J. Abbott, San Diego
Phillip S. Althoff, Martinez
Arthur H. Bredenbeck, Burlingame
Adryenn Cantor, Beverly Hills
Llewellyn P. Chin, Los Angeles
Nancy K. Chiu, Los Angeles
Donna M. Dell, Walnut Creek
Jose H. Garcia, San Francisco
James C. Hagedorn, Sacramento
John F. Hartigan, Los Angeles
Christina J. Imre, Encino
Craig Labadie, Oakland
Susan T. Levin, San Jose
Gerald F. Mohun, Jr., Mammoth Lakes
John W. Noonan, Pleasanton
Mary V. O'Hare, Burbank
Peter C. Pang, San Francisco
Thomas A. Papageorge, Los Angeles
Richard Pearl, San Francisco
John T. Philipsborn, San Francisco
Elaine M. Profant–Turner, Eureka
Bruce E. Ramsey, Modesto
James J. Scherer, South San Francisco
Anthony F. Sgherzi, Los Angeles
Willie J. Smith, Fresno
Richard Neil Snyder, San Francisco

EDUCATION OF THE BAR

June T. Summers, San Francisco
Timothy B. Taylor, San Diego
Stephen E. Traverse, Los Angeles
Leslie L. van Houten, Oakland
Gary L. Waldron, Fresno
Patricia A. Wilson, San Francisco
Debra W. Yang, Los Angeles
David M. Zeligs, Long Beach

Law School Dean Members
Dean Scott H. Bice, University of Southern California Law Center
Dean Paul A. Brest, Stanford University
Dean Benjamin Bycel, Ventura/Santa Barbara Colleges of Law
Dean Jesse H. Choper, University of California (Berkeley)
Dean Charles E. D'Arcy, Lincoln Law School of Sacramento
Dean Michael H. Dessent, California Western School of Law
Dean John A. FitzRandolph, Whittier College School of Law
Dean H. Jay Folberg, University of San Francisco
School of Law
Dean Nels B. Fransen, Humphreys College of Law
Dean Seymour Greitzer, Glendale University College of Law
Dean Kenneth Held, University of LaVerne/University of LaVerne at
San Fernando Valley Colleges of Law
Dean Joe H. Henderson, Empire College School of Law
Dean Fred Herro, Monterey College of Law
Dean Ellen Jordan, University of California (Davis)
Dean Chris Kanios, New College of California School of Law
Dean Gerald T. McLaughlin, Loyola Law School
Acting Dean Kenneth A. Meade, John F. Kennedy University School of Law
Dean Mark Owens, Jr., San Francisco Law School
Dean Anthony J. Pagano, Golden Gate University School of Law
Dean Janice L. Pearson, San Joaquin College of Law
Acting Dean Mary L. Perry, Western State University
College of Law of San Diego
Dean Ronald F. Phillips, Pepperdine University School of Law
Dean Perry Polski, University of West Los Angeles
School of Law
Dean Susan Westerberg Prager, University of California
(Los Angeles)
Dean Franklin Thompson Read, Hastings College of Law
Acting Dean John E. Ryan, McGeorge School of Law,
University of the Pacific
Dean Kristine Strachan, University of San Diego School of Law
Dean Leigh H. Taylor, Southwestern University School of Law
Dean William H. J. Tiernan, National University School of Law
Dean Gerald F. Uelmen, University of Santa Clara School of Law
Dean Marcia B. Wilbur, Western State University College of Law of
Orange County

Preface

This supplement, like most CEB publications, was produced by and for members of the California Bar. Members of the Bar wrote and edited it, and the problems were discussed with California lawyers.

We consider this supplement part of a dialogue with our readers. Another supplement next year, cumulative of this one, will give us an opportunity to make corrections and additions you suggest. If you know something we did not include, or if we erred, share your knowledge with other California lawyers. Send your comments to:

Update Editor
Continuing Education of the Bar—California
2300 Shattuck Avenue
Berkeley, California 94704

CEB thanks the author of this supplement, C. Darrell Sooy, of Tobin & Tobin, Walnut Creek. Gordon Graham, CEB attorney, served as consultant.

Copy editing and production were handled by Joanna Boudreaux. Legal research assistance was provided by Samuel R. Cacas, Glenn Robert Hodge, Suzanne Homer, and Kenneth Marr. The index was prepared by Robert W. Burke, Jr. Composition was performed by CEB's Electronic Publishing staff.

William A. Carroll
Director

Contents

Cutoff Dates

We completed legal editing on this supplement at the end of January 1992.

We have checked:

Case citations through:

—Shepard's California Cumulative Supplement vol 72, no. 10. Cutoffs were 53 C3d 441, 228 CA3d 1219, 112 L Ed 2d 1111, 928 F2d 412, 758 F Supp 742.

—Shepard's United States Cumulative Supplement vol 90, no. 2. Cutoffs were 112 L Ed 2d 709, 927 F2d 1228, 757 F Supp 1433.

—Shepard's Federal Cumulative Supplement vol 81, no. 4. Cutoffs were 112 L Ed 2d 709, 927 F2d 1228, 757 F Supp 1433.

California statutes for amendments and repeals through Stats 1991, ch 1231.

Federal statutes for amendments and repeals through 105 Stat 1627.

We try to add significant statutory and judicial developments, subsequent histories of cases, and other matters such as new forms and regulations after legal editing is done, but you should not assume that all developments after the listed cutoff dates have been included.

Selected Developments

CALIFORNIA REAL PROPERTY SALES TRANSACTIONS
Update May 1992

Since Previous Update: The appraisal subcommittee of the Federal Financial Institutions Examination Council, which has the power under Title XI of FIFREA to extend the deadline for the mandated federal requirements for appraisals on federally related transactions, has extended the deadline for enforcement of the federal requirements until December 31, 1992. See Update §1.35.

An inverse condemnation action can be used to attack a rent control ordinance that does not provide a just and reasonable return on property. See Update §8.41.

Several CAR forms have been revised: Exclusive Authorization and Right To Sell (see Update §2.60); Real Estate Purchase Contract and Receipt for Deposit, and Interim Occupancy Agreement (see Update §3.40); Seller Financing Disclosure Statement (see Update §5.1B).

The Office of Thrift Supervision has adopted a regulation that purports to preempt "any state law purporting to address the subject of the operations" of a federal savings institution. See Update §6.5.

Since Publication of the Book: Beginning January 1, 1991, federal standards will apply to appraisals performed in connection with real estate loans made by or sold to federally insured financial institutions. See Update §1.35 for discussion of the new Real Estate Appraisers' Licensing and Certification Law (Bus & P C §§11300–11422) and federal regulations.

An appellate court has held that a broker has a duty of disclosure to third parties who may foreseeably be harmed by the broker's action. See Update §2.113.

The statutory forms of certificates of acknowledgment found in former CC §§1189, 1190, 1190a, 1190.1, 1191, and 1192 have been combined into a single statutory form of certificate of acknowledgment in which the capacity of the person signing the documents is indicated below the signature. See Update §11.94.

New Civil Code §1057.3 requires all parties to execute documents required by the escrow holder within 30 days following demand to enable the release of any funds to the party entitled to them, if there is no good faith dispute relative to release of the funds. See Update §1.42.

For local ordinances enacted after June 1990, a new form has been provided for disclosures in connection with the sale of certain residential property. See Update §§1.69, 1.69B.

A real estate broker is not entitled to a commission from the seller if the only contractual obligation to pay that commission is contained in the sales agreement, but the property is sold in eminent domain proceedings rather than under the agreement. See Update §2.35.

The exception to the purchase-money antideficiency protection of CCP §580b announced in *Spangler v Memel* (1972) 7 C3d 603, 102 CR 807, is continually being expanded by the courts of appeal. See Update §5.39.

See Update §11.42 on new rules governing out-of-state bank checks.

Prospective transferees of real property must now be given notice by the owner of any lis pendens received. See Update §12.87.

The California Administrative Code has been renamed the California Code of Regulations. References cited in the supplement have been changed but portions of the book still refer to the California Administrative Code.

The duty to disclose an occupant's death on real property has been limited. See Update §1.69.

The California Supreme Court has maintained a distinction between an unlicensed finder and a licensed broker with respect to their abilities to collect fees based on an oral promise. See Update §§2.56–2.57.

It is now unlawful to discriminate on the basis of blindness or physical disability in renting, leasing, or otherwise providing real property. See Update §3.97.

See Update §7.18 on changes in the Probate Code that affect real property sales by a personal representative.

There have been changes in the standards for proving oppression, fraud, and malice. See Update §12.34.

The efficacy of a lis pendens expungement in protecting a subsequent buyer has been upheld. See Update §12.88.

Seeing a need to educate buyers and sellers of real property on the existence of various types of agency relationships that may occur in residential real property transactions, the legislature enacted CC §§2373–2382, inclusive, to be effective January 1, 1988, requiring disclosure to buyers and sellers by real estate agents, in defined sales transactions, of the various types of agency relationships that may occur. The disclosures are given in a statutorily mandated form to assure uniformity of disclosure in simple, comprehensible, and nontechnical terms. See Update §§2.20 and 2.20A. California has enacted the Lancaster-Montoya Appraisal Act (CC §§1922–1922.14) to legislate general standards for appraisals. See Update §1.35. The method of processing applications for recovery under the Real Estate Recovery Program (Bus & P C §§10470–10481) has been extensively revised effective January 1, 1986. See Update §2.109.

The legislature responded to the decision in *Easton v Strassburger* (1984) 152 CA3d 90, 199 CR 383 (see Update §2.89), by enacting CC §2079, effective January 1, 1986, which partially codifies the *Easton* decision, and CC §§1102–1102.13, operative January 1, 1987, which will require specific written disclosures in sales transactions of real property improved with one to four dwelling units (see Update §1.69).

Operative July 1, 1989, CCP §§1298, 1298.5, 1298.7, and 1298.8 require specified statutory language in certain real property contracts that are entered into on or after that date and that contain arbitration clauses. See Update §3.183.

Civil Code §2924.7, effective January 1, 1989, provides that a lender's right to accelerate the maturity date of any loan secured by a mortgage or deed of trust on real property and the lender's right to receive and control the disbursement of the proceeds of any insurance policy respecting the property are enforceable whether or not the lender's security interest has been impaired by the defaulting borrower. See Update §§6.45–6.46.

A major development since publication of the Book concerns the enforceability of due-on-sale clauses in mortgages and deeds of trust on California real property.

With enactment of the Garn-St. Germain Depository Institutions Act of 1982 (Pub L 97–320, 96 Stat 1469) on October 15, 1982, Congress preempted all state laws that limited or restricted enforcement of due-on-sale clauses. Effective October 15, 1982, the preemption applies to all real property loans, except for loans originated or transferred by other than a federal savings and loan association during a "window period." The starting date of the window period has not been determined, but it ended on October 14, 1982. For window-period loans the preemption did not become effective until October 15, 1985. Regulations were issued on the implementation of these rules. For discussion of due-on-sale clauses, see Update §5.24.

The Appendix, discussing which transactions trigger a reappraisal for real property tax purposes, incorporates the extensive revisions in the California Code of Regulations.

The Civil Code now regulates multiple listing services. See Update §2.26.

The statutes determining the damages recoverable by a buyer or seller after breach of a contract to sell real property have been amended. See Update §§12.13–12.14, 12.19.

The California homestead laws have been completely revised, effective July 1, 1983. See Update §§3.9, 3.15.

The California Home Loan Mortgage Association has been created to bolster the secondary mortgage market. See Update §6.11.

An "instrument" that is entitled to be recorded has been given a statutory definition by Govt C §27279, effective January 1, 1989. See Update §11.91.

Provisions concerning acknowledgments have been revised. See Update §11.94.

1

The Lawyer's Role in Real Property Sales

THE LAWYER AND REAL PROPERTY PRACTICE

[§§1.12–1.13] Possibility of Malpractice; Ethical Considerations

See *Gutierrez v Mofid* (1985) 39 C3d 892, 218 CR 313, in which the supreme court observed that "it is well settled that an attorney is liable for malpractice when his negligent investigation, advice, or conduct of the client's affairs results in loss of the client's meritorious claim."

The California Supreme Court revised and renumbered the Rules of Professional Conduct operative May 27, 1989. The substance of Cal Rules of Prof Cond 6–101, cited in Book §1.12, is in new Cal Rules of Prof Cond 3–110. The substance of Cal Rules of Prof Cond 5–101 and 5–102, cited in Book §1.13, is in new Cal Rules of Prof Cond 3–300 and 3–310.

Lawyer Participation in Transaction

[§§1.14–1.15] Duty to Client; Avoiding Conflict of Interest

Former CC §2235, expressing the presumption that transactions between a trustee and a beneficiary by which the trustee gains any advantage from the beneficiary are presumed to be under undue influence, has been repealed. Former CC §§2228–2239, requiring good faith and prohibiting personal interest and profit, have also been repealed. Probate Code §16004 now contains similar language, but the trustee's gain through the trust is expressed in terms of creating a presumption of a violation of the trustee's fiduciary duties.

The California Supreme Court revised and renumbered the Rules of Professional Conduct operative May 27, 1989. The substance of Cal Rules of Prof Cond 4–101, cited in Book §§1.14–1.15, is in new Cal Rules of Prof Cond 3–310.

[§1.18] Self-Education

The treatise by Miller & Starr, cited in the Book, has been replaced by Miller & Starr, California Real Estate (2d ed 1989).

The reference to Witkin in the Book should now be to 4 Witkin, Summary of California Law, *Real Property* (9th ed 1987).

Title Insurance & Trust Company, Title Handbook for Title Men (22d ed 1980) has been replaced by the 32d edition, published in 1990.

ATTORNEY-CLIENT RELATIONSHIP

Setting Fee

[§1.23] Negotiating Fee Agreement

Beginning January 1, 1987, matters that do not involve contingency fees are subject to Bus & P C §6148. Under §6148, a written contract for attorneys' services is required if it is reasonably foreseeable that the expense to the client will exceed $1000. The statute is framed in terms of "expenses to the client," not in terms of attorneys' fees. Therefore other fees or costs such as deposition expenses must be considered. Failure to provide a written contract when required permits the client to void the agreement with the attorney, and the attorney may recover reasonable fees only, not the amount provided for in the agreement.

There are four exceptions to the requirement for a written contract: (1) services rendered in an emergency to avoid foreseeable prejudice to the client's rights or when a writing is impractical; (2) services rendered that are of the same general kind as those previously paid for by the client; (3) when a client knowingly waives the Bus & P C §6148 provisions for providing a written contract; and (4) when the client is a corporation.

The contract must show the hourly rate or the standard rates, fees, and charges applicable to the matter. The general nature of the legal services and the respective responsibilities of the attorney and the client in pursuing the matter must also be set out. The State Bar of California has prepared sample contracts. They are available for $3.50 by writing to the State Bar of California, Fee Agreements, P.O. Box 24527, San Francisco, CA 94124–9959.

American Bar Association Code Prof Resp EC 2–19 has been superseded by ABA Model R of Prof Cond 1.5(b), which provides that fee information should be communicated to a new client before or within a reasonable time after beginning representation.

The California Supreme Court revised and renumbered the Rules of Professional Conduct operative May 27, 1989. The substance of Cal Rules of Prof Cond 2–107, cited in Book §1.23, is in new Cal Rules of Prof Cond 4–200.

[§1.24] Computing Fee

American Bar Association Code of Prof Resp DR 2–106 and EC 2–16 have been superseded by ABA Model R of Prof Cond 1.5(a), (d), and 6.1, 6.2(b), respectively.

The California Supreme Court revised and renumbered the Rules of Professional Conduct operative May 27, 1989. The substance of Cal Rules of Prof Cond 2–107, cited in Book §1.24, is in new Cal Rules of Prof Cond 4–200.

[§1.25] Equity Interests

American Bar Association Code of Prof Resp DR 2–106 has been superseded by ABA Model R of Prof Cond 1.5(a), (d).

The California Supreme Court revised and renumbered the Rules of Professional Conduct operative May 27, 1989. The substance of Cal Rules of Prof Cond 4–101, cited in Book §1.25, is in new Cal Rules of Prof Cond 3–310. The substance of Cal Rules of Prof Cond 2–107 is in new Cal Rules of Prof Cond 4–200.

HANDLING MECHANICS OF TRANSACTION

[§1.34] Publications

Several of the addresses noted in Book §1.34 have been changed as follows:

Aerial Photography Field Office, attn: User Services, P.O. Box 30010, U.S. Dept. of Agriculture, Salt Lake City, UT 84130; (801) 524–5856.

U.S. Geological Survey, Western Distribution Branch, Box 25286, Denver, CO 80225; (303) 236–7477.

Geological Survey, U.S. Dept. of the Interior, 555 Battery St., Room 504, San Francisco, CA 94111; (415) 705–1010. This office provides over-the-counter service; maps are listed by name of the quadrangle.

National Ocean Survey, Distribution Branch NCG 33, Riverdale, MD 20737–1199; (301) 436–6990. Free catalogs are available.

California Coastal Commission, 45 Fremont St., Suite 200, San Francisco, CA 94105; (415) 904–5200. Call the California Coastal Commission first to ascertain the number of the map(s) needed, and then contact the supplier: Blue Print Service Co., the address of which is listed in Book §1.34.

International Conference of Building Officials; (213) 699–0541.

John B. Reeves & Son, 8538 Warner Dr., Culver City, CA 90232 (for Uniform Plumbing Code); (213) 870–0321.

National Fire Protection Association, 1 Batterymarch Park, Quincy, MA 02269; (800) 344–3555.

[§1.35] Experts

California became one of the first states to legislate general standards for real property appraisals and appraisal reports with enactment of the Lancaster-Montoya Appraisal Act (CC §§1922–1922.14) operative January 1, 1988. Operative July 1, 1991, those sections of the Civil Code are repealed and replaced by the Real Estate Appraisers' Licensing and Certification Law (Bus & P C §§11300–11422). The new law authorizes issuance of legally defined "certified real estate appraisal reports" by "state certified real estate appraisers" and sets forth standards for each. The new law also creates an Office of Real Estate Appraisers within the Business, Transportation and Housing Agency to enforce its provisions. Bus & P C §§11301–11302. Under CC §1922.11 (repealed July 1, 1991), any person damaged by a violation of the Lancaster-Montoya Appraisal Act could bring an action for damages, equitable relief, or both, and the prevailing party in such an action could be awarded costs and reasonable attorney fees. Under Bus & P C §§11300–11422, however, there is no such provision. Instead, the new law creates a Real Estate Appraisers Regulation Fund and a Recovery Account, against which claims may be made under procedures "closely analogous to those which have been adopted for the Real Estate Recovery Fund." Bus & P C §§11411–11412.

Business and Professions Code §11321 provides that Federal National Mortgage Association (FNMA) and Federal Home Loan Mortgage Corporation (FHLMC) form appraisals on one to four residential units may be deemed "certified appraisals" when done by a state-certified appraiser and the approved federal form is completed in compliance with the rules and regulations of the agency adopting the form. Bus & P C §11302(l). See also former CC §1922.13 (repealed July 1, 1991).

The new law further applies federal standards to appraisals performed in federally related transactions as defined by Bus & P C §11302(l). Bus & P C §11302(k). Business and Professions Code §11325 states that regulations adopted by the Director of the Office of Real Estate Appraisers are to specify the types of federally related transactions that must be performed by licensed and certified real estate appraisers, and must be in conformity with §1112 of Title XI of the Financial Institutions Reform, Recovery and Enforcement Act of 1989 (FIRREA; Pub L 101–73, 103 Stat 183, 511). Title XI establishes an appraisal subcommittee of the Federal Financial Institutions Examinations Council to monitor appraisal standards in the United States, and requires the federal banking agencies and the Resolution Trust Corporation to establish proposed appraisal standards. The Real Estate Appraisers' Licensing and Certification Law is the California legislature's response to Title XI encouragement of the creation of state certification and licensing requirements for appraisers, and its requirement that certain appraisals be conducted by certified or licensed appraisers.

On August 23, 1990, federal regulations for savings and loan associations were published. See 55 Fed Reg 34532. The new regulations, 12 CFR pt 564, set appraisal standards for "federally related transactions," which include most real property loans made by insured financial institutions. The regulations (see 12 CFR §564.3) apply different appraisal standards to all loans of $50,000 or less and to different types of loans of more than $50,000:

Property Type and Loan Amount	*Type of Appraiser Needed for Appraisal*
All loans of $50,000 or less	Need not be certified or licensed
Multifamily under $250,000	Either certified or licensed
Noncomplex (subjective determination of lender) loan of over $250,000 but less than $1,000,000 secured by one-to-four-family residence	Either certified or licensed
Multifamily $250,000 or over	Certified
One-to-four-family over $250,000 complex loan	Certified
One-to-four-family $1,000,000 or over	Certified
Nonresidential over $250,000	Certified
Any loan of $1,000,000 or more	Certified

The deadline for enforcement of the mandated federal requirements for appraisals on federally related transactions has been extended to December 31, 1992. See Pub L 102–242, §472, 105 Stat 2236 (1991), amending 12 USC §3348(a)(1). The Office of Thrift Supervision, which adopted the new regulations (see 12 CFR §564), has proposed raising the $50,000 threshold in its regulations to $100,000. At the time this update went to press, it appeared likely that, by the time the regulations applied to federally related transactions, the threshold will be $100,000 instead of $50,000.

An appraiser may be liable on a negligent misrepresentation theory for rendering an erroneous opinion of value. However, recovery against an appraiser does not extend to all those who were foreseeably harmed, but only to those to whom or for whom the opinion of value was made. *Christiansen v Roddy* (1986) 186 CA3d 780, 231 CR 72. The judgment against the appraiser in *Christiansen* was reversed because the plaintiffs were investors who did not request the appraisal or even see the written appraisal. Instead the plaintiffs relied on a loan brochure prepared by the mortgage broker who had ordered the appraisal and used the opinion of value in the loan brochure.

The use of environmental experts is becoming commonplace in real estate transactions because of the increase in environmental laws that create liability for owners of contaminated real property. Among these laws are the Comprehensive Environmental Response, Compensation, and Liability Act of 1989 (CERCLA; 42 USC §§9601–9675); Resource Conservation and Recovery Act of 1976 (RCRA; 42 USC §§6901–6992k); Carpenter-Presley-Tanner Hazardous Substance Account Act (Health & S C §§25300–25395); Porter-Cologne Water Quality Control Act (Wat C §§13000–13999.18); and other Health & S C sections, including §§25100– 25210.1, 25220–25244.11, 25249.5–25249.13, and 25280–25299.6.

Ensuring Compliance With Government Requirements

Regulation of Development

State and Local Controls

[§1.43] General and Specific Plans

An amendment to Govt C §65453 effective January 1, 1986, provides that a specific plan may be repealed in the same manner as it is required to be amended. Before this amendment there was no statutory procedure for repealing a specific plan.

[§1.46] Environmental Controls

The regulations concerning enforcement of CEQA are now published in 14 Cal Code Regs §§15000–15387.

[§1.48] Other Statutes

The reference in Book §1.48(a)(3) to Air Pollution Control (Health & S C §§39000–43835) should now be to Air Resources (Health & S C §§39000–44210).

Effective January 1, 1986, the Municipal Organization Act of 1977 (Govt C §§35000–35500), the District Reorganization Act of 1965 (Govt C §§56000–56540), and the Knox-Nisbet Act (Govt C §§54773–54863) were repealed and replaced by the Cortese-Knox Local Government Reorganization Act of 1985 (Govt C §§56000–57550), which generally contains the provisions of those acts but in a substantially revised, consolidated, and reorganized format.

[§1.49] Federal Controls

The statutory citation to the National Environmental Policy Act (NEPA) in Book §1.49(1) should be 42 USC §§4321–4370.

The Noise Control Act of 1972, referred to in Book §1.49(4), is found at 42 USC §§4901–4918. The Noise Pollution and Abatement Act of 1970 is found at 42 USC §§7641–7642.

Title 42 USC §5320, which requires certain historic preservation measures for urban development action grants, may also affect some development projects.

Additional federal statutes that affect the ownership and possibly the development of real property include the Clean Water Act of 1977 (33 USC §§1251–1376), which prohibits any discharge of certain material into "navigable waters," and the Comprehensive Environmental Response, Compensation, and Liability Act of 1980 (42 USC §§9601–9675), which creates a mechanism for emergency response to dangerous conditions caused by past or present release of hazardous substances.

Consumer Legislation

[§1.50] Federal Truth in Lending Act

The Truth in Lending Act (15 USC §§1601–1681t) was substantially revised by the Truth in Lending Simplification and Reform Act (Pub L 96–221, 94 Stat 168 (1980)). A revised Regulation Z (12 CFR pt 226) was published April 7, 1981. The revised Truth in Lending Act was to have been effective starting March 31, 1982, but the effective date was delayed to October 1, 1982, by Pub L 97–110, 95 Stat 144 (1981). Creditors were allowed to voluntarily comply with the revised act before October 1, 1982. A further revision of Regulation Z was published on April 6, 1987. 52 Fed Reg 10875. These revisions were effective April 1, 1987; however, compliance was optional until October 1, 1987. 52 Fed Reg 10876.

Note that seller financing may now come within the coverage of the Truth in Lending Act if the credit is arranged by a real estate broker. See Coskran, *Brokers (and Salespersons) Arranging Seller Financing— Compliance with Truth in Lending*, 3 Real Prop News 6 (Winter 1982).

[§1.51] Federal Interstate Land Sales Full Disclosure Act

The address and telephone number of the Office of Interstate Land Sales Registration is now 451 Seventh Street, SW, Room 6264, Washington, DC 20410; (202) 708–0502.

[§1.53] California Subdivided Lands Act

The administrative regulations of the California Department of Real Estate are now found at 10 Cal Code Regs §§2705–3200. A conflict-of-interest code comprising former 10 Cal Adm C §§3200–3208 (now called the California Code of Regulations) (which was replaced by amended 10 Cal Code Regs §3200 and appendix) may now be obtained from that department.

COUNSELING SELLER

[§1.57] Checklist for Interviewing and Counseling Seller

The following item should be added to the checklist in Book §1.57 under "3. The property":

g. Property features that require disclosure (§§1.66–1.73).

Shaping Transaction To Meet Seller's Objectives

[§1.59] Tax-Deferred Exchange; Nontaxable Reinvestment

Nonsimultaneous exchanges are now specifically permitted under IRC §1031. The property to be transferred in the future must be identified by the taxpayer within 45 days after the transfer of the property relinquished in the exchange, and must be transferred no later than 180 days after that initial transfer or by the due date of the taxpayer's tax return, whichever is earlier. IRC §1031(a)(3).

To qualify for a tax-deferred exchange, the property must be held "for productive use in trade or business or for investment" within the meaning of IRC §1031(a). Despite the narrow interpretation by the Internal Revenue Service that the taxpayer first intend to keep property indefinitely, the Ninth Circuit has held that, if the taxpayer does not intend to liquidate or use the property for personal pursuits, the property qualifies under IRC §1031(a). The property thus may qualify for a tax-deferred exchange if a property owner initially acquires property with the intent to exchange it for like-kind property. *Bolker v Commissioner* (9th Cir 1985) 760 F2d 1039.

For extensive discussion of tax-deferred exchanges, see Real Property Exchanges (Cal CEB 1982).

[§1.65] Installment Land Contract; Buyer Financially Insecure

See Update §§5.5, 12.2, and 12.8 for recent restrictions on any benefit to the use of an installment land contract.

The cite to Bus & P C §§10230–10236.1 should now be to Bus & P C §§10230–10236.2.

Preventing Fraud

[§1.69] Nondisclosure

The material facts the seller must disclose to the buyer are not limited to physical characteristics of the property and should include the history associated with the property if that history could significantly depress the market value. In *Reed v King* (1983) 145 CA3d 261, 193 CR 130, a buyer who was not informed that multiple murders had occurred on the property was allowed to maintain an action for rescission and damages. The legislature has amended CC §1710.2 to provide that the failure to disclose the occurrence of an occupant's death on the real property or the manner of death when the death occurred more than three years before the date the transferee offers to purchase, lease, or rent the real property does not give rise to a cause of action against the property owner, his or her agent, or any agent of the buyer. This amendment does not shield an owner or his or her agent from intentional misrepresentations in response to a direct question from the transferee or prospective transferee concerning deaths on the real property.

Civil Code §1710.2 has also been amended to provide that during a sales transaction, the failure to disclose that an owner or occupant of real property was afflicted with the virus that causes acquired immune deficiency syndrome (AIDS) does not give rise to a cause of action against the property owner, his or her agent, or any buyer's ageny.

In a case denoted one of first impression in California, the court in *Heliotis v Schuman* (1986) 181 CA3d 646, 226 CR 509, held that an attorney representing the seller in a sales transaction was not liable to the buyer for failure to disclose the real property's allegedly poor underlying soil condition. The court found the attorney acted only as the seller's attorney and not in the capacity of a broker.

Civil Code §§1102–1102.15 require that specific written disclosures be made to prospective transferees of real property or residential stock cooperatives improved with one to four dwelling units under a sale transaction, exchange, installment land sale contract, lease with option to purchase, any other option to purchase, or ground lease coupled with improvements. The disclosure obligation is placed on the transferor by CC §1102.2. However, CC §1102.4 (errors and omissions in disclosure) refers to the transferor and his or her agent; a companion statute, Bus & P C §10176.5, also operative January 1, 1987, provides for the suspension or revocation of a real estate licensee's license for willful or repeated violations of CC §§1102–1102.15. The intent of the new statutes is apparently to have the real estate licensee ensure that the required disclosures are made by the transferor. For example, CC §1102.12(a) provides that, if more than one licensed real estate broker is acting as an agent in a transaction, the broker who obtained the offer made by the transferee must deliver the disclosure to the transferee unless the transferor has given other written instructions for delivery. Civil Code §1102.13 provides that any person who willfully or negligently violates or fails to perform any duty described by CC §§1102–1102.15 shall be liable for actual damages to the transferee.

The required disclosures are to be made on a form found at CC §1102.6, a copy of which is reproduced at Update §1.69A. If a local city and county government enacts an ordinance after June 1990 requiring disclosures in addition to those required by CC §1102.6, the additional disclosures must be incorporated into the form found at CC §1102.6a, reproduced at Update §1.69B. If the ordinance is adopted before July 1990, the local city and county governments may require real property sale disclosures on a form different from that found at CC §1102.6a and may thereafter amend those disclosure requirements. CC §1102.6a.

The real estate broker also has duties to inspect and disclose certain information to prospective purchasers of residential real property of four units or less. See CC §§2079–2079.7 and Update §2.89.

[§1.69A] Form: Real Estate Transfer Disclosure Statement

REAL ESTATE TRANSFER DISCLOSURE STATEMENT
THIS DISCLOSURE STATEMENT CONCERNS THE REAL PROPERTY SITUATED IN THE CITY OF _____, COUNTY OF _____, STATE OF CALIFORNIA, DESCRIBED AS _____. THIS STATEMENT IS A DISCLO-SURE OF THE CONDITION OF THE ABOVE DESCRIBED PROPERTY IN COMPLIANCE WITH SECTION 1102 OF THE CIVIL CODE AS OF _____, 19___. IT IS NOT A WARRANTY OF ANY KIND BY THE SELLER(S) OR ANY AGENT(S) REPRESENTING ANY PRINCIPAL(S) IN THIS TRANSACTION, AND IS NOT A SUBSTITUTE FOR ANY INSPEC-TIONS OR WARRANTIES THE PRINCIPAL(S) MAY WISH TO OBTAIN.

I

COORDINATION WITH OTHER DISCLOSURE FORMS

This Real Estate Transfer Disclosure Statement is made pursuant to Section 1102 of the Civil Code. Other statutes require disclosures, depending upon the details of the particular real estate transaction (for example: special study zone and purchase-money liens on residential property).

Substituted Disclosures: The following disclosures have or will be made in connection with this real estate transfer, and are intended to satisfy the disclosure obligations on this form, where the subject matter is the same:_____
_____
_____

(list all substituted disclosure forms to be used in connection with this transaction)

II

SELLERS INFORMATION

The Seller discloses the following information with the knowledge that even though this is not a warranty, prospective Buyers may rely on this information in deciding whether and on what terms to purchase the subject property. Seller hereby authorizes any agent(s) representing any principal(s) in this transaction to provide a copy of this statement to any person or entity in connection with any actual or anticipated sale of the property.

THE FOLLOWING ARE REPRESENTATIONS MADE BY THE SELLER(S) AND ARE NOT THE REPRESENTATIONS OF THE AGENT(S), IF ANY. THIS INFORMATION IS A DISCLOSURE AND IS NOT INTENDED TO BE PART OF ANY CONTRACT BETWEEN THE BUYER AND SELLER.

Seller _is _is not occupying the property.

A. The subject property has the items checked below (read across):

_Range	_Oven	_Microwave
_Dishwasher	_Trash Compactor	_Garbage Disposal
_Washer/Dryer Hookups	_Window Screens	_Rain Gutters
_Burglar Alarms	_Smoke Detector(s)	_Fire Alarm
_T.V. Antenna	_Satellite Dish	_Intercom
_Central Heating	_Central Air Cndtng.	_Evaporator Cooler(s)
_Wall/Window Air Cndtng.	_Sprinklers	_Public Sewer System
_Septic Tank	_Sump Pump	_Water Softener
_Patio/Decking	_Built-in Barbeque	_Gazebo
_Sauna	_Pool	_Spa _Hot Tub
_Security Gate(s)	_Automatic Garage Door Opener(s)*	_Number Remote Controls
Garage:_Attached	_Not Attached	_Carport
Pool/Spa Heater:_Gas	_Solar	_Electric
Water Heater:_Gas		_Private Utility or
Water Supply:_City	_Well	Other_____
Gas Supply:_Utility	_Bottled	

Exhaust Fan(s) in_____ 220 Volt Wiring in_____ Fireplace(s) in_____

Gas Starter_____ Roof(s): Type:_____ Age:_____ (approx.)

Other:_____

Are there, to the best of your (Seller's) knowledge, any of the above that are not in operating condition? _Yes _No. If yes, then describe.

*This garage door opener may not be in compliance with the safety standards relating to automatic reversing devices as set forth in Chapter 12.5 (commencing with Section 19890) of Part 3 of Division 13 of the Health and Safety Code.

(Attach additional sheets if necessary * * *):_____
_____
_____
_____

B. Are you (Seller) aware of any significant defects/malfunctions in any of the following? _Yes _No. If yes, check appropriate space(s) below.

_Interior Walls _Ceilings _Floors _Exterior Walls _Insulation _Roof(s) _Windows _Doors _Foundation _Slab(s) _Driveways _Sidewalks _Walls/Fences _Electrical Systems _Plumbing/Sewers/Septics _Other

Structural Components (Describe: _____)

If any of the above is checked, explain. (Attach additional sheets if necessary):_____
_____
_____
_____

C. Are you (Seller) aware of any of the following:

1. Substances, materials, or products which may be an environmental hazard such as, but not limited to, asbestos, formaldehyde, radon gas, lead-based paint, fuel or chemical storage tanks, and contaminated soil or water on the subject property . . . . _Yes   _No

2. Features of the property shared in common with adjoining landowners, such as walls, fences, and driveways, whose use or responsibility for maintenance may have an effect on the subject property . . . . _Yes   _No

3. Any encroachments, easements or similar matters that may affect your interest in the subject property . . . . _Yes   _No

4. Rooms additions, structural modifications, or other alterations or repairs made without necessary permits . . . . _Yes   _No

5. Rooms additions, structural modifications, or other alterations or repairs not in compliance with building codes . . . . _Yes   _No

6. Landfill (compacted or otherwise) on the property or any portion thereof   _Yes   _No

7. Any settling from any cause, or slippage, sliding, or other soil problems. .   _Yes   _No

8. Flooding, drainage or grading problems . . . . _Yes   _No

9. Major damage to the property or any of the structures from fire, earth-quake, floods, or landslides . . . . _Yes   _No

10. Any zoning violations, nonconforming uses, violations of "setback" requirements . . . . _Yes   _No

11. Neighborhood noise problems or other nuisances . . . . _Yes   _No

12. CC&R's or other deed restrictions or obligations . . . . _Yes   _No

13. Homeowners' Association which has any authority over the subject property . . . . _Yes   _No

14. Any "common area" (facilities such as pools, tennis courts, walkways, or other areas co-owned in undivided interest with others) . . . . _Yes   _No

15. Any notices of abatement or citations against the property . . . . _Yes   _No

16. Any lawsuits against the seller threatening to or affecting this real property . . . . _Yes   _No

If the answer to any of these is yes, explain. (Attach additional sheets if necessary.):_____
_____
_____

* * *

Seller certifies that the information herein is true and correct to the best of the Seller's knowledge as of the date signed by the Seller.

Seller _____ Date _____

Seller _____ Date _____

III

AGENTS INSPECTION DISCLOSURE

(To be completed only if the Seller is represented by an agent in this transaction.)

THE UNDERSIGNED, BASED ON THE ABOVE INQUIRY OF THE SELLER(S) AS TO THE CONDITION OF THE PROPERTY AND BASED ON A REASONABLY COMPETENT AND

DILIGENT VISUAL INSPECTION OF THE ACCESSIBLE AREAS OF THE PROPERTY IN CONJUNCTION WITH THAT INQUIRY, STATES THE FOLLOWING:

_____
_____
_____
_____

Agent (Broker
Representing Seller)_____ By_____ Date _____
     (Please Print)   (Associate Licensee
                           or Broker-Signature)

IV

AGENTS INSPECTION DISCLOSURE

(To be completed only if the agent who has obtained the offer is other than the agent above.) THE UNDERSIGNED, BASED ON A REASONABLY COMPETENT AND DILIGENT VISUAL INSPECTION OF THE ACCESSIBLE AREAS OF THE PROPERTY, STATES THE FOLLOWING:

_____
_____
_____

Agent (Broker
obtaining the Offer)_____ By _____ Date _____
     (Please Print)   (Associate Licensee
                           or Broker-Signature)

V

BUYER(S) AND SELLER(S) MAY WISH TO OBTAIN PROFESSIONAL ADVICE AND/OR INSPECTIONS OF THE PROPERTY AND TO PROVIDE FOR APPROPRIATE PROVISIONS IN A CONTRACT BETWEEN BUYER AND SELLER(S) WITH RESPECT TO ANY ADVICE/INSPECTIONS/DEFECTS.

I/WE ACKNOWLEDGE RECEIPT OF A COPY OF THIS STATEMENT.

Seller_____Date_____Buyer_____Date_____
Seller_____Date_____Buyer_____Date_____

Agent (Broker
Representing Seller)_____ By_____ Date _____
                              (Associate Licensee
                              or Broker-Signature)

Agent (Broker
obtaining the Offer)_____ By _____ Date _____
                              (Associate Licensee
                              or Broker-Signature)

A REAL ESTATE BROKER IS QUALIFIED TO ADVISE ON REAL ESTATE. IF YOU DESIRE LEGAL ADVICE, CONSULT YOUR ATTORNEY.

Comment: The above form for transfer disclosure statements is required by CC §1102.6.

[§1.69B] Form: Real Estate Transfer Disclosure Statement (After June 1990)

LOCAL OPTION

REAL ESTATE TRANSFER DISCLOSURE STATEMENT

THIS DISCLOSURE STATEMENT CONCERNS THE REAL PROPERTY SITUATED IN THE CITY OF _____, COUNTY OF _____, STATE OF CALIFORNIA, DESCRIBED AS _____. THIS STATEMENT IS A DISCLOSURE OF THE CONDITION OF THE ABOVE DESCRIBED PROPERTY IN COMPLIANCE WITH ORDINANCE NO. _____ OF THE _____ CITY OR COUNTY CODE AS OF _____, 19___. IT IS NOT A WARRANTY OF ANY KIND BY THE SELLER(S) OR ANY AGENT(S) REPRESENTING ANY PRINCIPAL(S) IN THIS TRANSACTION, AND IS NOT A SUBSTITUTE FOR ANY INSPECTIONS OR WARRANTIES THE PRINCIPAL(S) MAY WISH TO OBTAIN.

I

SELLERS INFORMATION

The Seller discloses the following information with the knowledge that even though this is not a warranty, prospective Buyers may rely on this information in deciding whether and on what terms to purchase the subject property. Seller hereby authorizes any agent(s) representing any principal(s) in this transaction to provide a copy of this statement to any person or entity in connection with any actual or anticipated sale of the property.

THE FOLLOWING ARE REPRESENTATIONS MADE BY THE SELLER(S) AS REQUIRED BY THE CITY OR COUNTY OF _____. AND ARE NOT THE REPRESENTATIONS OF THE AGENT(S), IF ANY, THIS INFORMATION IS A DISCLOSURE AND IS NOT INTENDED TO BE PART OF ANY CONTRACT BETWEEN THE BUYER AND SELLER.

1. _____

_____

_____

_____

2. _____

_____

_____

_____

(Example: Adjacent land is zoned for timber production which may be subject to harvest.)

Seller certifies that the information herein is true and correct to the best of the Seller's knowledge as of the date signed by the Seller.

Seller _____ Date _____

Seller _____ Date _____

II

BUYER(S) AND SELLER(S) MAY WISH TO OBTAIN PROFESSIONAL ADVICE AND/OR IN-SPECTIONS OF THE PROPERTY AND TO PROVIDE FOR APPROPRIATE PROVISIONS IN A CONTRACT BETWEEN BUYER AND SELLER(S) WITH RESPECT TO ANY ADVICE/INSPEC-TIONS/DEFECTS.

I/WE ACKNOWLEDGE RECEIPT OF A COPY OF THIS STATEMENT.

Seller _____ Date _____ Buyer _____ Date _____

Seller _____ Date _____ Buyer _____ Date _____

Agent (Broker
Representing Seller) _____ By _____ Date _____
                                            (Associate Licensee
                                            or Broker-Signature)

Agent (Broker
Obtaining the Offer) _____ By _____ Date _____
                                            (Associate Licensee
                                            or Broker-Signature)

A REAL ESTATE BROKER IS QUALIFIED TO ADVISE ON REAL ESTATE. IF YOU DESIRE LEGAL ADVICE, CONSULT YOUR ATTORNEY.

Comment: If a local city and county government enacts an ordinance after June 1990 requiring disclosures in addition to those required by CC §1102.6, the additional disclosures must be incorporated into the form found at CC §1102.6a, reproduced above. If the ordinance is adopted before July 1990, the local city and county governments may require real property sale disclosures on a form different from that found at CC §1102.6a and may thereafter amend those disclosure requirements. CC §1102.6a.

Common Fraud Situations

[§1.73] Number of Units and Legality of Additions

Between July 1, 1985, and December 31, 1986, former CC §1134.5 provided that a transferor of real property containing one to four residential units must disclose to the transferee in writing whether structural additions, other significant changes that were made while the transferor owned the property, or changes the transferor knows about were made under an appropriate permit. Civil Code §1134.5 was repealed effective January 1, 1987, and the disclosure is now substantially made under the Real Estate Transfer Disclosure Statement required by CC §§1102–1102.15. See Update §1.69.

COUNSELING BUYER

[§1.79] Attorney's Role

When the seller is a foreign investor and the property is other than a single-family residence the purchase price of which does not exceed $300,000, the buyer's attorney should be familiar with the Foreign Investment in Real Property Tax Act of 1980 (FIRPTA; Pub L 96–499, §§1121–1125, 94 Stat 2682) and the requirements regarding withholding by the buyer. When there is a question whether a foreign investor may be involved, counsel should require delivery of a nonforeign affidavit by the seller (IRC §1445(b)(2)) in all real property transactions subject to FIRPTA.

Avoiding Fraud

[§1.82] Of Buyer

The buyer in *Nussbaum v Weeks* (1989) 214 CA3d 1589, 263 CR 360, was held not to have a duty to disclose to the seller that an upcoming change in water district policy would increase the value of the real property purchased. The buyer was the general manager of the water district and knew that a change in policy that was forthcoming would allow more water for the property and consequently increase its value. The court held that the buyer did not have a fiduciary or confidential relationship with the seller merely because he was a public officer. The court then analyzed the extent of a buyer's duty to disclose material facts to the seller. The court found that the duty to disclose existed only in limited circumstances described in Restatement Second of Torts §551. These circumstances include those in which (1) a fiduciary or confidential relationship exists, (2) a partial or misleading disclosure is made, or (3) the buyer knows that the seller would reasonably expect a disclosure to be made. The court found none of these circumstances present.

2

The Broker

REGULATION OF BROKERS

[§2.1] Statutory Requirements

See also the reporting of real estate transactions required of real estate brokers added by the Tax Reform Act of 1986 (Pub L 99–514, 100 Stat 2085) IRC §6045(e).

Specialized Licensees

[§2.3] Mortgage Loan Brokers

The amendment to Cal Const art XV, §1, exempting real estate brokers who make or arrange loans secured by real property from usury limitations, was given retroactive effect in *Chapman v Farr* (1982) 132 CA3d 1021, 183 CR 606, thus protecting those brokers from liability for usury in transactions before the amendment. See Harroch & Dana, *The Real Estate Broker Exemption From the California Usury Law,* 4 CEB Real Prop L Rep 137 (Oct. 1981).

The term "make or arrange" includes loans in which the broker is a lender or a third party acting for others for compensation or is soliciting a loan with an expectation of compensation, but it does not include a loan in which the broker is merely a borrower. CC §1916.1; *Winnett v Roberts* (1986) 179 CA3d 909, 225 CR 82; *Green v Future Two* (1986) 179 CA3d 738, 225 CR 3. The expected compensation may be a share in the entity obtaining the loan. *Stickel v Harris* (1987) 196 CA3d 575, 242 CR 88. See CC §§2956–2967 on disclosure requirements that apply to brokers and other "arrangers of credit" (as defined in CC §2957) on purchase money liens on residential property.

Effective January 1, 1986, Bus & P C §§10242–10248.3 have been limited in application to loans secured by a dwelling. Bus & P C §10240.1.

The limitation expressly does not apply to Bus & P C §10240, discussed in Book §2.3. A dwelling is defined as a single dwelling unit in a condominium or cooperative, or any parcel of residential real property containing one to four units that is owned by the signatory on the mortgage or deed of trust at the time of its execution. Bus & P C §10240.2. Business and Professions Code §10242(a) has been amended to provide that the charge that may be imposed for brokerage costs and expenses exclusive of actual title charges and recording fees is limited to the greater of 5 percent of the principal amount of the loan or $390, but may in no event exceed $700.

Effective January 1, 1991, Bus & P C §10245 was amended to provide that most of the provisions of the Real Property Loan Law apply only to loans of less than $30,000 secured by first deeds of trust or to loans of less than $20,000 secured by junior liens.

See Bus & P C §10240 limiting the application of §§10240–10248.3 to certain brokers.

The provisions of Bus & P C §§10248.7–10248.9, cited in Book §2.3, have been repealed and replaced by new advertising and reporting restrictions in Bus & P C §§10232.1–10232.5.

The exemption from the usury limitations of Cal Const art XV, §1 for loans arranged by real estate brokers has been limited further by an amendment to CC §1916.1, effective January 1, 1986, to restrict the exemptions to situations in which the broker

(1) acts for compensation or in expectation of compensation for soliciting, negotiating, or arranging the loan for another, (2) acts for compensation or in expectation of compensation for selling, buying, leasing, exchanging, or negotiating the sale, purchase, lease, or exchange of real property or a business for another and (A) arranges a loan to pay all or any portion of the purchase price of, or of an improvement to, that property or business or (B) arranges a forbearance, extension, or refinancing of any loan in connection with that sale, purchase, lease, exchange of, or an improvement to, real property or a business, or (3) arranges or negotiates for another a forbearance, extension, or refinancing of any loan secured by real property in connection with a past transaction in which the broker had acted for compensation or in expectation of compensation for selling, buying, leasing, exchanging, or negotiating the sale, purchase or exchange of real property or a business.

Title 10 Cal Adm C (now called the California Code of Regulations) §2849.7 has been repealed.

According to the court in *Stephens, Partain & Cunningham v Hollis* (1987) 196 CA3d 948, 242 CR 251, the fiduciary duty owed by a mortgage loan broker to the borrower terminates when the agency relationship terminates (CC §2355) and does not prevent the broker, who is the trustee of the deed of trust securing the arranged loan, from purchasing the real property security at a trustee's foreclosure sale.

[§2.4] Business Opportunity Brokers

Effective January 1, 1991, Bus & P C §10133.3 was added to provide that the provisions of Bus & P C §§10131 and 10131.2 on business opportunities do not apply to any person or legal entity that for another buys or sells or offers to buy or sell or performs other specified services concerning transfers of radio, television, or cable enterprises that are licensed by the FCC, if the purchase, sale, or exchange of the enterprise is not in substance a transfer of real property.

[§2.5] Real Property Securities Dealers

Effective January 1, 1986, Bus & P C §10237.5 has been repealed.
Title 10 Cal Adm C §2980 (now called the California Code of Regulations) also has been repealed.

[§2.7] Exemptions From Licensing Requirements

Effective January 1, 1991, Bus & P C §10131.1 was amended to add an exemption to the broker licensing requirement for a person engaged as a principal in the business of buying, selling, or exchanging with the public real property sale contracts or notes secured by liens on real property. The new provision exempts from the definition of "sale, resale, and exchange" the original issuance of a promissory note by a borrower or a real property sales contract by a vendor, either of which is to be secured directly by a lien on real property owned by the borrower or vendor.

The subsections of Bus & P C §10133, cited in Book §2.7, have been renumbered effective January 1, 1986, as follows:

Former	Current
Bus & P C §10133(a)	Bus & P C §10133(a)(1)
Bus & P C §10133(b)	Bus & P C §10133(a)(2)
Bus & P C §10133(c)	Bus & P C §10133(a)(3)
Bus & P C §10133(d)	Bus & P C §10133(a)(4)
Bus & P C §10133(e)	Bus & P C §10133(a)(5)

Also effective January 1, 1986, the legislature added an exception from the licensing requirements for a general partner dealing with partnership property without expectation of special compensation. Bus & P C §10133(a)(1). These changes in Bus & P C §10133 omitted the previous reference to dealing with one's own property.

In *Sheetz v Edmonds* (1988) 201 CA3d 1432, 247 CR 776, an unlicensed property manager obtained powers of attorney from all her clients for whom she performed services that otherwise would have required her to be licensed. The court held that the power-of-attorney exemption applied only to those powers of attorney created because of personal necessity in a particular or isolated transaction. Thus, the court held that the power-of-attorney exemption could not be used to conduct a business that otherwise would require a license. See Bus & P C §10133(b).

The subsections of Bus & P C §10133.1, cited in Book §2.7, have also been renumbered as follows:

Former	*Current*
Bus & P C §10133.1(a)	Bus & P C §10133.1(a)(1)
Bus & P C §10133.1(b)	Deleted
Bus & P C §10133.1(c)	Bus & P C §10133.1(a)(2)
Bus & P C §10133.1(d)	Bus & P C §10133.1(a)(3)
Bus & P C §10133.1(e)	Bus & P C §10133.1(a)(4)
Bus & P C §10133.1(f)	Bus & P C §10133.1(a)(5)
Bus & P C §10133.1(g)	Bus & P C §10133.1(a)(6)
Bus & P C §10133.1(h)	Bus & P C §10133.1(a)(7)

To the list of exemptions under Bus & P C §10133.1 have been added the following:

Agents of savings institutions acting under written authority (Bus & P C §10133.1(a)(8));

Licensed securities brokers and dealers and their employees, officers, and agents in transactions involving a pool of promissory notes secured by a lien on real property (Bus & P C §10133.1(a)(9));

Certain persons who collect payments or perform services for lenders or on notes of owners in connection with loans secured by real property (Bus & P C §10133.1(b)).

[§2.8] Licensing Qualifications

Beginning January 1, 1983, at least 3 of the 45 hours of continuing education required of real estate licensees must cover the professional ethics and legal aspects of being a real estate broker or salesperson. Bus & P C §10170.5.

Beginning July 1, 1987, Bus & P C §10170.5 also requires that not less than 18 of the 45 hours of continuing education be in courses or programs related to consumer protection, and that 3 hours be in a course in agency relationships and duties in a real estate brokerage practice. This course must include instruction in the disclosures to be made and the confidences to be kept in the various agency relationships between licensees and parties to real estate transactions. See also Update §2.20 on agency disclosures.

Effective January 1, 1992, Bus & P C §10171.6 was repealed.

[§2.9] Corporations and Partnerships as Licensees

Title 10 Cal Adm C §2732 (now called California Code of Regulations) has been repealed. Title 10 Cal Code Regs §2731, providing that a licensee cannot do business under a fictitious name unless the license was issued in that name, remains in effect.

Title 10 Cal Adm C Regs §2741.5 was repealed. Now see 10 Cal Code Regs §2740.

[§2.10] Brokers Distinguished From Finders

The treatise by Miller & Starr, cited in the Book, has been replaced by 2 Miller & Starr, California Real Estate §§4.15–4.16 (2d ed 1989).

Broker's Relationship With Salespersons

[§2.12] Employee or Independent Contractor

The court in *Payne v White House Props., Inc.* (1980) 112 CA3d 465, 169 CR 373, held that as a matter of law, a real estate salesperson cannot be an independent contractor, but is an agent of the broker. Whether the salesperson is an employee of the broker for worker's compensation purposes is a question of fact to be determined at trial.

For a recent California Supreme Court analysis of the employee versus independent contractor issue in a worker's compensation action concerning migrant agricultural workers, see *S.G. Borello & Sons v Department of Indus. Relations* (1989) 48 C3d 341, 256 CR 543.

The citation in Book §2.12 to IRC §3306(i)(1) was an error. See instead IRC §3401(d).

The treatise by Miller & Starr, cited in the Book, has been replaced by 2 Miller & Starr, California Real Estate §3.11 (2d ed 1989).

Broker as Escrow Agent

[§2.13] License Requirements

Title 10 Cal Adm C §2833 (now called California Code of Regulations) cited in Book §2.13, was repealed and replaced by 10 Cal Code Regs §2951, which specifies the regulations that apply to real estate brokers who act as escrow holders.

The California Escrow Law is now found at Fin C §§17000–17701.

RETAINING A BROKER

Appointment of an Agent

[§2.18] Agency Versus Contract Law

Former CC §1624(5), cited in Book §2.18, now is designated as CC §1624(d).

Creation of the Agency

[§2.20] Agency by Express or Implied Agreement

Effective January 1, 1988, CC §§2373–2382 require one acting as a real estate agent in sales transactions (including leases for more than one year) involving residential property of one to four units and mobile homes to provide written disclosures to both the buyer and seller concerning the agency relationship options that are available and to have the principals confirm in writing the particular agency relationship selected (see Update §2.20B). Under CC §2378 an agent may select, as a condition of employment, a form of agency not specifically prohibited by CC §§2373–2382 if the requirements of CC §§2374 and 2375.5 are met.

The delivery of the completed disclosure form embodied in CC §2375 (see Update §2.20A) must be made by the listing agent to the seller before entering into the listing agreement, by the selling agent to the seller as soon as practical before presenting an offer, and by the selling agent to the buyer as soon as practical before execution of the buyer's offer. Minor exceptions exist in situations in which the selling agent is not dealing directly with the seller or buyer. Except in a few minor situations, the disclosure form must be signed by the seller or buyer, acknowledging receipt. CC §2374. Confirmation of the type of agency relationship that exists must be made in a form prescribed by CC §2375.5. See Update §2.20B.

Civil Code §2376 prohibits a selling agent from acting only for the buyer when the selling agent is also the listing agent. Civil Code §2377 provides that the payment or obligation to pay compensation to an agent by the seller or buyer is not necessarily determinative of a particular agency relationship between an agent and the seller or buyer. Under CC §2379, a dual agent must not disclose to a seller that a buyer is willing to pay more than the offering price nor disclose to a buyer that the seller is willing to take less than the listing price unless the express written consent for such disclosure is given by the applicable party.

[§2.20A] Form: Disclosure Regarding Real Estate Agency Relationship

DISCLOSURE REGARDING
REAL ESTATE AGENCY RELATIONSHIP

(As required by the Civil Code)

When you enter into a discussion with a real estate agent regarding a real estate transaction, you should from the outset understand what type of agency relationship or representation you wish to have with the agent in the transaction.

SELLER'S AGENT

A Seller's agent under a listing agreement with the Seller acts as the agent for the Seller only. A Seller's agent or a subagent of that agent has the following affirmative obligations:

To the Seller:

(a) A fiduciary duty of utmost care, integrity, honesty, and loyalty in dealings with the Seller.

To the Buyer and the Seller:

(a) Diligent exercise of reasonable skill and care in performance of the agent's duties.

(b) A duty of honest and fair dealing and good faith.

(c) A duty to disclose all facts known to the agent materially affecting the value or desirability of the property that are not known to, or within the diligent attention and observation of, the parties.

An agent is not obligated to reveal to either party any confidential information obtained from the other party which does not involve the affirmative duties set forth above.

BUYER'S AGENT

A selling agent can, with a Buyer's consent, agree to act as agent for the Buyer only. In these situations, the agent is not the Seller's agent, even if by agreement the agent may receive compensation for services rendered, either in full or in part from the Seller. An agent acting only for a Buyer has the following affirmative obligations:

To the Buyer:

(a) A fiduciary duty of utmost care, integrity, honesty, and loyalty in dealings with the Buyer.

To the Buyer and the Seller:

(a) Diligent exercise of reasonable skill and care in performance of the agent's duties.

(b) A duty of honest and fair dealing and good faith.

(c) A duty to disclose all facts known to the agent materially affecting the value or desirability of the property that are not known to, or within the diligent attention and observation of, the parties. An agent is not obligated to reveal to either party any confidential information obtained from the other party which does not involve the affirmative duties set forth above.

AGENT REPRESENTING BOTH SELLER AND BUYER

A real estate agent, either acting directly or through one or more associate licensees, can legally be the agent of both the Seller and the Buyer in a transaction, but only with the knowledge and consent of both the Seller and the Buyer.

In a dual agency situation, the agent has the following affirmative obligations to both the Seller and the Buyer:

(a) A fiduciary duty of utmost care, integrity, honesty and loyalty in the dealings with either Seller or the Buyer.

(b) Other duties to the Seller and the Buyer as stated above in their respective sections.

In representing both Seller and Buyer, the agent may not, without the express permission of the respective party, disclose to the other party that the Seller will accept a price less than the listing price or that the Buyer will pay a price greater than the price offered.

The above duties of the agent in a real estate transaction do not relieve a Seller or Buyer from the responsibility to protect their own interests. You should carefully read all agreements to assure that they adequately express your understanding of the transaction. A real estate agent is a person qualified to advise about real estate. If legal or tax advice is desired consult a competent professional.

Throughout your real property transaction you may receive more than one disclosure form, depending upon the number of agents assisting in the transaction. The law requires each agent with whom you have more than a casual relationship to present you with this disclosure form. You should read its contents each time it is presented to you, considering the relationship between you and the real estate agent in your specific transaction.

This disclosure form includes the provisions of Article 2.5 (commencing with Section 2373) of Chapter 2 of Title 9 of Part 4 of Division 3 of Civil Code set forth on the reverse hereof. Read it carefully.

Agent	Buyer/Seller (date) (Signature)
Associate Licensee (date) (Signature)	Buyer/Seller (date) (Signature)

Comment: The form set out above is required by CC §2375. For discussion, see Update §2.20.

[§2.20B] Form: Confirmation of Agency Relationship

_ _[*Name of Listing Agent*]_ _ **is the agent of (check one):**

[ ] the seller exclusively; or
[ ] the buyer and seller.

_ _[*Name of Selling Agent if not the same as the Listing Agent*]_ _ **is the agent of (check one):**

[ ] the buyer exclusively; or
[ ] the seller exclusively; or
[ ] both the buyer and seller.

Comment: The form set out above is required by CC §2375.5. It must be included in the contract to purchase and sell real property or in a separate writing executed or acknowledged before or coincident with the execution of the contract. If the listing agent's confirmation is a separate writing, it must be executed or acknowledged by the seller and the listing agent. CC §2375.5(b). If the selling agent's confirmation is a separate writing, it must be executed by the seller, the buyer, and the selling agent. CC §2375.5(a).

[§2.21] Agency by Ratification

The reference to Witkin in the Book should now be to 2 Witkin, Summary of California Law, *Agency and Employment* §39 (9th ed 1987).

Broker's Authority To Appoint Subagents

[§2.26] Subagents Through Multiple Listing Services

Restricting access to the residential listings of a multiple listing service to members of a local board was held an illegal group boycott in *People v National Ass'n of Realtors* (1981) 120 CA3d 459, 174 CR 728. The court held that the board's refusal to accept any but an exclusive right to sell listings was also an illegal group boycott because it defeated the broker's right to negotiate other types of listings. Board encouragement of equal commission splits and disapproval of those brokers who attempted to negotiate different arrangements was held to be price fixing in violation of the Cartwright Anti-Trust Act (Bus & P C §§16700–16758) and the unlawful competition statutes. In *Feldman v Sacramento Bd. of Realtors* (1981) 119 CA3d 739, 174 CR 231, the court held that, even if the fees for use of a multiple listing service are the same for members and nonmembers, the fees may violate the Cartwright Act if they unreasonably restrict competition. The *National Ass'n of Realtors* and *Feldman* cases are discussed further in 4 CEB Real Prop L Rep 127 (Oct. 1981) and 106 (Aug. 1981) respectively.

Access to the multiple listing service may be restricted to licensed brokers and salespersons. *Derish v San Mateo-Burlingame Bd. of Realtors* (1982) 136 CA3d 534, 186 CR 390.

The Civil Code now regulates multiple listing services. See CC §§1086–1090, effective January 1, 1983. Civil Code §1086 defines various terms, including three types of listing agreements—exclusive right to sell, exclusive agency, and open.

[§2.27] Conflict of Interest

The treatise by Miller & Starr, cited in the Book, has been replaced by 2 Miller & Starr, California Real Estate §3.7 (2d ed 1989).

[§2.28] Extent of Broker's Authority

Title 10 Cal Adm C §§2833 and 2835 (now called the California Code of Regulations) have been repealed.

Broker's Compensation

[§2.29] Prerequisites to Broker's Right to Commission

Former CC §1624(5), cited in Book §2.29, now is designated as CC §1624(d).

Ready, Willing, and Able Buyer

[§2.35] Offer Accepted; Sale Not Completed

A real estate broker is not entitled to a commission from the seller if the only contractual obligation to pay that commission is contained in the sales agreement, but the property is sold in eminent domain proceedings rather than under the agreement. *City of Turlock v Paul M. Zagaris,*

Inc. (1989) 209 CA3d 189, 256 CR 902. The court held that, when the written agreement for a broker commission is contained only in the sales agreement, the sale contemplated by that agreement must be consummated before the commission becomes due. It should be noted that through no fault of the seller or buyer conditions precedent to the consummation of the sale were not satisfied because of the intervening eminent domain action. The same result would apparently not have been reached if the reason for the failure of the sale to be consummated was an unjustified refusal of the seller to perform. See *Collins v Vickter Manor, Inc.* (1957) 47 C2d 875, 306 P2d 783.

[§2.37] Conditional Commission Provision

The treatise by Miller & Starr, cited in the Book, has been replaced by 1 Miller & Starr, California Real Estate §2.25 (2d ed 1989).

Sale After the Listing Period

[§2.40] The Safety Clause

The treatise by Miller & Starr, cited in the Book, has been replaced by 1 Miller & Starr, California Real Estate §2.27 (2d ed 1989).

[§2.41] Amount of Commission

Allegations that the publication and promotion by the California Association of Realtors of a widely used form contract for employment of a salesperson by a broker as an independent contractor provided for a fixed commission rate were held insufficient to support a cause of action for an antitrust civil conspiracy in *Bartley v California Ass'n of Realtors* (1980) 115 CA3d 930, 173 CR 284. See discussion in §2.12 on whether a salesperson can be an independent contractor.

Recovery of Commission From Buyer

[§2.44] Interference With Prospective Economic Advantage

A broker's cause of action against the buyer for tortious interference with prospective economic advantage will not lie when the prospective economic advantage itself is fraudulent, as from a secret commission payable by the seller and not disclosed to the buyer. *Renaissance Realty, Inc. v Soriano* (1981) 120 CA3d Supp 13, 174 CR 837.

For a recent example of the use by a broker of a cause of action for interference with prospective economic advantage in order to sue a buyer for a commission when no written commission agreement existed, see *Deeter v Angus* (1986) 179 CA3d 241, 224 CR 801.

Contracting With the Broker

Elements Applicable to Both Sellers and Buyers

[§2.45] Essentials of Contract

Title 10 Cal Adm C §2902 (now called the California Code of Regulations) was repealed and not replaced. However, Bus & P C §10142 still requires that a copy of any agreement authorizing or employing a real estate licensee must be delivered to the person signing it when the signature is obtained.

Statute of Frauds

[§§2.46–2.47] Writing Required; Exceptions

Former CC §1624(5), cited in Book §2.46, now is designated as CC §1624(d).

Although a broker's or finder's agreement with a seller or buyer must be in writing (see *Tenzer v Superscope, Inc.* (1985) 39 C3d 18, 216 CR 130, discussed at Update §§2.56–2.57), the statute of frauds (CC §1624(d)) does not require that an agreement between a finder and a broker providing for a fee to the finder for introducing the broker to prospective sellers or buyers be in writing, because no buyer or seller is a party to the agreement. *Grant v Marinell* (1980) 112 CA3d 617, 169 CR 414.

In *Hughes v Morrison* (1984) 160 CA3d 103, 206 CR 321, the brokers were allowed to recover a commission on a subsequent sale that closely followed a prior sale between the same seller and buyer. The buyer had defaulted after the first sale, and the seller had foreclosed. The brokers had a written commission agreement for the first sale and participated in the second sale, but had no new written agreement for the second sale. The original commission agreement provided for payment at 5 percent as installment payments were made to the sellers. Because the second sale also involved installment payments, the court ruled that the orginal agreement applied to the second sale and that the 5 percent commission should be applied as the payments were received. The court's ruling allowed the brokers not two full commissions on two sales, but what in effect was one full commission on two sales.

[§§2.49, 2.51] Employment of Broker; Execution

Former CC §1624(5), cited in Book §2.49, is now designated as CC §1624(d).

In *Rader Co. v Stone* (1986) 178 CA3d 10, 223 CR 806, a broker in a lease transaction was able to satisfy the subscription requirement of the statute of frauds for purposes of a demurrer because a landlord's agent had signed a Realtor Registration Form, completed by the broker, which was held one of a series of papers constituting the written contract for a commission.

[§§2.56–2.57] Principal's Misrepresentation Theory; Estoppel Theory

The supreme court in *Tenzer v Superscope, Inc.* (1985) 39 C3d 18, 216 CR 130, affirmed the rule that a finder's fee agreement with a seller or buyer must be in writing to be enforceable under former CC §1624(5) (now CC §1624(d)). However, the court held that the unenforceability of an allegedly fraudulent unwritten promise as a contract does not preclude an action for fraud. The court reversed the opposite rule announced in *Kroger v Baur* (1941) 46 CA2d 801, 117 P2d 50, cited in Book §2.56, that an action for fraud may not be maintained when the allegedly fraudulent promise is unenforceable because of the statute of frauds. Consequently, the court disapproved the cases following *Kroger,* including *Keely v Price* (1972) 27 CA3d 209, 103 CR 531, also cited in Book §2.56. The supreme court also held that mere proof that a promise was made but was not fulfilled would not be enough to prove fraud and that something more than nonperformance would be required to prove an intent not to perform the promise. *Tenzer* involved the reversal of a grant of summary judgment for defendants that was based on the statute of frauds; the matter was remanded for trial on the issue of fraud and on the issue of whether the finder, under the facts of the case, could invoke the equitable doctrine of estoppel to avoid the statute of frauds defense.

On the issue of estoppel, the supreme court held that a finder, who need not be a licensed real estate broker, is entitled to invoke the doctrine of estoppel to plead the statute of frauds. The supreme court distinguished a line of cases, including *Keely v Price, supra; King v Tilden Park Estates* (1958) 156 CA2d 824, 320 P2d 109; *Hicks v Post* (1908) 154 C 22, 96 P 878; and *Augustine v Trucco* (1954) 124 CA2d 229, 268 P2d 780; all cited in Book §§2.56–2.57, that held an estoppel to plead the statute of frauds may not be predicated on the refusal to comply with an oral promise to pay a commission to a licensed real estate broker. Those cases involved only licensed real estate brokers, who are assumed to be knowledgeable regarding the laws relating to real estate and apparently better able to protect their interests. However, the court noted that this rule for actual licensed brokers has been vigorously criticized but was not before the court.

Two years after the *Tenzer* decision, the supreme court in *Phillippe v Shapell Indus.* (1987) 43 C3d 1247, 241 CR 22, decided that a licensed broker could not invoke equitable estoppel to avoid the statute of frauds. The supreme court rejected the broker's argument that the party from whom the commission was claimed was prohibited from asserting the statute of fraud as a defense because the broker had changed his position by performing services in reliance on the other party's oral promise to pay a commission. It did note that estoppel is proper to avoid unconscionable injury or unjust enrichment that would result from the refusal to enforce an oral promise, but found that licensed brokers, because of the educational requirements to become and continue as licensed professionals, cannot reasonably rely on such oral promises, because they should know that commission agreements must be in writing. The court disapproved of *Le Blond v Wolfe,* cited in Book §2.57, to the extent it allowed a licensed broker to assert equitable estoppel.

Seller-Broker Agreements; Types of Listing Agreements

Exclusive Right To Sell

[§2.59] General Characteristics

Requiring a buyer of a subdivision lot to enter an exclusive listing agreement for the lot's resale as a condition to the purchase agreement may violate antitrust laws. See *Classen v Weller* (1983) 145 CA3d 27, 192 CR 914.

[§2.60] Form: CAR Exclusive Authorization and Right To Sell Listing Agreement

The form in Book §2.60 has been replaced by the form reprinted on the following pages.

EXCLUSIVE AUTHORIZATION AND RIGHT TO SELL
MULTIPLE LISTING AUTHORIZATION
THIS IS INTENDED TO BE A LEGALLY BINDING AGREEMENT — READ IT CAREFULLY
CALIFORNIA ASSOCIATION OF REALTORS® (CAR) STANDARD FORM

1. **EXCLUSIVE RIGHT TO SELL:** I hereby employ and grant _____
hereinafter called "Broker," the exclusive and irrevocable right commencing on _____, 19_____, and expiring at
midnight on _____, 19_____, to sell or exchange the real property situated in the City of _____
County of _____, California described as follows _____

2. **TERMS OF SALE:** The purchase price shall be _____
_____ ($_____), to be paid as follows _____

The following items of personal property are included in the above stated price: _____

3. **MULTIPLE LISTING SERVICE (MLS):** Broker is a Participant of _____
ASSOCIATION/BOARD OF REALTORS® Multiple Listing Service (MLS) and this listing information will be provided to the MLS to be published and disseminated to its Participants in accordance with its Rules and Regulations. Broker is authorized to cooperate with other real estate brokers, to appoint subagents and to report the sale, its price, terms and financing for the publication, dissemination, information and use by authorized Association/Board members, MLS Participants and Subscribers.

4. **TITLE INSURANCE:** Evidence of title shall be a California Land Title Association policy of title insurance in the amount of the selling price.

Notice: The amount or rate of real estate commissions is not fixed by law. They are set by each Broker individually and may be negotiable between the Seller and Broker.

5. **COMPENSATION TO BROKER:** I hereby agree to compensate Broker, irrespective of agency relationship(s), as follows:
   (a) _____ percent of the selling price, or $_____, if the property is sold during the term hereof, or any extension thereof, by Broker or through any other person, or by me on the terms herein set forth, or any other price and terms I accept, or _____ percent of the price shown in 2, or $_____, if said property is withdrawn from sale, transferred, conveyed, leased, or rented without the consent of Broker, or made unmarketable by my voluntary act during the term hereof or any extension thereof.
   (b) The compensation provided for in subparagraph (a) above if property is sold, conveyed or otherwise transferred within _____ calendar days after the termination of this authority or any extension thereof to anyone with whom Broker has had negotiations prior to final termination, provided I have received notice in writing, including the names of the prospective purchasers, before or upon termination of this agreement or any extension hereof. However, I shall not be obligated to pay the compensation provided for in subparagraph (a) if a valid listing agreement is entered into during the term of said protection period with another licensed real estate broker and a sale, lease or exchange of the property is made during the term of said valid listing agreement.
   (c) I authorize Broker to cooperate with other brokers, to appoint subagents, and to divide with other brokers such compensation in any manner acceptable to brokers.
   (d) In the event of an exchange, permission is hereby given Broker to represent all parties and collect compensation or commissions from them, provided there is full disclosure to all principals of such agency. Broker is authorized to divide with other brokers such compensation or commissions in any manner acceptable to brokers.
   (e) Seller shall execute and deliver an escrow instruction irrevocably assigning Broker compensation in an amount equal to the compensation provided in subparagraph (a) (above) from the Seller's proceeds.

6. **DEPOSIT:** Broker is authorized to accept and hold on Seller's behalf a deposit to be applied toward purchase price.

7. **HOME PROTECTION PLAN:** Seller is informed that home protection plans are available. Such plans may provide additional protection and benefit to a Seller and Buyer. Cost and coverage may vary.

8. **KEYBOX:** I authorize Broker to install a KEYBOX.
   Refer to reverse side for important keybox information.   (Initial) YES (_____/_____) NO (_____/_____)

9. **SIGN:** Authorization to install a FOR SALE/SOLD sign on the property.   (Initial) YES (_____/_____) NO (_____/_____)

10. **PEST CONTROL:** Seller shall furnish a current Structural Pest Control Report on the main building and all structures of the property, except _____

11. **DISCLOSURE:** Unless exempt, Seller shall provide a Real Estate Transfer Disclosure Statement concerning the condition of the property. I agree to save and hold Broker harmless from all claims, disputes, litigation and/or judgments arising from any incorrect information supplied by me, or from any material fact known by me which I fail to disclose.   (Initial) (_____/_____)

12. **TAX WITHHOLDING:** Seller agrees to perform any act reasonably necessary to carry out the provisions of FIRPTA (Internal Revenue Code §1445) and California Revenue and Taxation Code §§18805 and 26131, and regulations promulgated thereunder. Refer to the reverse side for withholding provisions and exemptions.

13. **EQUAL HOUSING OPPORTUNITY:** This property is offered in compliance with federal, state, and local anti-discrimination laws.

14. **ARBITRATION OF DISPUTES:** Any dispute or claim in law or equity arising out of this contract or any resulting transaction shall be decided by neutral binding arbitration in accordance with the rules of the American Arbitration Association, and not by court action except as provided by California law for judicial review of arbitration proceedings. Judgment upon the award rendered by the arbitrator(s) may be entered in any court having jurisdiction thereof. The parties shall have the right to discovery in accordance with Code of Civil Procedure §1283.05. The following matters are excluded from arbitration hereunder: (a) a judicial or non-judicial foreclosure or other action or proceeding to enforce a deed of trust, mortgage, or real property sales contract as defined in Civil Code §2985, (b) an unlawful detainer action, (c) the filing or enforcement of a mechanic's lien, (d) any matter which is within the jurisdiction of a probate court, or (e) an action for bodily injury or wrongful death, or for latent or patent defects to which Code of Civil Procedure §337.1 or §337.15 applies. The filing of a judicial action to enable the recording of a notice of pending action, for order of attachment, receivership, injunction, or other provisional remedies, shall not constitute a waiver of the right to arbitrate under this provision.

"NOTICE: BY INITIALLING IN THE SPACE BELOW YOU ARE AGREEING TO HAVE ANY DISPUTE ARISING OUT OF THE MATTERS INCLUDED IN THE 'ARBITRATION OF DISPUTES' PROVISION DECIDED BY NEUTRAL ARBITRATION AS PROVIDED BY CALIFORNIA LAW AND YOU ARE GIVING UP ANY RIGHTS YOU MIGHT POSSESS TO HAVE THE DISPUTE LITIGATED IN A COURT OR JURY TRIAL. BY INITIALLING IN THE SPACE BELOW YOU ARE GIVING UP YOUR JUDICIAL RIGHTS TO DISCOVERY AND APPEAL, UNLESS THOSE RIGHTS ARE SPECIFICALLY INCLUDED IN THE 'ARBITRATION OF DISPUTES' PROVISION. IF YOU REFUSE TO SUBMIT TO ARBITRATION AFTER AGREEING TO THIS PROVISION, YOU MAY BE COMPELLED TO ARBITRATE UNDER THE AUTHORITY OF THE CALIFORNIA CODE OF CIVIL PROCEDURE. YOUR AGREEMENT TO THIS ARBITRATION PROVISION IS VOLUNTARY."

"WE HAVE READ AND UNDERSTAND THE FOREGOING AND AGREE TO SUBMIT DISPUTES ARISING OUT OF THE MATTERS INCLUDED IN THE 'ARBITRATION OF DISPUTES' PROVISION TO NEUTRAL ARBITRATION."

(Initial) BROKER (_____) SELLER (_____)

15. **ATTORNEY'S FEES:** In any action, proceeding or arbitration arising out of this agreement, the prevailing party shall be entitled to reasonable attorney's fees and costs.

16. **ADDITIONAL TERMS:** _____

17. **ENTIRE AGREEMENT:** I, the Seller, warrant that I am the owner of the property or have the authority to execute this agreement. The Seller and Broker further intend that this agreement constitutes the complete and exclusive statement of its terms and that no extrinsic evidence whatsoever may be introduced in any judicial or arbitration proceeding, if any, involving this agreement.

I acknowledge that I have read and understand this agreement, including the information on the reverse side, and have received a copy.

Date _____, 19_____   _____, California
Seller _____   Address _____
Seller _____   City _____ State _____ Zip _____
In consideration of the above, Broker agrees to use diligence in procuring a purchaser.   Phone _____
Real Estate Broker _____   By _____
Address _____   City _____ Date _____

THIS STANDARDIZED DOCUMENT FOR USE IN SIMPLE TRANSACTIONS HAS BEEN APPROVED BY THE CALIFORNIA ASSOCIATION OF REALTORS® IN FORM ONLY. NO REPRESENTATION IS MADE AS TO THE APPROVAL OF THE FORM OF ANY SUPPLEMENTS NOT CURRENTLY PUBLISHED BY THE CALIFORNIA ASSOCIATION OF REALTORS® OR THE LEGAL VALIDITY OR ADEQUACY OF ANY PROVISION IN ANY SPECIFIC TRANSACTION. IT SHOULD NOT BE USED IN COMPLEX TRANSACTIONS OR WITH EXTENSIVE RIDERS OR ADDITIONS.
A REAL ESTATE BROKER IS THE PERSON QUALIFIED TO ADVISE ON REAL ESTATE TRANSACTIONS. IF YOU DESIRE LEGAL OR TAX ADVICE, CONSULT AN APPROPRIATE PROFESSIONAL.

This form is available for use by the entire real estate industry. The use of this form is not intended to identify the user as a REALTOR®. REALTOR® is a registered collective membership mark which may be used only by real estate licensees who are members of the NATIONAL ASSOCIATION OF REALTORS® and who subscribe to its Code of Ethics.

* REFER TO REVERSE SIDE FOR ADDITIONAL INFORMATION

The copyright laws of the United States (17 U.S. Code) forbid the unauthorized reproduction of this form by any means including facsimile or computerized formats.
Copyright© 1988, CALIFORNIA ASSOCIATION OF REALTORS®
525 South Virgil Avenue, Los Angeles, California 90020
REVIEWED 2/91   **FORM A-14**

OFFICE USE ONLY
Reviewed by Broker or Designee _____
Date _____

THIS FORM CONTINUED ON
FOLLOWING PAGE →

8 KEYBOX: A keybox designed as a repository of a key to the above premises, will permit access to the interior of the premises by Participants of the Multiple Listing Service (MLS), their authorized licensees and prospective buyers. If property is not seller occupied, seller shall be responsible for obtaining occupants' written permission for use of the keybox. Neither listing nor selling broker, MLS or Board of REALTORS® is an insurer against theft, loss, vandalism or damage attributed to the use of keybox. SELLER is advised to verify the existence of, or obtain appropriate insurance through their own insurance broker.

12 TAX WITHHOLDING: (a) Under the Foreign Investment in Real Property Tax Act (FIRPTA), IRC §1445, every Buyer of U.S. real property must, unless an exemption applies, deduct and withhold from Seller's proceeds 10% of the gross sales price. The primary FIRPTA exemptions are: No withholding is required if (i) Seller provides Buyer with an affidavit under penalty of perjury, that Seller is not a "foreign person," or (ii) Seller provides Buyer with a "qualifying statement" issued by the Internal Revenue Service, or (iii) Buyer purchases real property for use as a residence and the purchase price is $300,000 or less and Buyer or a member of Buyer's family has definite plans to reside at the property for at least 50% of the number of days it is in use during each of the first two 12-month periods after transfer. (b) In addition, under California Revenue and Taxation Code §§18805 and 26131, every Buyer must, unless an exemption applies, deduct and withhold from the Seller's proceeds 3⅓% of the gross sales price if the Seller has a last known street address outside of California, or if the Seller's proceeds will be paid to a financial intermediary of the Seller. The primary exemptions are: No withholding is required if (i) the Seller has a homeowner's exemption for the subject property, for local property taxes, for the year in which the title transfers, or (ii) the property is selling for $100,000 or less, or (iii) the Franchise Tax Board issues a certificate authorizing a lower amount or no withholding, or (iv) the Seller signs an affidavit stating that the Seller is a California resident or a corporation qualified to do business in California. (c) Seller and Buyer agree to execute and deliver as directed any instrument, affidavit, or statement reasonably necessary to carry out these statutes and regulations promulgated thereunder.

14 ARBITRATION: Arbitration is the referral of a dispute to one or more impartial persons for final and binding determination. It is private and informal, designed for quick, practical, and inexpensive settlements. Arbitration is an orderly proceeding, governed by rules of procedure and standards of conduct prescribed by law.

ENFORCEMENT OF ARBITRATION AGREEMENTS
UNDER CALIFORNIA CODE OF CIVIL PROCEDURE SECTIONS 1281, 1282.4, 1283.1, 1283.05, 1287.4 & 1287.6

§ 1281. A written agreement to submit to arbitration an existing controversy or a controversy thereafter arising is valid, enforceable and irrevocable, save upon such grounds as exist for the revocation of any contract.

§ 1282.4. A party to the arbitration has the right to be represented by an attorney at any proceeding or hearing in arbitration under this title. A waiver of this right may be revoked; but if a party revokes such waiver, the other party is entitled to a reasonable continuance for the purpose of procuring an attorney.

§ 1283.1. (a) All of the provisions of Section 1283.05 shall be conclusively deemed to be incorporated into, made a part of, and shall be applicable to, every agreement to arbitrate any dispute, controversy, or issue arising out of or resulting from any injury to, or death of, a person caused by the wrongful act or neglect of another.
   (b) Only if the parties by their agreement so provide, may the provisions of Section 1283.05 be incorporated into, made a part of, or made applicable to, any other arbitration agreement.

§ 1283.05. To the extent provided in Section 1283.1 depositions may be taken and discovery obtained in arbitration proceedings as follows:
   (a) After the appointment of the arbitrator or arbitrators, the parties to the arbitration shall have the right to take depositions and to obtain discovery regarding the subject matter of the arbitration, and, to that end, to use and exercise all of the same rights, remedies, and procedures, and be subject to all of the same duties, liabilities, and obligations in the arbitration with respect to the subject matter thereof, as provided in Chapter 2 (commencing with Section 1985) of, and Article 3 (commencing with Section 2016) of Chapter 3 of, Title 3 of Part 4 of this code, as if the subject matter of the arbitration were pending in a civil action before a superior court of this state, subject to the limitations as to depositions set forth in subdivision (e) of this section.
   (b) The arbitrator or arbitrators themselves shall have power, in addition to the power of determining the merits of the arbitration, to enforce the rights, remedies, procedures, duties, liabilities, and obligations of discovery by the imposition of the same terms, conditions, consequences, liabilities, sanctions, and penalties as can be or may be imposed in like circumstances in a civil action by a superior court of this state under the provisions of this code, except the power to order the arrest or imprisonment of a person.
   (c) The arbitrator or arbitrators may consider, determine, and make such orders imposing such terms, conditions, consequences, liabilities, sanctions, and penalties, whenever necessary or appropriate at any time or stage in the course of the arbitration, and such orders shall be as conclusive, final, and enforceable as an arbitration award on the merits, if the making of any such order that is equivalent to an award or correction of an award is subject to the same conditions, if any, as are applicable to the making of an award or correction of an award.
   (d) For the purpose of enforcing the duty to make discovery, to produce evidence or information, including books and records, and to produce persons to testify at a deposition or at a hearing, and to impose terms, conditions, consequences, liabilities, sanctions, and penalties upon a party for violation of any such duty, such party shall be deemed to include every affiliate of such party as defined in this section. For such purpose:
   (1) The personnel of every such affiliate shall be deemed to be the officers, directors, managing agents, agents, and employees of such party to the same degree as each of them, respectively, bears such status to such affiliate; and
   (2) The files, books, and records of every such affiliate shall be deemed to be in the possession and control of, and capable of production by, such party. As used in this section, "affiliate" of the party to the arbitration means and includes any party or person for whose immediate benefit the action or proceeding is prosecuted or defended, or an officer, director, superintendent, member, agent, employee, or managing agent of such party or persons.
   (e) Depositions for discovery shall not be taken unless leave to do so is first granted by the arbitrator or arbitrators.

§ 1287.4. If an award is confirmed, judgment shall be entered in conformity therewith. The judgment so entered has the same force and effect as, and is subject to all the provisions of law relating to, a judgment in a civil action; and it may be enforced like any other judgment of the court in which it is entered.

§ 1287.6. An award that has not been confirmed or vacated has the same force and effect as a contract in writing between the parties to the arbitration.

Provisions in Listing Agreements

[§2.68] Form: Property To Be Sold

Former CC §1624(5), cited in Book §2.68, is now designated as CC §1624(d).

[§2.69] Form: Purchase Price

Chapter 5 does not discuss exchanges. See instead Real Property Exchanges (Cal CEB 1982).

Buyer's Deposit

[§2.71] Form: Handling of Deposits

A broker is required to deposit funds into an interest-bearing account if the owner of the funds or principals in the transaction so request. Bus & P C §10145(d).

The treatise by Miller & Starr, cited in the Book, has been replaced by 1 Miller & Starr, California Real Estate §2.9 (2d ed 1989).

[§2.82] Execution

Former CC §1624(5), cited in Book §2.82, now is designated as CC §1624(d).

Buyer-Broker Agreements

[§2.83] General Considerations

See discussion of *Renaissance Realty, Inc. v Soriano* (1981) 120 CA3d Supp 13, 174 CR 837, in Update §2.44.

DUTIES AND LIABILITIES

Broker to Principal

[§2.86] Broker's Fiduciary Duty

Former CC §§2228–2240, on the obligations of a trustee, have been repealed. Trustees' duties to beneficiaries are now defined by Prob C §§16000–16015.

For a discussion of real estate brokers' fiduciary duty, see *Jorgensen v Beach 'N' Bay Realty, Inc.* (1981) 125 CA3d 155, 177 CR 882, discussed in Update §2.94.

[§2.88] Expiration May Survive Closing

The citation to *Beeler v West Am. Fin. Co.* (1962) 201 CA2d 702, 20 CR 190, in Book §2.88, is incorrect; the agency in that case had not expired when the broker violated the confidential relationship. Nevertheless, brokers are under a duty to deal fairly and honestly with their principals (Bus & P C §10176(i)), and this duty could well be held to require that after expiration of the agency the broker not take advantage of confidential information acquired during the agency. 2 Witkin, Summary of California Law, *Agency & Employment* §43 (9th ed 1987); Restatement (Second) of Agency §396 (1958). See also *Realty Projects, Inc. v Smith* (1973) 32 CA3d 204, 108 CR 71 (mortgage loan broker's duty of fair and honest dealing arises when the borrower is only prospective and before any loan documents have been executed).

[§2.89] Duty To Disclose

A broker's duty to disclose was expanded from a duty to disclose material facts known to the broker to an affirmative duty to conduct a reasonably competent and diligent inspection of the residential property listed for sale and to disclose to prospective purchasers all facts revealed by the investigation that materially affect the value or desirability of the property. *Easton v Strassburger* (1984) 152 CA3d 90, 199 CR 383. *Easton* concerned a landslide, and one or more agents of the broker knew that the residence was built on landfill, which often leads to settlement and erosion problems. Moreover, one agent observed an "uneven floor," which is considered a "red flag" indicator of soil problems. For a form containing a provision for a broker's required disclosure of material facts revealed by a reasonable inspection, see Update §1.69A.

Civil Code §2079, effective January 1, 1986, partially codifies the *Easton* decision by creating a duty of real estate brokers to prospective purchasers of real property comprising from one to four residential units to conduct a reasonably competent and diligent visual inspection of property offered for sale and to disclose to prospective purchasers all facts materially affecting the value or desirability of the property. See also Update §1.69 regarding new specific written disclosures required in sales transactions involving real property improved with one to four dwelling units.

The real estate broker may satisfy the requirement that he or she inform prospective purchasers of common environmental hazards by delivering to the transferee a booklet on that subject that the Department of Real Estate has been instructed to prepare under Bus & P C §10084.1. CC §2079.7. A broker or seller may satisfy the requirement to inform prospective purchasers of geologic or seismic hazards in general by delivering to the transferee a booklet on earthquake preparedness described in Bus & P C §10149.

In *Smith v Rickard* (1988) 205 CA3d 1354, 254 CR 633, the broker inspection and disclosure duties in CC §§2079–2079.7 and *Easton v Strassburger, supra,* were held not to apply to the sale of a 50-acre commercial orchard property that contained a single family residence, because the undisclosed defect related to the commercial portion of the property (diseased orchard trees) only.

Unless the property has been previously occupied, the disclosure duty imposed on real estate brokers by CC §2079 does not apply to transfers required to be preceded by a public report under Bus & P C §11018.1 or to transfers that can be made without a public report under Bus & P C §11010.4. CC §2079.6.

A broker should always disclose knowledge of substantial damage noted in a termite report. *Godfrey v Steinpress* (1982) 128 CA3d 154, 180 CR 95. In *Godfrey* the broker failed to disclose a second termite report indicating $1155 of needed repairs. The buyers won a judgment against him for $81,800, including punitive damages and damages for emotional distress.

A broker may have a duty to advise a lessee client of the lessor's actual ownership interest in the leased premises. See *George Ball Pac., Inc. v Coldwell Banker & Co.* (1981) 117 CA3d 248, 172 CR 597, discussed in 4 CEB Real Prop L Rep 85 (July 1981).

A broker may have a duty to disclose certain information regarding seller financing, as an "arranger of credit" under CC §§2956–2967. See Update §5.1A for discussion of those sections. See the discussion of *Gray v Fox* (1984) 151 CA3d 482, 198 CR 720, in Update §2.109.

[§2.90] Dual Representation

Former CC §2230, prohibiting a trustee from holding an interest adverse to the beneficiary, has been repealed. Substantially similar language is now found in Prob C §16004. See Bus & P C §10177(o), discussed in Update §2.110.

[§2.94] Speculative Purchases and Resales

In *Jorgensen v Beach 'N' Bay Realty, Inc.* (1981) 125 CA3d 155, 177 CR 882, the court held that a prima facie case of fraud, misrepresentation, and breach of fiduciary duty is stated when an agent who represents both buyer and seller fails to disclose to the seller that the buyer is an investor who intends to quickly resell the property. That may be a material fact that could have affected seller's decision to sell. The property had been listed at $214,500 and sold for $200,000, and immediately resold for $227,000. The court noted that the immediate resale at a higher price strongly suggested that the original sale price was below comparable values and held that expert testimony is not required to establish that the agent was negligent in setting the sale price.

[§§2.95–2.96] Brokers' Purchase of Principal's Property; Disclosure Requirements; Indirect Sales

Former CC §2235, expressing the presumption that transactions between a trustee and a beneficiary by which the trustee gains any advantage from the beneficiary are presumed to be under undue influence, has been repealed. Probate Code §16004(c) now contains similar language but is expressed in terms of creating a presumption of a violation of the trustee's fiduciary duties. Former CC §2230, requiring full disclosure and the consent of beneficiaries when the trustee deals with trust property, has also been repealed. Similar disclosure is now required by Prob C §16463.

See Bus & P C §10177(o), discussed in Update §2.110.

[§2.100] Duty To Exercise Reasonable Care

The citation in Book §2.100 to Bus & P C §§10170–10170.6 should now be to Bus & P C §§10170–10170.5.

[§2.102] Duty To Account

Title 10 Cal Adm C §§2833 and 2835 (now called the California Code of Regulations) have been repealed.

Remedies Against Broker

[§2.104] Damages for Breach of Fiduciary Duty

On the damages obtainable when a broker negligently misrepresents to a buyer that the seller has accepted the purchase offer, see *Gray v Don Miller & Assoc.* (1984) 35 C3d 498, 198 CR 551. *Gray* held that a broker who has committed fraud is not liable for the defrauded party's attorneys' fees absent any exception to the general rule that each party bear his or her own attorneys' fees. In so holding, the court disapproved that portion of *Walters v Marler* (1978) 83 CA3d 1, 147 CR 655, cited in Bock §2.104, upholding a fee award.

[§2.107] Punitive Damages

Civil Code §3294 has been amended to provide that oppression, fraud, or malice must be proved by clear and convincing evidence. The amendment also changed the definition of malice so that the defendant's conduct must be despicable and done with a willful and conscious disregard of the rights or safety of others. The definition of oppression was changed to mean despicable conduct that subjects a person to cruel and unjust hardship in conscious disregard of that person's rights. The amendments apply to all actions in which the initial trial has not commenced before January 1, 1988.

[§2.109] Recovery of Unsatisfied Judgments From the Real Estate Fund

Business and Professions Code §§10470–10483 were repealed operative January 1, 1987, and replaced by new Bus & P C §§10470–10481 (Real Estate Recovery Program). The change concerns the process by which application is made to the Department of Real Estate for recovery, including use of a prescribed form (see Update §2.109A for a copy of the form) and the placing of additional duties on both the applicant and the Real Estate Commissioner. The intent of the legislation apparently is to have the Department of Real Estate determine claims against the recovery fund instead of the courts. The legislation provides that former law will prevail for applications filed before January 1, 1987, regarding any inconsistencies between the old law and the new legislation. Stats 1985, ch 690, §4. Business and Professions Code §10471 was further amended effective January 1, 1988, to allow recovery from the real estate fund following an arbitration award that has been confirmed and reduced to judgment under CCP §1287.4.

The new legislation renumbers some sections as follows:

Former *Bus & P C §*	*Bus & P C §* *(Operative Jan. 1, 1987)*
10471	10471, 10471.1, 10474
10472	10471, 10472.1
10474	10473, 10474
10483	10481

The limitations on recovery for each "transaction" in former Bus & P C §10471 are found in new Bus & P C §10474, and the one-year statute of limitations in former Bus & P C §10472 is found in new Bus & P C §10471(b).

When a party applies for payment from the real estate fund of an uncollected judgment against a licensee, the Commissioner of the Department of Real Estate may relitigate material and relevant issues determined in the underlying action, but the licensee is severely restricted in what he or she may relitigate. Bus & P C §§10473–10473.1. But see *Deas v Knapp* (1981) 29 C3d 69, 171 CR 823, in which the court held that in an action for recovery against the real estate fund, the underlying judgment for damages resulting from fraud, misrepresentation, deceit, or conversion of trust funds, if contested by the broker (see Bus & P C §10473), creates only a rebuttable presumption of the broker's fraud, misrepresentation, deceit, or conversion of trust funds. The broker is entitled to present evidence in the action for recovery against the fund to rebut that presumption. In the action for recovery, the broker may not relitigate issues other than whether his or her actions were fraud, misrepresentation, deceit, or conversion. The determination in the underlying action of who is entitled to judgment was held to be res judicata in the subsequent appellate decision. *Deas v Knapp* (1982) 129 CA3d 443, 181 CR 76. If the trial court makes no finding that the broker committed fraud, but renders a judgment against the broker for simple breach of contract, the judgment creditor cannot raise the issue of fraud in the action for recovery against the fund; it is res judicata. *Stuart v Department of Real Estate* (1983) 148 CA3d 1, 195 CR 524.

The amount awarded to the applicant from the fund must be reduced by any monetary income tax benefits the applicant received as a result of the transaction. *Froid v Fox* (1982) 132 CA3d 832, 183 CR 461. In *Froid*, the applicants, who were held entitled to recover from the fund, had their awards reduced by the amount of reduction in their federal income tax attributable to the investment tax shelter provided in the underlying transaction.

When a broker agrees to accept a commission as part of a sales transaction in which he is also a buyer and intends to immediately resell the property to third parties at a higher price, he assumes all the fiduciary duties to the seller that brokers usually have, including the duty to disclose all facts known to him that are material to the sale. When the broker breaches those duties, and the sellers suffer damages, the sellers are entitled to reimbursement from the Real Estate Fund. *Gray v Fox* (1984) 151 CA3d 482, 198 CR 720.

In *Gray*, a licensed broker was obtaining a split of the listing broker's commission (which was disclosed to the sellers) and was buying the property for himself. He offered $120,000, and the sellers accepted. Without informing the sellers, the broker arranged to immediately resell the property for $144,000. In escrow, the sellers became concerned that the broker was trying to cheat them and got the broker to sign cancellation papers. Under pressure to make the sale quickly, the sellers accepted a cash offer of $115,000. Sellers sought reimbursement for the difference between what they would have received, had the broker not breached his fiduciary duties and informed them of the third party buyers ($144,000), and the $115,000 they received. The court held that, because the transaction was one for which a real estate license was required and because the sellers were damaged as a result of the broker's conduct, they were entitled to recover $5000 from the fund. This was the difference between the price the broker agreed to pay ($120,000) and the price the sellers finally received ($115,000).

This holding and the award of $5000 appear to be in error. The causes of action sellers pursued at trial against the broker were fraud, deceit, negligent misrepresentation, and breach of contract. A default judgment was entered for $5000. Although the opinion does not state the basis for the trial court's decision, $5000 would logically be the amount of a judgment only for breach of the contract to buy the property. If this was so, the appellate court should not have awarded any recovery from the fund, because Bus & P C §10471(a) permits recovery only when a final judgment on the grounds of fraud, misrepresentation, deceit, or conversion of trust funds is obtained. If the trial court had found fraud, it should have awarded $29,000 ($144,000 minus $115,000), and the appellate court could then have awarded the maximum $10,000 recovery from the fund. Note that for causes of action occurring after 1980, the maximum recovery is $20,000. Bus & P C §10474(c).

Interestingly, former Bus & P C §10471(a) provided only that the final judgment based on grounds of fraud, misrepresentation, deceit, or conversion of trust funds arises "directly out of any transaction when the [broker] was licensed and performed acts for which a license is required." That section did not explicitly require that the broker's misconduct be proved the cause of the damages. The court, however, held that the sellers were damaged as a result of the broker's fraudulent conduct. Based on the award of $5000, it appears that the court found that the sellers were damaged by the broker's breach of contract instead.

The language from Bus & P C §10471(a) quoted above was first changed in 1986 and again in 1987, effective January 1, 1988; it reads, "directly out of any transaction not in violation of Section 10137 or 10138 in which the defendant, while licensed under this part, performed acts for which that license was required." The changes appear to follow the court's reasoning in *Merrifield v Edmonds* (1983) 146 CA3d 336, 194 CR 104, in which a judgment against a real estate salesperson for failure to pay back two personal loans was found not to have arisen "directly" from a real estate transaction, so recovery from the fund was denied. Additionally, recovery from the fund was not permitted based on a judgment for losses arising from the saleperson's nonresident property management. The court found that a broker's license, not just a salesperson's license, was required for nonresident property management and held that former Bus & P C §10471 required the loss to arise from a transaction in which a licensed judgment debtor had performed acts for which the judgment debtor's license was required. The judgment creditor in *Merrifield* could have entered into a valid nonresident property management contract only with a licensed broker. Therefore, the court reasoned, the judgment creditor was not protected by the fund as an "innocent member of the public," because he entered into an illegal contract with the salesperson. The court noted that, under Bus & P C §10138, the judgment creditor committed a misdemeanor by paying the salesperson.

Merrifield was distinguished in *Vinci v Edmonds* (1986) 185 CA3d 1251, 230 CR 308. In *Vinci* a salesperson misrepresented that he was a licensed broker and defrauded plaintiffs in a short term swing loan transaction for which a broker's license is required. Although the salesperson was not licensed for the acts performed, the court in *Vinci* held that the plaintiffs were innocent members of the public who were within the class of individuals the Real Estate Recovery Program was intended to benefit. The court found that the plaintiffs in *Vinci* had been deceived about the salesperson's status and were free from any wrongdoing themselves, unlike the plaintiff in *Merrifield* who knew the true status of the salesperson and was wrong in paying the salesperson. It appears that the language of new Bus & P C §10471(a) will prevent a ruling such as that in *Vinci*.

In *Dierenfield v Stabile* (1988) 198 CA3d 126, 243 CR 598, the court distinguished *Merrifield* on a basis similar to that in *Vinci*. In *Dierenfield*, a salesperson's employment with a broker was necessary if secured real property loans that the salesperson was arranging for a lender were to be exempt from usury prohibitions. The salesperson fraudulently concealed from the lender the fact that the salesperson had ended his employment with the broker. The appellate court held that because of this concealment the lender qualified as an innocent member of the public and thus could recover from the recovery fund. However, the lender, who settled with his borrowers after they filed a complaint for usury, was denied the difference between the interest he received and the interest agreed to be paid by the borrowers because such benefit-of-the-bargain damages were not "actual and direct loss" as provided in Bus & P C §10471.

A finding of negligent misrepresentation is sufficient for recovery from the fund, according to the court in *Andrepont v Meeker* (1984) 158 CA3d 878, 204 CR 887. Recovery of damages for emotional distress, punitive damages, and attorneys' fees has not been allowed from the fund. *Temple v Kerwin* (1989) 209 CA3d 1087, 257 CR 651; *Lewis v Edmonds* (1987) 190 CA3d 1101, 235 CR 835; *Acebo v Real Estate Educ., Research & Recovery Fund* (1984) 155 CA3d 907, 202 CR 518.

A party defrauded as part of a scheme involving multiple licensees may be entitled to recovery from the account of any licensed judgment debtor. *Edmonds v Augustyn* (1987) 193 CA3d 1056, 238 CR 704. The holding in *Edmonds* was codified in Bus & P C §10474(d), operative August 23, 1988. The legislature declared that the new subsection was not intended to overturn the cases of *Fox v Prime Ventures, Ltd.* (1978) 86 CA3d 333, 150 CR 202 (when transaction from which judgments arose required only one license, limit of liability of fund was $20,000, although both judgment debtors, the corporation and its designated officer, were licensees), and *Deas v Knapp, supra*.

The burden of proof requirement of Bus & P C §10472(b)(6) requires parties attempting to recover from the real estate fund to demonstrate that they acted with due diligence in pursuing their remedies against all persons liable to them in the transaction. In *Fine v Southern Cal. Business Sales, Inc.* (1987) 190 CA3d 480, 235 CR 489, recovery from the real estate fund was denied because the party seeking recovery failed to sue the officers and employees of the broker individually after it filed for bankruptcy.

An amendment to Bus & P C §10471, effective January 1, 1988, requires a claimant to represent that the underlying judgment and debt were not discharged in bankruptcy, or, in the case of a still open bankruptcy proceeding, that the payment and discharge have been declared nondischargeable. The court in *Rogers v Edmonds* (1988) 200 CA3d 1237, 248 CR 15, held that the amendment did not apply retroactively.

The separate account for research, education, and recovery has been divided into two accounts, the recovery account and the education and research account. Bus & P C §10450.6.

[§2.109A] Form: Application for Payment From Recovery Account of Real Estate Fund; Instructions for Application

Form 2.109A–1

State of California   Department of Real Estate
                                                                       Recovery Account Unit
**RECOVERY ACCOUNT —
APPLICATION FOR PAYMENT**

RE 808 (Rev. 1/88)

General Information

- Section 10471.1(a) of the Business and Professions Code requires that a copy of both sides of the Notice (RE 809) and a copy of this Application, be served on the judgment debtor.

- Notice to claimant regarding bankruptcy required by Section 10471(d) of the Business and Professions Code: The claimant must protect the underlying debt and judgment from discharge in bankruptcy. That means that the underlying debt and judgment must not have been discharged in a completed bankruptcy; or in the case of a bankruptcy open at the time of filing the Application, the claimant must demonstrate that the judgment and debt have been declared to be nondischargeable.

- To expedite handling, send the application by certified mail to: Department of Real Estate
                                                                      Recovery Account Unit
                                                                      P. O. Box 187000
                                                                      Sacramento, CA 95818-7000

- Attach extra paper if more space is needed.

PART I — INFORMATION REQUIRED BY STATUTE

- Submission of all of the following information requested in this Part is required by Section 10471(c) of the Business and Professions Code (attach extra paper if more space is needed).

- Be sure to notify the Department of any change in address or telephone.

1. Claimant's Name

Street Address			Telephone Number
City	State	Zip Code	

Attorney's Name (complete only if represented by an attorney in this recovery application)

Street Address			Telephone Number
City	State	Zip Code	

2. List the Name and Address of Judgment Debtor(s). If the addresses of any of the judgment debtors is unknown, the names and addresses of persons who may know the judgment debtor(s) present whereabouts must be provided.

Name	Address

3. IDENTIFICATION OF THE JUDGMENT	A1. Date of Judgment	A2. Court and Court File Number

B. Itemized Amount of Judgment (list the basis and amount of each element of compensatory damages awarded):

_____

_____

_____

_____

_____

_____

1) Court-Awarded Costs: $ _____

2) Interest Awarded, if any : * $ _____

3) Punitive Damages, if any: $ _____

4) Attorney's Fees, if any: $ _____

* Explain below, from what date, at what rate, and on what amounts the interest was computed:

_____

_____

_____

_____

C. Attach to the Application a copy of the *Judgment* bearing the court's file stamp.

4. Amount of Claim Against the Recovery Account: $_____

☞ By statute and decisional case law, only a claimant's "actual and direct loss," plus interest at the legal rate from the date of loss, and court costs, are payable from the Recovery Account. Therefore the actual and direct loss may differ from the amounts awarded in the judgment. Actual and direct loss usually does not include such things as loss of anticipated profits and attorneys fees, and never includes punitive damages. The following questions must be answered in order that it may be determined whether the amounts sought to be paid from the Recovery Account are allowable.

A. Itemize and explain how the amount of the claim was computed:

_____

_____

_____

_____

_____

_____

_____

_____

5. Itemize and explain the actual out of pocket loss upon which the claim against the Recovery Account is based:

_____

_____

_____

_____

_____

_____

_____

_____

_____

_____

_____

_____

_____

C. Itemize and explain any amount being claimed above and beyond the actual and direct loss and explain why it is believed that those amounts are collectible from the Recovery Account. Punitive damages are not collectible from the Recovery Account, and loss of anticipated profits and attorneys fees are also normally not collectible, so if anything is claimed for those items be sure to explain why it is asserted that those items are collectible.

_____

_____

_____

_____

_____

_____

_____

_____

_____

_____

_____

§2.109A   48

5. Answer the following questions and provide the following information:

A. Is the claimant a spouse of the judgment debtor or a personal representative of the spouse? ❑ Yes ❑ No

B. Is the judgment upon which this claim is made a final judgment in a court of competent jurisdiction? ❑ Yes ❑ No

C. Is the judgment based upon the defendant's fraud, misrepresentation, deceit, made with intent to defraud; or conversion of trust funds? ❑ Yes ❑ No

D. Did the conduct of the defendant upon which the judgment is based arise directly out of a transaction in which the defendant was licensed by the Department of Re Estate? ❑ Yes ❑ No

E. In the transaction referred to in "D" above, was the defendant performing acts for which the license held by the defendant was required? ❑ Yes ❑ No

F. Is there attached to the Application a description of all searches and inquiries conducted by or on behalf of the claimant with respect to the judgment debtor's assets liable to be sold or applied to satisfaction of the judgment, an itemized valuation of any assets discovered, and a description of the results of actions by the claimant to have the assets applied to satisfaction of the judgment? ❑ Yes ❑ No

G. Has the claimant diligently pursued collection efforts against other judgment debtors and all other persons liable to the claimant in the transaction that is the basis for the underlying judgment? ❑ Yes ❑ No

H. Was the Application mailed or delivered to the Department no later than one year after the underlying judgment became final? ❑ Yes ❑ No

I. Is the underlying judgment one based upon a determination of nondischargeability in a bankruptcy proceeding filed by the judgment debtor? ❑ Yes ❑ No

   a. If yes to Item I, proceed to Item #6.
   b. If no to Item I, did the judgment debtor file a bankruptcy? ❑ Yes ❑ No

      1) If no to Item Ib, proceed to Item #6.
      2) If yes to Item Ib, please answer the following:

         a) When did the judgment debtor file bankruptcy? _____

         b) Did the claimant file a claim in the bankruptcy? ❑ Yes ❑ No

         If no, please explain why not.

c) Was any attempt made to have the debt to the claimant determined to be nondischargeable? .... ❑ Yes ❑ No

If no, please explain why not.
If yes, what was the result?

_____

_____

_____

_____

_____

d) Was the debt underlying the judgment, and/or the judgment, discharged in the bankruptcy proceeding? .... ❑ Yes ❑ No

If yes, when? .... _____

6. Attach to the Application a detailed narrative statement of facts, signed under penalty of perjury, explaining the allegations of the complaint upon which the judgment is based. This should be a coherent explanation of the claimant's relationship with the licensee, the nature of the transaction or transactions in which the claimant was involved with the licensee, and the nature of the involvement of any other person, particularly anyone else named as a plaintiff, defendant, cross-complainant, or cross-defendant. A *chronological* description is usually best.

7. Attach to the Application a statement by the claimant, signed under penalty of perjury, that the complaint upon which the underlying judgment is based was prosecuted conscientiously and in good faith. "Conscientiously and in good faith" means that no party potentially liable to the claimant in the underlying transaction was intentionally and without good cause omitted from the complaint, that no party named in the complaint who otherwise reasonably appeared capable of responding in damages was dismissed from the complaint intentionally and without good cause, and that the claimant employed no other procedural tactics contrary to the diligent prosecution of the complaint in order to provide access to the Recovery Account.

PART II — ADDITIONAL INFORMATION

As indicated in the Instructions to this Application, there are two ways an Application can be made substantially complete:

A. By submitting *all* information listed in the Recovery Account statutes and regulations. This approach would be accomplished if:

1) Part I of this form is completed and served upon the Department; and

2) *All* of the information required by Regulation 3102 is supplied with the Application.

B. By submitting *all* information required by statute, but less than all the items listed in Regulation 3102. This approach would be accomplished if:

1) Part I of this form is completed and served upon the Department; and

2) Enough information is submitted for the Department to make a determination whether the application qualifies, though not necessarily all the items listed in Regulation 3102, and the Department is allowed to notify the claimant if what was submitted is sufficient.

Therefore, to follow the second approach, after completing Part I of the Application, please answer the following questions and provide the following information:

1. Attach proof of service of the Notice and Application on the judgment debtor. The Application will *not* be treated as substantially complete without this item. See the Instructions or Section 10471.1(b) of the Business and Professions Code for what constitutes proper service.

2. Attach a copy of the Complaint, Cross-Complaint, or the amended version of those documents upon which the judgment is based, and a copy of any minute order, statement of decision, or other statement by the court explaining the basis for the judgment.

3. Explain the basis of the contention that the defendant was performing acts for which the license held by the defendant was required.

_____

_____

_____

_____

_____

4. If the judgment debtor was licensed only as a salesperson at the time of the transaction, was the broker who employed the judgment debtor at the time sued? .... ❑ Yes ❑ No
   If not, why not? _____

_____

_____

_____

_____

_____

_____

5. Was any person liable or potentially liable to the claimant in the transaction either not sued or dismissed from the lawsuit? .... ❑ Yes ❑ No
   If so, explain why, and itemize any funds or other consideration received from that person or persons in settlement of the potential liability of that person or persons.

_____

_____

_____

_____

_____

_____

6. Did any other person or persons liable or potentially liable to the claimant in the transaction
   file bankruptcy? .... ❑ Yes   ❑ No

   a. If no, proceed to Item #7.
   b. If yes, please answer the following.

   1) What is the name of the person or persons? .... _____

   2) When did the person file bankuptcy? .... _____

   3) Did the claimant file a claim in the bankruptcy? .... ❑ Yes   ❑ No

       If no, please explain why not.

       _____

       _____

       _____

       _____

       _____

       _____

   4) Was any attempt made to have the debt to the claimant determined to be nondis-
       chargeable? .... ❑ Yes   ❑ No

       If no, please explain why not.
       If yes, what was the result?

       _____

       _____

       _____

       _____

       _____

   5) Was the debt underlying the judgment, and/or the judgment, discharged in the bank-
       ruptcy proceeding? .... ❑ Yes   ❑ No

       If yes, when? .... _____

7. Attach copies of abstracts of judgment bearing evidence of having been recorded in the county or counties in which the
   judgment debtor may possibly have assets.

☞ If the information supplied in PART II is insufficient for the Department to determine whether the Application qualifies
   for payment, you will receive an itemized list of any deficiencies.

PART III — VERIFICATION

VERIFICATION BY CLAIMANT

STATE OF CALIFORNIA, COUNTY OF _____

    I am the Claimant in this Application; I have read the Application and all attachments thereto and know the contents thereof; and I certify that the same is true of my own knowledge, except as to those matters which are therein stated upon my information or belief, as to which matters I believe them to be true; and I further certify that all documents attached to the Application are true and correct copies of the originals, and if such documents purport to be copies of documents filed in court, they are true and correct copies of the originals filed with the court.

Executed on _____ ____ at _____, California.

I declare, under penalty of perjury, that the foregoing is true and correct.

_____
Signature

VERIFICATION BY ATTORNEY

    I am the attorney for the Claimant in this Application. The Claimant is absent from the County where I have my offices, and I make this verification for and on behalf of the Claimant for that reason. I have read the Application and all attachments thereto and know the contents thereof; and I certify that the same is true of my own knowledge, except as to those matters which are therein stated upon my information or belief, as to which matters I believe them to be true; and I further certify that all documents attached to the Application are true and correct copies of the originals, and if such documents purport to be copies of documents filed in court, they are true and correct copies of the originals filed with the court.

Executed on _____ at _____, California.

I declare, under penalty of perjury, that the foregoing is true and correct.

_____
Signature

VERIFICATION BY OUT-OF-STATE CLAIMANT

STATE OF _____ COUNTY OF_____

    I am the Claimant in the Application; I have read the Application and all attachments thereto and know the contents thereof; and I certify that the same is true of my own knowledge, except as to those matters which are therein stated upon my information or belief, as to which matters I believe them to be true; and I further certify that all documents attached to the Application are true and correct copies of the originals, and if such documents purport to be copies of documents filed in court, they are true and correct copies of the originals filed with the court.

I declare under penalty of perjury under the laws of the State of California that the foregoing is true and correct.

_____   _____
Date   *Signature*

PART IV — SUMMARY

A. At this point, the Application must, at a minimum, contain all the information required in Part I, which would include as attachments the first three items listed below.

    1. A copy of the judgment bearing the court's file stamp.

    2. The detailed narrative statement of the facts referred to in Part I, Item 6.

    3. The description of searches and inquiries referred to in Part I, Item 5F.

B. The Application should also contain as attachments all documents submitted in support of the Application, which may be all of the items listed in Regulation 3102, but in no event will the Application be treated as substantially complete until proof has been supplied that the judgment debtor was served with the Notice and Application.

C. As to the Application and all documentation submitted with it, the appropriate Verification must be signed.

Form 2.109A–2

State of California

RECOVERY ACCOUNT –
INSTRUCTIONS TO CLAIMANTS

RE 807 (Rev. 1/88)

Department of Real Estate
Recovery Account Unit

INSTRUCTIONS TO CLAIMANTS

❖ Note: In order to qualify for payment from the Recovery Account, the claimant must protect the underlying debt and judgment from discharge in bankruptcy. See Part IX, General Requirements and Restrictions, for further information.

❖ The Application for Payment (RE 808) and the enclosed Notice to Judgment Debtor (RE 809) must be served on the judgment debtor before the Application can be made substantially complete.

❖ As explained below, the Application may be served on the Department either by certified mail or personal delivery at an office of the Department. To expedite handling of the Application and minimize the chances of it being misplaced, it is recommended that the Application be served on the Department by sending it certified mail to:

> Department of Real Estate
> Recovery Account Unit
> P.O. Box 187000
> Sacramento, CA 95818-7000

PART I.   GENERAL INFORMATION

A. Before attempting to fill out the Application, you should read the description of general requirements and restrictions contained in Part IX.

B. Description of Approaches to Making An Application "Substantially Complete".

As mentioned in the attached cover letter, the Department will have 90 days from the receipt of a "substantially complete" application in which to evaluate the Application, make a determination as to whether it qualifies for payment, and if so, for how much. If the Department does not act within the 90 days, the Application is automatically denied. It is the applicant's responsibility to supply sufficient information and documentation for the application to be evaluated, i.e., to make the Application "substantially complete". Under the Regulations governing Recovery Account Applications (see attached copies of Regulations 3101 and 3102), there are two ways to make the Application substantially complete:

1. Meet all the requirements of Part I of the Application (this much is required by law), and meet all the requirements of Regulation 3102. If these require-

ments are met, the Department is required to treat the Application as substantially complete, the 90 days within which the Department must act starts running, and the Department must notify all parties of the date on which the substantially complete application was received. If there are any deficiencies in what is submitted, the Department must provide the claimant with an itemized list of deficiencies within 15 days after the Application is submitted. However, in recognition of the fact that in less complicated cases, not all the information required by Regulation 3102 may be necessary, the Regulations provide the following alternative approach.

2. Regulation 3101 allows the Department to treat an Application as substantially complete if less than all the information required by Regulation 3102 is submitted, but enough information is provided for the Department to determine whether the Application qualifies for payment. If what is submitted is sufficient, the Department will notify the parties that the application is substantially complete, and the 90 days will start running from the date the substantially complete application was received. If what is submitted is insufficient for the Department to evaluate the application, the Department must provide the claimant with an itemized list of deficiencies within 15 days after submission. Part II of the Application can serve as a guide to what should suffice in most cases.

☛   *Part I of the Application must be completed under either approach.*

PART II.   COMPLETING THE APPLICATION

A. Complete Part I of the Application. This much is required by Section 10471(c) of the Business and Professions Code.

B. Decide whether to make the Application substantially complete by meeting all the requirements of Regulation 3102, or complete Part II of the Application and submit enough supporting documentation and additional information for the Application to be evaluated.

☛   Be sure to make enough copies of the Application and supporting documents, since a copy of the Notice and Application with its supporting documentation must be served on the judgment debtor or debtors, and you will want a copy for your own records.

PART III   **SERVING THE NOTICE AND**
                 APPLICATION

A. *On the Department of Real Estate.* The original Application and supporting documentation (including proof of service of the Notice and Application on the judgment debtor) must be served on the Department of Real Estate within one year after the judgment becomes final. Note that the original Notice to Judgment Debtor (RE 809) *(front and back)* must be served on the judgment debtor. The law allows service to be by certified mail or by personal delivery to an office of the Department of Real Estate.

   1. **Certified Mail.** As noted elsewhere, to expedite handling of the Application it is recommended that it be served by certified mail at the address listed at the beginning of these instructions. Service by other means is risky because if the Application is substantially complete, but is lost, it will be automatically denied after 90 days.

   2. **Personal Delivery.** Service can be effected by personal delivery at an office of the Department of Real Estate. If this option is chosen, make sure that the Departmental employee to whom it is handed understands that it is a Recovery Account application. It is recommended that the claimant bring along his or her copy at the time of delivery and make sure the employee stamps both the original and the copy as "received".

B. *On the judgment Debtor(s).* **Both** the original Notice to the Judgment Debtor (RE 809), *front and back*, (enclosed after page 9 of the application) **and** a *copy* of the Application and its supporting documentation must be served on all judgment debtors whose activity as real estate licensees is the basis for the Recovery Account claim. Service may be accomplished in three ways:

   1. **By Registered Mail.** A judgment debtor may be served by registered mail if the judgment debtor holds a current license issued by the Department. Service is accomplished by mailing the Notice, Application, and supporting documentation by registered mail addressed to the judgment debtor at the latest business or residence address on file with the Department. Current licensing information can be obtained by calling the Department at 916-739-3758, or writing to the Department. If you write for the information, be sure to give the judgment debtor's full name, license identification number (if known), and the city where the judgment debtor was last known to reside or do business and address the inquiry to: Department of Real Estate, Licensing Information, P.O. Box 187000, Sacramento, CA 95813-7000.

☞   Service by registered mail is effective only if the judgment debtor holds a current license issued by the Department.

Proof of Service: Proof of service by this means may be accomplished by completing the attached Proof of Service – Registered Mail (RE 811).

   2. **By Personal Service.** A judgment debtor may be served with the Notice and Application by personally delivering a copy of each to the judgment debtor. Personal service may be effected by any person who is at least 18 years of age and not a party to the application proceeding.

Proof of service: Proof of service by this means may be accomplished by completing the attached Proof of Service – Personal (RE 810).

   3. **Service by Publication.** If the judgment debtor does not hold a current license issued by the Department and personal service cannot be effected through the exercise of reasonable diligence, the claimant can serve the judgment debtor by one publication of the Notice (first page of RE 809 only)* in each of two successive weeks in a newspaper of general circulation published in the county in which the judgment debtor was last known to reside. Note that this form of service is effective only if service by the other two means listed above is not possible. Service by publication is deemed complete on the date of last publication.

*   Be sure to include the names of all judgment debtors against whom application is being made.

Proof of service: Proof of service by this means may be accomplished by following the instructions on the attached Proof of Service – Publication (RE 812).

PART IV. RESPONSE BY THE JUDGMENT DEBTOR

The judgment debtor has 30 days after personal service, mailing, or final publication of the Notice within which to file a written response contesting the Application. Any such response must be served on both the claimant and the Department. If the judgment debtor does not file a timely response, he or she will not be entitled to any further notice of any action taken or proposed to be taken with respect to the Application.

If the judgment debtor does file a timely response to the Application, both the judgment debtor and the claimant will be given the opportunity to submit written argument. The Department will notify all parties of the appropriate time to submit argument.

PART V. DETERMINATION WHETHER APPLICATION IS SUBSTANTIALLY COMPLETE

The Department will notify the claimant within 15 days after service of the Application on the Department of any deficiencies in the application. If there are no deficiencies, or any deficiencies previously noted are corrected, the claimant, and any judgment debtor who has filed a timely response, will be notified of the date when the substantially complete Application was received. That date is the date from which the 90 days is computed within which the Department must act on the Application. If the Department does not act within that 90 days, the Application is automatically denied.

If the Department notifies the claimant of any deficiencies in the Application, and the claimant does not respond within a reasonable period of time (which is not less than six months), the Department will notify the claimant that the Application must be made substantially complete within a specified period of time (at least 30 days after mailing of the notice) or the Application will be denied.

Any documentation submitted in response to a list of deficiencies must be accompanied by:

1. the certification as to the authenticity of the documents as specified in Regulation 3102(s); and

2. proof that the documentation was also served on any judgment debtor who filed a response.

PART VI. ACTION ON THE APPLICATION

The Department will notify the claimant, and any judgment debtor who has filed a timely response, of the decision on the Application.

A. Decision to Make Payment. If the decision is to make a payment to the claimant out of the Recovery Account, a judgment debtor who filed a response will have 30 days following receipt of the notice of the decision to file a writ of mandamus for judicial review of the suspension of his or her license(s) and license rights which would result from a payment.

B. Decision to Deny the Application. If the decision is to deny payment on the Application, the claimant may pursue the Application in the court which rendered the underlying judgment. To do so, the claimant must file the application with the court not later than six months after receipt of the notice of denial of the Application.

PART VII. SUBSEQUENT SERVICE OF CORRESPONDENCE AND NOTICES

After initial service of the Application on the Department and of the Notice and Application on the judgment debtor, the parties must be served with subsequent correspondence and notices by first class mail as follows:

A. The Department must be served at:
   Department of Real Estate
   Recovery Account Unit
   P.O. Box 187000
   Sacramento, CA 95818-7000.

B. The claimant must be served at his or her address as specified in the Application, or if represented by an attorney, at the address of the attorney as specified in the Application.

C. A judgment debtor who has filed a timely response must be served at his or her address as specified in the response, or if represented by an attorney, at the address of the attorney as specified in the response.

☞ Any party having a change of address should notify the other parties of the new address. Failure to do so will result in correspondence and notices being legally served at the old address.

PART VIII. PRORATION

As noted in the following part, the maximum liability of the Recovery Account for any one licensee is limited. At any time prior to the rendering of a decision on a claim, if the Department determines that the aggregate valid claims of all aggrieved persons against that licensee are likely to exceed that limit, in lieu of further administrative proceedings the Department will terminate the application procedure and initiate a proceeding in court to prorate the funds available among the claimants.

Applications received by the Department relating to a particular judgment debtor subsequent to the filing of a proration action as to that judgment debtor will be returned to the claimant with a notification that the Application must be filed in the proration proceeding.

PART IX.   GENERAL REQUIREMENTS AND
            RESTRICTIONS

The rules governing applications for payment from the Recovery Account, both those filed with the Department and applications denied by the Department and refiled in court, are set forth in Sections 10470-10481 of the Business and Professions Code and in Sections 3100-3109 of the Regulations of the Real Estate Commissioner. They include the following:

A. The cause of action must have occurred after July 1, 1964.

B. The claimant must have obtained a final judgment against a real estate licensee based upon that person's fraud, misrepresentation, deceit, made with intent to defraud; or conversion of trust funds.

C. The fraud, etc., must have arisen directly out of a transaction in which the judgment debtor:

    1   was properly licensed at the time; and
    2   was performing acts for which that license was required.

Note: If a judgment is against a person licensed only as a salesperson, and at the time of the acts underlying the judgment the salesperson was not employed by a broker, or was acting outside the scope of employment of a broker, the judgment against that salesperson cannot form a basis for payment from the Recovery Account. See Section 10471(a) of the Business and Professions Code, which requires that the underlying transaction not be in violation of Section 10137 or 10138 of the Business and Professions Code. Those sections are reproduced in the enclosed form, Recovery Account – Regulation and Code Excerpts (RE 813).

D. Applications must be filed on the form prescribed by the Department and must be filed not later than one year after the underlying judgment became final.

    Applications filed with the court following a denial of an application by the Department must be filed with the court which rendered the underlying judgment within six months of receipt of notice of denial of the Application by the Department.

E. The judgment debtor must be served with the Application and both sides of the Notice (RE 809), and proper proof of service must be supplied to the Department.

F. The claimant must have diligently pursued collection efforts against the judgment debtor and all other persons liable to the claimant in the transaction that is the basis for the underlying judgment.

G. For any one transaction the liability of the Recovery Account is limited as follows:

    1. $20,000.00 per transaction for causes of action occurring on or after January 1, 1980;

    2. $10,000.00 per transaction for causes of action occurring before January 1, 1980.

H. For any one licensee the liability of the Recovery Account is limited as follows:

    1. $20,000.00 per licensee for causes of action occurring from July 1, 1964, to December 31, 1974;

    2. $40,000.00 per licensee for causes of action occurring from January 1, 1975, to December 31, 1979;

    3. $100,000.00 per licensee for causes of action occurring on and after January 1, 1980.

I. The claimant must protect the underlying debt and judgment from discharge in bankruptcy. That means that the underlying debt and judgment must not have been discharged in a completed bankruptcy; or in the case of a bankruptcy open at the time of filing the Application, the claimant must demonstrate that the judgment and debt have been declared to be nondischargeable.

J. The claimant must provide a statement, signed under penalty of perjury, that the complaint upon which the underlying judgment is based was prosecuted conscientiously and in good faith. "Conscientiously and in good faith" means that no party potentially liable to the claimant in the underlying transaction was intentionally and without good cause omitted from the complaint, that no party named in the complaint who otherwise reasonably appeared capable of responding in damages was dismissed from the complaint intentionally and without good cause, and that the claimant employed no other procedural tactics contrary to the diligent prosecution of the complaint in order to provide access to the Recovery Account.

[§2.109B] Notice of Application for Payment From Recovery Account of Real Estate Fund; Proof of Service

Form 2.109B–1

State of California

Department of Real Estate
Recovery Account Unit

NOTICE TO JUDGMENT DEBTOR
(Recovery Account Claim)

RE 809 (Rev. 1/88)

TO: *(Print names of all Judgment Debtors.)*

_____

NOTICE: Based upon a judgment entered against you in favor of _____

_____ ,
                            (Name of Claimant)
application for payment from the Recovery Account of the Real Estate Fund is being made to the Department
of Real Estate.

If payment is made from the Recovery Account, all licenses and license rights that you have under the
Real Estate Law will be automatically suspended on the date of payment and cannot be reinstated until the
Recovery Account has been reimbursed for the amount paid plus interest at the prevailing rate.

If you wish to contest payment by the Real Estate Commissioner, you must file a written response to the
application addressed to the Department of Real Estate at:

> Department of Real Estate
> Recovery Account Unit
> P.O. Box 187000
> Sacramento, CA 95818-7000

within 30 days after mailing, delivery, or publication of this notice and send a copy of that response to the
claimant. If you fail to do so, you will have waived your right to present your objections to payment.

☛ *See further instructions on the reverse of this Notice.*

INSTRUCTIONS TO JUDGMENT DEBTOR ON FILING A RESPONSE

A. The written response must contain a verification that a copy of the response was sent to the claimant, or if the claimant is represented by an attorney, to the claimant's attorney, at the address specified in the Application for the claimant or his attorney.

B. If you wish to file a response and will not be represented by an attorney, the response must contain your name, the address at which you wish to receive correspondence and notices relating to the Application, and a telephone number where you can be reached during regular business hours. If you are going to be represented by an attorney in objecting to the Application, the response must contain the name, business address, and telephone number of the attorney.

C. All parties must be served with subsequent correspondence and notices by first class mail as follows:

   1. The Department shall be served at:

      Department of Real Estate
      Recovery Account Unit
      P.O. Box 187000
      Sacramento, CA 95818-7000

   2. The claimant shall be served at his or her address as specified in the Application, or if the claimant is represented by an attorney, at the address of the attorney as specified in the Application.

   3. The judgment debtor shall be served at his or her address as specified in the response, or if represented by an attorney, at the address of the attorney as specified in the response.

D. NOTE: As the judgment debtor you are entitled to submit written argument and to receive notice of subsequent correspondence and notices only if a timely written response is filed. Such notices and correspondence would include copies of any further documentation submitted by the claimant, any notification that the Application has been determined to be substantially complete, copies of any argument submitted by the claimant, and notification of the final decision of the Department whether or not to pay the claim.

Form 2.109B–2

State of California

PROOF OF SERVICE — PERSONAL

RE 810 (Rev. 4/87)

Department of Real Estate
Recovery Account Unit

I served the following:

☐ Notice to Judgment Debtor (RE 809)

☐ Recovery Account – Application for Payment (RE 808)

☐ All attachments to the Recovery Account application

by personally delivering them as follows:

1. Person Served:

2. Date and Time of Delivery:

3. Place of Delivery (Address):

At the time of service I was at least 18 years of age and not a party to the Application for Payment from the Recovery Account.

I declare under penalty of perjury that the foregoing is true and correct, and that this declaration was executed on

_____ at _____, California.
(Date) *(Place)*

_____
(Signature)

Form 2.109B–3

STATE OF CALIFORNIA   DEPARTMENT OF REAL ESTATE
                                                       RECOVERY ACCOUNT UNIT

PROOF OF SERVICE – REGISTERED MAIL

RE 811 (Rev. 6/89)

I served the following:

    ☐ Notice to Judgment Debtor (RE 809)

    ☐ Recovery Account – Application for Payment (RE 808)

    ☐ All attachments to the Application,

by placing true copies enclosed in a sealed envelope with the postage thereon fully prepaid and registered, in the United States

Mail on _____ ____ at ____ ___ ___ __ _____ _____ ,
            (Date)   (Place)
California, addressed as follows:

_____

_____

_____

_____

_____

At the time of service I was at least 18 years of age and not a party to the Application for Payment from the Recovery

Account.

I declare under penalty of perjury that the foregoing is true and correct, and that this declaration was executed on

_____ _____ _____ at ___ _____ __ _____ ____, California.
        (Date)   (Place)

                                               _____
                                                     (Signature)

Comment: Under Bus & P C §10471.1, the person applying for payment from the recovery account of the real estate fund must serve, by personal service or registered mail, a copy of the application and a notice including the language in Form 2.109B–1.

Disciplinary Proceedings by the Real Estate Commissioner

[§2.110] Grounds for Imposing Discipline

In *Chodur v Edmonds* (1985) 174 CA3d 565, 220 CR 80, the term "dishonest dealing," a ground for imposing discipline under Bus & P C §10177(j), was held to not be unconstitutionally vague either on its face or as applied. The broker in *Chodur* had intentionally omitted to make payments on an underlying note, although he received payments from his borrowers under his all-inclusive promissory note, and then used the payments received for his own benefit.

Effective January 1, 1991, Bus & P C §10177(o) was added to provide that a ground for suspension or revocation of a real estate license is the failure of a licensee, as an agent for the buyer of real property, to disclose to the buyer the nature and extent of the agent's direct or indirect ownership interest in the property. Direct or indirect ownership interest in the property by a person related to the agent by blood or marriage, by an entity in which the agent has an ownership interest, or by any other person with whom the agent occupies a special relationship must be disclosed to the buyer.

[§2.111] Procedures and Remedies

Effective January 1, 1986, Bus & P C §10175.2 was enacted to give the Real Estate Commissioner the authority to impose or accept a monetary penalty instead of the suspension of a licensee's license. The amount may not exceed $250 for each day of suspension or $10,000 for each decision. The money is deposited in the recovery account of the real estate fund.

California Administrative Mandamus (Cal CEB 1966) has been replaced by California Administrative Mandamus (2d ed Cal CEB 1989).

Broker to Third Parties

[§2.112] Secret Profits

A broker who fails to transmit a third party's written offer to purchase to the broker's principal (the seller), but instead buys the property himself at a lower price, has breached his duty of honesty and truthfulness to the third party prospective purchaser. If the broker still owns the property he can be obligated, as a constructive trustee, to transfer the property to the prospective purchaser on tender of the consideration the broker paid his principal and assumption by the prospective purchaser of any obligations the broker owed his principal. *Nguyen v Scott* (1988) 206 CA3d 725, 253 CR 800.

[§2.113] Misrepresentation and Failure To Disclose

The court in *Norman I. Krug Real Estate Inv., Inc. v Praszker* (1990) 220 CA3d 35, 269 CR 228, held that a broker has a duty of disclosure to third parties who may foreseeably be harmed by the broker's action. The broker knew of an unrecorded deed of trust in favor of a former owner of real property listed for sale by the broker. The broker had previously notified the lien holder to record the deed of trust because a sale was pending and advised the prospective buyer of the unrecorded lien. However, after this sale fell through, a later sale closed without the broker's notifying the former owner of the new sale or the new buyer of the unrecorded lien. The latter sale extinguished the unrecorded lien because the buyer was a bona fide purchaser for value. The court found that there was substantial evidence to support a determination that the broker breached his duty to the former owner but reversed with directions to the trial court to make new findings on the comparative negligence of the former owner in not recording the lien.

[§2.116] Housing Discrimination

The Rumford Fair Housing Act is properly referred to as the California Fair Employment and Housing Act (Govt C §§12900–12996).

Principal to Third Parties for Broker's Acts

[§2.119] Failure To Disclose

See also discussion on failure to disclose in §2.89 and Real Estate Transfer Disclosure Statement and Comment in Update §1.69A.

[§2.120] Effect of Exculpatory Provision

The treatise by Miller & Starr, cited in the Book, has been replaced by 2 Miller & Starr, California Real Estate §§3.26–3.27 (2d ed 1989).

[§2.121] Liability to Subsequent Purchasers

The holding in *Cohen v Citizens Nat'l Trust & Sav. Bank* (1956) 143 CA2d 480, 300 P2d 14, that a subsequent purchaser could not sue the builder for the builder's failure to disclose building code violations to the original purchaser, absent an assignment of the cause of action from the original purchaser, was criticized in *Barnhouse v City of Pinole* (1982) 133 CA3d 171, 183 CR 881. The court in *Barnhouse* allowed a subsequent purchaser to bring a direct action against the builder for failure to disclose underground seeps, springs, and slides to the original purchaser.

3

The Purchase and Sale Agreement

Drafting Considerations
Essential Elements of the Agreement

Use and Development of Property

DRAFTING CONSIDERATIONS

[§§3.3, 3.7] Resolving Conflicting Interests; Use of Printed Forms

See Update §3.8 for discussion of home equity sales contracts.

Preparation and Format of the Agreement

[§3.5] Language of the Agreement

There is now a second edition of Wydick, Plain English for Lawyers, published in 1985.

ESSENTIAL ELEMENTS OF THE AGREEMENT

[§3.8] Requisites for Enforceability

Civil Code §§2945–2945.9 concern mortgage foreclosure consultants. One requirement is that a contract between a foreclosure consultant and a trustor can be canceled by the trustor for three business days following execution. CC §2945.2.

Major legislation concerning home equity sales contracts appears in CC §§1695–1695.17. The statutes apply to the sale of any one-to-four-family, owner-occupied residence that is sold by the trustor ("equity seller") within one year after a notice of default has been recorded.

Operative July 11, 1980, it is unlawful for anyone to take unconscionable advantage of an owner whose residential property is in foreclosure, *e.g.,* by purchasing it for little or no money with the promise to reconvey later if the debt is paid. CC §1695.13. This kind of transaction may be rescinded within two years by the record title owner of the property at the time the notice of default was recorded, except as against a bona fide purchaser or encumbrancer for value when the purchase or encumbrance occurred before the notice of rescission was recorded. CC §1695.14. Exempted transactions also include a trustee sale, acquisition of title by in lieu deed, and transactions in which the "equity purchaser" is a spouse or blood relative or is purchasing the property as a personal residence. CC §1695.1(a).

The sales contract must state in bold print that the equity seller has a five-day right of cancellation (CC §1695.4) and cannot be asked to sign any other document during that period; there must also be attached to the contract a form notice of cancellation for the equity seller to use. CC §1695.5. During the five-day period, the equity purchaser may not take any deed from the seller, record any document, transfer or encumber the property, or pay the seller any consideration. CC §1695.6(b). Forms for required contract notice provisions are provided in Update §3.8A.

When the equity purchaser has given the equity seller an option to repurchase, he may not encumber or transfer the property without the seller's consent. CC §1695.6(e). A purchaser who violates any of the provisions of CC §§1695–1695.4 may be liable for actual and punitive damages as well as attorneys' fees (CC §1695.7); he is also subject to fine and imprisonment (CC §1695.8). However, bona fide purchasers from the equity purchaser are protected. CC §1695.12.

The reference in Book §3.8 to 3 Witkin, California Procedure, *Pleading* §645 (2d ed 1971) should now be to 5 Witkin, California Procedure, *Pleading* §739 (3d ed 1985).

Former CC §1624(4) has been redesignated CC §1624(c), and former CC §1624(7) has been redesignated CC §1624(f).

[§3.8A] Form: Equity Seller's Right of Cancellation

Form 3.8A–1

[*Insert in purchase-and-sale agreement directly above space reserved for equity seller's signature*]

You may cancel this contract for the sale of your house without any penalty or obligation at any time before ___ [*date and time of day: midnight of the fifth business day following the day on which the equity seller signs the contract or 8 a.m. on the day scheduled for the sale of the property pursuant to a power of sale conferred in a deed of trust, whichever occurs first*] ___. **See the attached notice of cancellation for an explanation of this right.**

Form 3.8A–2

[*Attach to purchase-and-sale contract*]

NOTICE OF CANCELLATION

[*Date contract was signed*]

You may cancel this contract for the sale of your house, without any penalty or obligation, at any time before ___ [*date and time of day: midnight of the fifth business day following the day on which the equity seller signs the contract or 8:00 a.m. on the day scheduled for the sale of the property pursuant to a power of sale conferred in a deed of trust, whichever occurs first*] ___

To cancel this transaction, personally deliver a signed and dated copy of this cancellation notice, or send a telegram to ___ [*name of purchaser*] **___, at ___** [*street address of purchaser's place of business*] **___ NOT LATER THAN ___** [*date and time of day: midnight of the fifth business day following the day on which the equity seller signs the contract or 8:00 a.m. on the day scheduled for the sale of property pursuant to a power of sale conferred in a deed of trust, whichever occurs first*] ___

_____
[*Signature of seller*]
[*Typed name*]
Seller

Form 3.8A–3

[Insert in purchase-and-sale agreement immediately above Form 3.8A–1]

NOTICE REQUIRED BY CALIFORNIA LAW

Until your right to cancel this contract has ended, ___ [*purchaser's name*] ___ or anyone working for ___ [*purchaser's name*] ___ CANNOT ask you to sign or have you sign any deed or any other document.

Comment: Form 3.8A–1 and the words "NOTICE OF CANCELLATION" in Form 3.8A–2 must be in 12-point boldface type in printed contracts or in capital letters in typed contracts. The remainder of Form 3.8A–2 must be in at least 10-point type if the contract is printed or in capital letters if typed. CC §1695.5. Form 3.8A–3 must be in 14-point boldface type in printed contracts or in capital letters in typed contracts, as required by CC §1695.3 (listing required contract terms). The notice of cancellation given by the equity seller is not required to be in the form provided by the contract and is effective, however expressed, if it indicates the intention of the equity seller not to be bound by the contract. CC §1695.4.

Parties

[§3.9] Necessary Parties as Sellers

Civil Code §§1237–1304, relating to declared homesteads, were repealed, effective July 1, 1983, and superseded by CCP §§704.710–704.850 (claimed homestead exemption) and 704.910–704.990 (declared homesteads). The homestead laws no longer provide that the spouse has an interest in the other spouse's homesteaded separate property under former CC §§1242 and 1265, as stated in Book §3.9(b). See new CCP §704.940. The revision of the homestead laws did not, however, affect the restriction of the right to convey or encumber community property found in the Civil Code (see, *e.g.,* CC §§5102, 5127–5128; see also §3.15). The substance of former CC §1265 is continued in part in new CCP §704.960(a).

On sale of real property of a decedent by the personal representative, now see 1 California Decedent Estate Practice §§13.14–13.60 (Cal CEB 1986), replacing California Decedent Estate Administration (Cal CEB 1971), cited in Book §3.9.

The reference in the Book to California Mortgage and Deed of Trust

Practice (Cal CEB 1979) should now be to California Mortgage and Deed of Trust Practice §§7.12–7.13 (2d ed Cal CEB 1990).

Capacity To Contract

[§3.11] Minors

Civil Code §63 has been amended and subparagraph (g) renumbered CC §63(b)(2). Under CC §63(b)(2) the emancipated minor may buy, sell, lease, encumber, exchange, or transfer any interest in real or personal property.

[§3.13] Guardianship or Conservatorship for Persons Under Disability

California Conservatorships §§5.43–5.60 (Cal CEB 1968) have been replaced by California Conservatorships and Guardianships §§12.82–12.101 (Cal CEB 1990).

Married Persons as Sellers

[§3.15] Buyer's Need for Certainty

Spouses holding homesteaded property can unilaterally alter the form of ownership from joint tenancy to tenancy in common without affecting the homestead. *Estate of Grigsby* (1982) 134 CA3d 611, 184 CR 886 (spouse severed joint tenancy by transfer to straw man, who transferred property back). For further discussion regarding amendments to homestead law, see Update §3.9.

Effective July 1, 1983, CC §1242 was repealed. New CCP §704.940 provides that a homestead declaration does not restrict any right to convey or encumber the property; and CCP §704.980(b) allows a declaration of abandonment of homestead to be recorded by one holding a power of attorney. Therefore, a power of attorney can probably be used after July 1, 1983, to transfer homesteaded property.

If a buyer knows that property is the community property of the sellers and only one spouse signs the sale contract, the buyer is not entitled to specific performance of the contract, including the one-half interest owned by the spouse who signed. *Andrade Dev. Co. v Martin* (1983) 138 CA3d 330, 187 CR 863, discussed further at 6 CEB Real Prop L Rep 62 (Apr. 1983).

[§3.17] Trustees

Numerous sections of the Civil Code that dealt with trusts have been repealed effective July 1, 1987, and the substance of the sections have been placed in the Trust Law (Division 9 of the Probate Code, §§15000–18201). The Trust Law in Prob C §15003 provides that the repeal of former CC §§2215–2290.12 is not intended to alter the rules applied by the courts to fiduciary and confidential relationships, except for express trusts governed by the Trust Law.

The changes from the Civil Code sections cited in Book §3.17 to the Probate Code are as follows:

Former	Current
CC §852	Prob C §15206
CC §869	Prob C §18103
CC §869a	Prob C §18104
CC §2243	Prob C §18100

The most important section of the Trust Law concerning Book §3.17 is Prob C §18100. Probate Code §18100 appears to change the rules found in several of the former Civil Code sections, particularly CC §870. Section 18100 provides protection for a third person dealing with a trustee by, in effect, giving a third person who acts in good faith for valuable consideration and without actual knowledge that the trustee is exceeding the trustee's powers or improperly exercising them, the status of a bona fide purchaser. The section provides that such third person is not bound to inquire whether the trustee has power to act or is properly exercising a power and may assume without inquiry the existence of a trust power and its proper exercise. Former CC §870 provided that, when an instrument creates a trust interest in real property, any conveyance in contravention of the trust is absolutely void. Under Prob C §18100, a good faith purchaser for value without actual notice that the trustee was transferring the property in contravention of the trust would now retain the property. This is apparently true even if the trustee converts the funds paid for the property by the good faith purchaser to his or her own use, because new Prob C §18101 provides that a third person who acts in good faith is not bound to ensure the proper application of trust property paid or delivered to the trustee.

[§3.18] Sales by Agents and Attorneys-in-Fact

California has enacted a new Uniform Durable Power of Attorney Act (CC §§2400–2423) under which a power of attorney does not automatically expire one year after a disability or incapacity occurs. Because a power of attorney drawn for real property transaction purposes should be of limited duration, as discussed in Book §3.18, the new durable power will rarely be used for that purpose. For further discussion of the new durable power, see Spitler, *California's "New" Durable Power of Attorney Act—The Second Time Around,* 3 CEB Est Plan Rep 41 (Dec. 1981). If the power of attorney may be used to transfer, counsel should first ascertain, if appropriate, whether the intended lender will lend and whether the title company will issue a policy on real property transferred by the attorney-in-fact.

Buyer's Use of Agents or Nominees

[§3.20] Agents as Buyers

The reference in Book §3.20(3) to 18 Cal Adm C §462(*l*) (now called the California Code of Regulations) should be to 18 Cal Code Regs §462(m)(1).

On the liability of an undisclosed principal, now see 2 Witkin, Summary of California Law, *Agency and Employment* §§107–109 (9th ed 1987).

[§3.22] Partnerships

A provision in a recorded statement of partnership that limits the authority of any one partner to convey partnership property has been held not to give "knowledge" (as that term is used in Corp C §15009(1)) to a buyer (who has not actually seen the statement of partnership) that the partner he had dealt with did not have authority to bind the partnership. *Owens v Palos Verdes Monaco* (1983) 142 CA3d 855, 191 CR 381.

In reaction to *Owens,* Corp C §15010.7 was added, effective January 1, 1985. This section provides that a recorded copy of a statement of partnership that is signed, acknowledged, and verified by one partner constitutes constructive notice of restrictions on the authority of individual partners to convey an interest in the partnership property. The constructive notice extends only to property in the county or counties where the statement of partnership is recorded.

On statements for the conveyance of real property by a partnership, now see Advising California Partnerships §§4.123–4.124 (2d ed Cal CEB 1988), which replaces the edition cited in Book §3.22.

The reference to Witkin in the Book should now be to 9 Witkin, Summary of California Law, *Partnership* §38 (9th ed 1989).

[§3.23] Limited Partnerships

On July 1, 1984, California's Uniform Limited Partnership Act was repealed and replaced by a new comprehensive law, the California Revised Limited Partnership Act (Corp C §§15611–15723). Corporations Code §15502 has been replaced by new Corp C §15621. Under Corp C §15621(b) the limited partnership is formed when the certificate of limited partnership is filed with the Secretary of State. Recordation still creates the same presumption as the statement of partnership. See Corp C §15621(d), replacing Corp C §15502(4).

The escape clause referred to in Book §3.23 is now in Corp C §15633, which replaced Corp C §15511 on July 1, 1984.

Note that the California Uniform Limited Partnership Act, including Corp C §15502, continues in effect for limited partnerships formed before July 1, 1984, that do not elect to be governed by the revised act. Corp C §§15711–15712.

See Advising California Partnerships, chap 5 (2d ed Cal CEB 1988), which replaces the edition, cited in Book §3.23, on limited partnerships.

The reference to Witkin in the Book should now be to 9 Witkin, Summary of California Law, *Partnership* §§61–108 (9th ed 1989).

[§3.26] Corporations

Agents of corporations entering into agreements that are made "subject to board of directors approval" have a duty to act in good faith in seeking board approval, and the board must consider the proposal in good faith. *Jacobs v Freeman* (1980) 104 CA3d 177, 163 CR 680.

The various statutory forms of acknowledgment by different types of entities have been deleted from the Civil Code and replaced by a single form of acknowledgment for general use. See CC §1189.

Manner of Holding Title

[§3.27] Importance of Ownership Form

California Will Drafting (Cal CEB 1965) has been replaced by California Will Drafting (3d ed Cal CEB 1992).

[§3.28] Cotenancies

For a case holding, as did *Riddle v Harmon* (1980) 102 CA3d 524, 162 CR 530, that a joint tenant may unilaterally sever the joint tenancy without the use of a straw man or notice to the other joint tenant, see *Estate of Carpenter* (1983) 140 CA3d 709, 189 CR 651.

Effective January 1, 1985, CC §683.2(a) provides that a joint tenant may sever his or her joint tenancy interest without the consent of the other joint tenant by execution and delivery of a deed conveying legal title of the interest to a third person or by execution of a written instrument evidencing the intent to sever the joint tenancy. The first method of severing the joint tenancy has been the law for some time. See *Delanoy v Delanoy,* cited in Book §3.28. As first enacted, CC §683.2 did not require recordation of the severance document. This probable oversight was corrected by an amendment effective January 1, 1986. Now a document effecting a severance under CC §683.2(a) must be either recorded before the death of the severing joint tenant or executed and acknowledged before a notary public by the severing joint tenant not earlier than three days before the death of that joint tenant and recorded not later than seven days after his or her death. CC §683.2(c)(2). These recordation requirements do not apply to or affect a severance made before January 1, 1986.

Civil Code §683.2 contains a further provision that the statute does not authorize severance of a joint tenancy contrary to a written agreement of the joint tenants, indicating that joint tenants can agree to a joint tenancy that can be severed only by death or mutual agreement. However, the fact that a severance is contrary to a written agreement does not defeat the rights of a good faith purchaser or encumbrancer without knowledge of the written agreement. CC §683.2(b).

On the nature of joint tenancy and the right of survivorship, now see Witkin, Summary of California Law, *Real Property* §§256–257 (9th ed 1987), which replaces the eighth edition cited in Book §3.28.

[§3.29] Partnership Compared With Tenancy in Common

See the Appendix to this Update for discussion of which transfers result in a reappraisal.

[§3.30] Husband and Wife as Buyers

The presumption that a single-family residence of a husband and wife is their community property if acquired by them during marriage as joint tenants was deleted from CC §5110, effective January 1, 1984. In its place, CC §4800.1 was enacted to provide that property acquired in joint tenancy by the parties during their marriage is presumed to be community property unless rebutted by a clear statement in the deed (or other documentary evidence of title) or by proof that the parties have made a written agreement that the property is separate property.

Civil Code §4800.1, as originally enacted, was effective January 1, 1984, and purported to apply to all proceedings for division of property (in dissolution) begun after 1983 or not yet final on January 1, 1984. The retroactive effect of CC §4800.1 was held unconstitutional by the supreme court in *Marriage of Buol* (1985) 39 C3d 751, 218 CR 31, in which an oral agreement that the couple's home was the wife's separate property was enforced in a case pending but not final before the effective date of CC §4800.1.

Civil Code §4800.2, effective January 1, 1984, also purports to apply (as did CC §4800.1) to proceedings not yet final on January 1, 1984. Civil Code §4800.2 provides that a party shall be reimbursed for that party's separate property contributions to the acquisition of the property being divided unless that party has made a written waiver of that reimbursement right. The retroactive effect of CC §4800.2 also was held unconstitutional by the supreme court in *Marriage of Fabian* (1986) 41 C3d 440, 224 CR 333.

In an effort to reinstate a limited retroactive effect of CC §§4800.1

and 4800.2, the legislature amended §4800.1, effective January 1, 1987, by adding a statement of legislative intent to support a finding that a compelling state interest exists to have both the statutes apply to jointly held property, regardless of the date of acquisition of the property or the date of any agreement affecting the character of the property, in all proceedings commenced on or after January 1, 1984, except when property settlement agreements were executed or judgments were entered before January 1, 1987. The statement of legislative intent has been ignored by the courts, which continue to deny retroactive effect to at least CC §4800.2 if the property had been acquired before 1984. See, *e.g., Marriage of Cairo* (1988) 204 CA3d 1255, 251 CR 731 (First District); *Marriage of Lockman* (1988) 204 CA3d 782, 251 CR 434 (Fifth District); *Marriage of Bankovich* (1988) 203 CA3d 49, 249 CR 713 (Fourth District).

The newly amended CC §4800.1 also extends its application beyond property acquired in joint tenancy form to property held in tenancy in common, joint tenancy, tenancy by the entirety, and community property.

The addition of CC §§4800.1 and 4800.2 in effect abrogated that portion of the holding of *Marriage of Lucas* (1980) 27 CA3d 808, 166 CR 853, described in Book §3.30. See 16 Cal L Rev'n Comm'n Reports 2165 (1982). For further discussion of these changes, see 2 California Marital Dissolution Practice Update §18.28 (Cal CEB).

The community property provisions of the Family Law Act (CC §§5100–5119) apply to a putative marriage under CC §4452. See *Marriage of Monti* (1982) 135 CA3d 50, 185 CR 72. The statement in Book §3.30 that these provisions apply only to valid marriages should have stated "valid or putative marriages" instead.

California Marital Termination Settlements (Cal CEB 1971) has been superseded by California Marital Termination Agreements (Cal CEB 1988). The effect of form of title of property ownership by husband and wife is discussed in 1 California Marital Dissolution Practice, chap 7 (Cal CEB 1981).

[§3.31] Entity To Be Formed

The former relative advantage of depreciating "new" rather than "old" property under IRC §167 mentioned in Book §3.31(4), has been eliminated for property placed in service after December 31, 1980, by the adoption of the Accelerated Cost Recovery System (ACRS) in IRC §168 by the Economic Recovery Tax Act of 1981 (Pub L 97–34, 95 Stat 172). Before the enactment of the Tax Reform Act of 1984 (Pub L 98–369, 98 Stat 494), a 15-year recovery period was assigned to improved real property placed in service after December 31, 1980, and recovery deductions were based on the 175-percent declining-balance method in the early years and the straight-line method in the later years. The 175-percent declining-balance method was retained under the Tax Reform Act of 1984, but the minimum recovery period was increased from 15 to 18 years for most improved real property placed in service after March 15, 1984.

The minimum recovery period was increased again, from 18 to 19 years for most improved real property placed in service after May 8, 1985, by the Imputed Interest Simplification Act (Pub L 99–121, 99 Stat 505). Instead of the declining-balance method, the taxpayer was entitled to claim straight-line recovery deductions over the 19-year period or over a 35- or 45-year period.

The Accelerated Cost Recovery System was substantially modified by the Tax Reform Act of 1986 (Pub L 99–514, 100 Stat 2085). Under these changes, real property generally is classified as either nonresidential real property or residential rental property under revised IRC §168(e)(2). The recovery period for nonresidential real property is 31.5 years, and the recovery period for residential rental property is 27.5 years. IRC §168(c). The straight-line depreciation method is mandatory for all nonresidential property and residential rental property. IRC §168(b)(3). The revised ACRS rules generally are effective for property placed in service after December 31, 1986. A taxpayer may elect to have the revised rules apply to property placed in service after July 31, 1986, and before January 1, 1987. TRA 1986 §203.

On July 1, 1984, Corp C §15621 replaced Corp C §15502. See Update §3.23.

[§3.33] Description of Property

Former CC §1624(4) has been redesignated as CC §1624(c).

Writing

[§3.36] General Rules

See Update §3.8 for discussion of home equity sales contracts.

Former CC §1624(4) has been redesignated as CC §1624(c).

The eighth edition of Witkin, Summary of California Law, is in the process of being replaced by a ninth edition. On the enforceability of an oral contract subject to the statute of frauds, now see 1 Witkin, Summary of California Law, *Contracts* §263 (9th ed 1987). On contracts that concern real property but that do not require a writing, now see 1 Witkin, Summary, *Contracts* §302.

[§3.38] Reformation

The reference to Witkin in the Book should now be to 1 Witkin, Summary of California Law, *Contracts* §§382–391 (9th ed 1987).

DRAFTING THE BASIC PURCHASE AND SALE AGREEMENT

California Association of Realtors Real Estate Purchase Contract and Receipt for Deposit

[§3.39] Major Revisions

See Update §3.8 for discussion of home equity sales contracts. See §3.40 for supplementary forms referred to in paragraph 4 of the CAR Real Estate Purchase Contract and Receipt for Deposit.

[§3.40] Form: CAR Real Estate Purchase Contract and Receipt for Deposit

The form in Book §3.40 has been replaced by the form reprinted below.

The supplements listed in paragraph 3 of this form are reproduced in this section. They are: Interim Occupancy Agreement (CAR form 10A–14); Residential Lease Agreement After Sale (CAR form RLAS–11); and VA and FHA Amendments (CAR form VA/FHA–11). The Addendum at paragraph 16E and 16F, Special Studies Zone and Flood Hazard Disclosure, is also reproduced in this section. They are reprinted by permission of the California Association of Realtors. Endorsement is not implied. The address of the California Association of Realtors is now 525 South Virgil Ave., Los Angeles, CA 90076.

Form 3.40–1

REAL ESTATE PURCHASE CONTRACT AND RECEIPT FOR DEPOSIT
THIS IS MORE THAN A RECEIPT FOR MONEY IT IS INTENDED TO BE A LEGALLY BINDING CONTRACT READ IT CAREFULLY
CALIFORNIA ASSOCIATION OF REALTORS' (CAR) STANDARD FORM

_____, California, _____, 19____

Received from _____

herein called Buyer, the sum of _____ Dollars $_____

evidenced by ☐ cash, ☐ cashier's check, ☐ personal check or ☐ _____, payable to _____

_____, to be held uncashed until acceptance of this offer as deposit on account of purchase price of

_____ Dollars $_____

for the purchase of property, situated in _____, County of _____, California,

described as follows _____

1. **FINANCING:** The obtaining of Buyer's financing is a contingency of this agreement.
   A. DEPOSIT upon acceptance, to be deposited into _____ $_____
   B. INCREASED DEPOSIT within _____ days of acceptance to be deposited into _____ $_____
   C. BALANCE OF DOWN PAYMENT to be deposited into _____ on or before _____ $_____
   D. Buyer to apply, qualify for and obtain a NEW FIRST LOAN in the amount of _____ $_____
      payable monthly at approximately $_____ including interest at origination not to exceed _____%,
      ☐ fixed rate, ☐ other _____ all due _____ years from date of origination. Loan fee not to
      exceed _____ Seller agrees to pay a maximum of _____ FHA/VA discount points.
      Additional terms _____

   E. Buyer ☐ to assume, ☐ to take title subject to an EXISTING FIRST LOAN with an approximate balance of _____ $_____
      in favor of _____ payable monthly at $_____ including interest at _____% ☐ fixed rate,
      ☐ other _____ Fees not to exceed _____
      Disposition of impound account _____
      Additional terms _____

   F. Buyer to execute a NOTE SECURED BY a ☐ first, ☐ second, ☐ third DEED OF TRUST in the amount of _____ $_____
      IN FAVOR OF SELLER payable monthly at $_____ or more, including interest at _____% all due
      _____ years from date of origination, ☐ or upon sale or transfer of subject property. A late charge of _____
      _____ shall be due on any installment not paid within _____ days of the due date.
      ☐ Deed of Trust to contain a request for notice of default or sale for the benefit of Seller. Buyer ☐ will, ☐ will not execute a request
      for notice of delinquency. Additional terms _____

   G. Buyer ☐ to assume, ☐ to take title subject to an EXISTING SECOND LOAN with an approximate balance of _____ $_____
      in favor of _____ payable monthly at _____ including interest at _____%
      ☐ fixed rate, ☐ other _____ Buyer fees not to exceed _____
      Additional terms _____

   H. Buyer to apply, qualify for and obtain a NEW SECOND LOAN in the amount of _____ $_____
      payable monthly at approximately $_____ including interest at origination not to exceed _____% ☐ fixed rate,
      ☐ other _____ all due _____ years from date of origination.
      Buyer's loan fee not to exceed _____ Additional terms _____

   I. In the event Buyer assumes or takes title subject to an existing loan, Seller shall provide Buyer with copies of applicable notes and Deeds
      of Trust. A loan may contain a number of features which affect the loan, such as interest rate changes, monthly payment changes, balloon
      payments, etc. Buyer shall be allowed _____ calendar days after receipt of such copies to notify Seller in writing of disapproval.
      FAILURE TO NOTIFY SELLER IN WRITING SHALL CONCLUSIVELY BE CONSIDERED APPROVAL. Buyer's approval shall not be
      unreasonably withheld. Differences in existing loan balances shall be adjusted in ☐ Cash, ☐ Other _____

   J. Buyer agrees to act diligently and in good faith to obtain all applicable financing. _____

   K. ADDITIONAL FINANCING TERMS: _____
      _____
      _____

   L. TOTAL PURCHASE PRICE _____ $_____

2. **OCCUPANCY:** Buyer ☐ does, ☐ does not intend to occupy subject property as Buyer's primary residence.

3. **SUPPLEMENTS:** The ATTACHED supplements are incorporated herein:
   ☐ Interim Occupancy Agreement (CAR FORM IOA-11)   ☐ _____
   ☐ Residential Lease Agreement after Sale (CAR FORM RLAS-11) ☐ _____
   ☐ VA and FHA Amendments (CAR FORM VA/FHA-11)   ☐ _____

4. **ESCROW:** Buyer and Seller shall deliver signed instructions to _____ the escrow holder, within _____ calendar days
   of acceptance of the offer which shall provide for closing within _____ calendar days of acceptance. Escrow fees to be paid as follows: _____
   _____
   _____

Buyer and Seller acknowledge receipt of copy of this page, which constitutes Page 1 of _____ Pages.
Buyer's Initials (_____) (_____)   Seller's Initials (_____) (_____)

THIS STANDARDIZED DOCUMENT FOR USE IN SIMPLE TRANSACTIONS HAS BEEN APPROVED BY THE CALIFORNIA ASSOCIATION OF REALTORS® IN FORM ONLY. NO REPRESENTATION
IS MADE AS TO THE APPROVAL OF THE FORM OR ANY SUPPLEMENTS NOT CURRENTLY PUBLISHED BY THE CALIFORNIA ASSOCIATION OF REALTORS® OR THE LEGAL VALIDITY OR
ADEQUACY OF ANY PROVISION IN ANY SPECIFIC TRANSACTION. IT SHOULD NOT BE USED IN COMPLEX TRANSACTIONS OR WITH EXTENSIVE RIDERS OR ADDITIONS.

A REAL ESTATE BROKER IS THE PERSON QUALIFIED TO ADVISE ON REAL ESTATE TRANSACTIONS. IF YOU DESIRE LEGAL OR TAX ADVICE, CONSULT AN APPROPRIATE PROFESSIONAL.

The copyright laws of the United States (17 U.S. Code) forbid the unauthorized
reproduction of this form by any means including facsimile or computerized formats.

Copyright © 1989. CALIFORNIA ASSOCIATION OF REALTORS®
525 South Virgil Avenue, Los Angeles, California 90020
REVISED 2/91

---- OFFICE USE ONLY ----
Reviewed by Broker or Designee _____
Date _____

REAL ESTATE PURCHASE CONTRACT AND RECEIPT FOR DEPOSIT (DLF-14 PAGE 1 OF 4)

☐
Subject Property Address

5. **TITLE:** Title is to be free of liens, encumbrances, easements, restrictions, rights and conditions of record or known to Seller, other than the following (a) Current property taxes, (b) covenants, conditions, restrictions, and public utility easements of record, if any, provided the same do not adversely affect the continued use of the property for the purposes for which it is presently being used, unless reasonably disapproved by Buyer in writing within _____ calendar days of receipt of a current preliminary report furnished at _____ expense, and (c) _____

Seller shall furnish Buyer at _____ expense a California Land Title Association policy issued by _____ _____ Company, showing title vested in Buyer subject only to the above. If Seller is unwilling or unable to eliminate any title matter disapproved by Buyer as above, Buyer may terminate this agreement. If Seller fails to deliver title as above, Buyer may terminate this agreement, in either case, the deposit shall be returned to Buyer.

6. **VESTING:** Unless otherwise designated in the escrow instructions of Buyer, title shall vest as follows _____
_____

(The manner of taking title may have significant legal and tax consequences. Therefore, give this matter serious consideration.)

7. **PRORATIONS:** Property taxes, payments on bonds and assessments assumed by Buyer, interest, rents, association dues, premiums on insurance acceptable to Buyer, and _____ shall be paid current and prorated as of ☐ the day of recordation of the deed; or ☐ _____ Bonds or assessments now a lien shall be ☐ paid current by Seller, payments not yet due to be assumed by Buyer, or ☐ paid in full by Seller, including payments not yet due, or ☐ _____ County Transfer tax shall be paid by _____ The _____ transfer tax or transfer fee shall be paid by _____ **PROPERTY WILL BE REASSESSED UPON CHANGE OF OWNERSHIP. THIS WILL AFFECT THE TAXES TO BE PAID.** A Supplemental tax bill will be issued, which shall be paid as follows: (a) for periods after close of escrow, by Buyer (or by final acquiring party if part of an exchange), and (b) for periods prior to close of escrow, by Seller. TAX BILLS ISSUED AFTER CLOSE OF ESCROW SHALL BE HANDLED DIRECTLY BETWEEN BUYER AND SELLER.

8. **POSSESSION:** Possession and occupancy shall be delivered to Buyer, ☐ on close of escrow, or ☐ no later than _____ days after close of escrow, or ☐ _____

9. **KEYS:** Seller shall, when possession is available to Buyer, provide keys and/or means to operate all property locks and alarms, if any.

10. **PERSONAL PROPERTY:** The following items of personal property, free of liens and without warranty of condition, are included: _____
_____

11. **FIXTURES:** All permanently installed fixtures and fittings that are attached to the property or for which special openings have been made are included in the purchase price, including electrical, light, plumbing and heating fixtures, built-in appliances, screens, awnings, shutters, all window coverings, attached floor coverings, TV antennas, air cooler or conditioner, garage door openers and controls, attached fireplace equipment, mailbox, trees and shrubs, and _____ except _____

12. **SMOKE DETECTOR(S):** State law requires that residences be equipped with operable smoke detector(s). Local law may have additional requirements. Seller shall deliver to Buyer a written statement of compliance in accordance with applicable state and local law prior to close of escrow.

13. **TRANSFER DISCLOSURE:** Unless exempt, Transferor (Seller), shall comply with Civil Code §§1102 et seq., by providing Transferee (Buyer) with a Real Estate Transfer Disclosure Statement: (a) ☐ Buyer has received and read a Real Estate Transfer Disclosure Statement; or (b) ☐ Seller shall provide Buyer with a Real Estate Transfer Disclosure Statement within _____ calendar days of acceptance of the offer, after which Buyer shall have three (3) days after delivery to Buyer, in person, or five (5) days after delivery by deposit in the mail, to terminate this agreement by delivery of a written notice of termination to Seller or Seller's Agent.

14. **TAX WITHHOLDING:** (a) Under the Foreign Investment in Real Property Tax Act (FIRPTA), IRC §1445, every Buyer of U.S. real property must, unless an exemption applies, deduct and withhold from Seller's proceeds 10% of the gross sales price. Three primary FIRPTA exemptions are: No withholding is required if (i) Seller provides Buyer with an affidavit under penalty of perjury, that Seller is not a "foreign person," or (ii) Seller provides Buyer with a "qualifying statement" issued by the Internal Revenue Service, or (iii) Buyer purchases real property for use as a residence and the purchase price is $300,000 or less and Buyer or a member of Buyer's family has definite plans to reside at the property for at least 50% of the number of days it is in use during each of the first two 12-month periods after transfer. (b) In addition, under California Revenue and Taxation Code §§1880.5 and 26131, every Buyer must, unless an exemption applies, deduct and withhold from the Seller's proceeds 3⅓% of the gross sales price if the Seller has a last known address outside of California, or if the Seller's proceeds will be paid to a financial intermediary of the Seller. The primary exemptions are: No withholding is required if (i) the Seller has a homeowner's exemption for the subject property, for local property taxes, for the year in which the title transfers, or (ii) the property is selling for $100,000 or less, or (iii) the Franchise Tax Board issues a certificate authorizing a lower amount or no withholding, or (iv) the Seller signs, in its escrow, stating that the Seller is a California resident or a corporation qualified to do business in California. (c) Seller and Buyer agree to execute and deliver as directed any and all instrument, affidavit, or statement reasonably necessary to carry out those statutes and regulations promulgated thereunder.

15. **MULTIPLE LISTING SERVICE:** If Broker is a Participant of an Association/Board multiple listing service ("MLS"), the Broker is authorized to report the sale, its price, terms, and financing for the publication, dissemination, information, and use of the authorized Board members, MLS Participants and Subscribers.

16. **ADDITIONAL TERMS AND CONDITIONS:**
ONLY THE FOLLOWING PARAGRAPHS 'A' THROUGH 'K' WHEN INITIALLED BY BOTH BUYER AND SELLER ARE INCORPORATED IN THIS AGREEMENT.
Buyer's Initials   Seller's Initials

_____/_____   _____/_____   **A. PHYSICAL AND GEOLOGICAL INSPECTION:** Buyer shall have the right, at Buyer's expense, to select a licensed contractor and/or other qualified professional(s) to make "Inspections" (including tests, surveys, other studies, inspections, and investigations) of the subject property, including but not limited to structural, plumbing, sewer/septic system, well, heating, electrical, built-in appliances, roof, soils, foundation, mechanical systems, pool, pool heater, pool filter, air conditioner, if any, possible environmental hazards such as asbestos, formaldehyde, radon gas and other substances/products, and geologic conditions. Buyer shall keep the subject property free and clear of any liens, indemnify and hold Seller harmless from all liability, claims, demands, damages, or costs, and repair all damages to the property arising from the "Inspections." All claimed defects concerning the condition of the property that adversely affect the continued use of the property for the purposes for which it is presently being used (☐ _____) shall be in writing, supported by written reports, if any, and delivered to Seller within _____ calendar days FOR "INSPECTIONS" OTHER THAN GEOLOGICAL, and/or within _____ calendar days FOR GEOLOGICAL "INSPECTIONS," **of acceptance of the offer.** Buyer shall furnish Seller copies, at no cost, of all reports concerning the property obtained by Buyer. When such reports disclose conditions or information unsatisfactory to the Buyer, which the Seller is unwilling or unable to correct, Buyer may cancel this agreement. Seller shall make the premises available for all Inspections. BUYER'S FAILURE TO NOTIFY SELLER IN WRITING SHALL CONCLUSIVELY BE CONSIDERED APPROVAL.
Buyer's Initials   Seller's Initials

_____/_____   _____/_____   **B. CONDITION OF PROPERTY:** Seller warrants, through the date possession is made available to Buyer: (1) property and improvements, including landscaping, grounds and pool/spa, if any, shall be maintained in the same condition as upon the date of acceptance of the offer, and (2) the roof is free of all known leaks, and (3) built-in appliances, and water, sewer/septic, plumbing, heating, electrical, air conditioning, pool/spa systems, if any, are operative, and (4) Seller shall replace all broken and/or cracked glass; (5) _____
Buyer's Initials   Seller's Initials

_____/_____   _____/_____   **C. SELLER REPRESENTATION:** Seller warrants that Seller has no knowledge of any notice of violations of City, County, State, Federal, Building, Zoning, Fire, Health Codes or ordinances, or other governmental regulation filed or issued against the property. This warranty shall be effective until the date of close of escrow.

Buyer and Seller acknowledge receipt of copy of this page, which constitutes Page 2 of _____ Pages.
Buyer's Initials (_____) (_____)   Seller's Initials (_____) (_____)

OFFICE USE ONLY
Reviewed by Broker or Designee _____
Date _____

REAL ESTATE PURCHASE CONTRACT AND RECEIPT FOR DEPOSIT (DLF-14 PAGE 2 OF 4)

Subject Property Address _____

Buyer's Initials   **Seller's Initials**

_____ / _____   _____ / _____   **D. PEST CONTROL:** (1) Within _____ calendar days of acceptance of the offer, Seller shall furnish Buyer at the expense of ☐ Buyer, ☐ Seller, a current written report of an inspection by _____ a licensed Structural Pest Control Operator, of the main building, ☐ detached garage(s) or carport(s), if any, and ☐ the following other structures on the property: _____

(2) If requested by either Buyer or Seller, the report shall separately identify each recommendation for corrective measures as follows:

"Section 1": Infestation or infection which is evident.

"Section 2": Conditions that are present which are deemed likely to lead to infestation or infection.

(3) If no infestation or infection by wood destroying pests or organisms is found, the report shall include a written Certification as provided in Business and Professions Code § 8519(a) that on the date of inspection "no evidence of active infestation or infection was found."

(4) All work recommended to correct conditions described in "Section 1" shall be at the expense of ☐ Buyer, ☐ Seller.

(5) All work recommended to correct conditions described in "Section 2," if requested by Buyer, shall be at the expense of ☐ Buyer, ☐ Seller.

(6) The repairs shall be performed with good workmanship and materials of comparable quality and shall include repairs of leaking showers, replacement of tiles and other materials removed for repairs. It is understood that exact restoration of appearance or cosmetic items following all such repairs is not included.

(7) Funds for work agreed to be performed after close of escrow, shall be held in escrow and disbursed upon receipt of a written Certification as provided in Business and Professions Code § 8519(b) that the inspected property "is now free of evidence of active infestation or infection."

(8) Work to be performed at Seller's expense may be performed by Seller or through others, provided that (a) all required permits and final inspections are obtained, and (b) upon completion of repairs a written Certification is issued by a licensed Structural Pest Control Operator showing that the inspected property "is now free of evidence of active infestation or infection."

(9) If inspection of inaccessible areas is recommended by the report, Buyer has the option to accept and approve the report, or within _____ calendar days from receipt of the report to request in writing further inspection be made. BUYER'S FAILURE TO NOTIFY SELLER IN WRITING OF SUCH REQUEST SHALL CONCLUSIVELY BE CONSIDERED APPROVAL OF THE REPORT. If further inspection recommends "Section 1" and/or "Section 2" corrective measures, such work shall be at the expense of the party designated in subparagraph (4) and/or (5), respectively. If no infestation or infection is found, the cost of inspection, entry and closing of the inaccessible areas shall be at the expense of the Buyer.

(10) Other _____
_____

Buyer's Initials   **Seller's Initials**

_____ / _____   _____ / _____   **E. FLOOD HAZARD AREA DISCLOSURE:** Buyer is informed that subject property is situated in a "Special Flood Hazard Area" as set forth on a Federal Emergency Management Agency (FEMA) "Flood Insurance Rate Map" (FIRM), or "Flood Hazard Boundary Map" (FHBM). The law provides that, as a condition of obtaining financing on most structures located in a "Special Flood Hazard Area," lenders require flood insurance where the property or its attachments are security for a loan.

The extent of coverage and the cost may vary. For further information consult the lender or insurance carrier. No representation or recommendation is made by the Seller and the Broker(s) in this transaction as to the legal effect or economic consequences of the National Flood Insurance Program and related legislation.

Buyer's Initials   **Seller's Initials**

_____ / _____   _____ / _____   **F. SPECIAL STUDIES ZONE DISCLOSURE:** Buyer is informed that subject property is situated in a Special Studies Zone as designated under §§ 2621-2625, inclusive, of the California Public Resources Code and, as such, the construction or development on this property of any structure for human occupancy may be subject to the findings of a geologic report prepared by a geologist registered in the State of California, unless such a report is waived by the City or County under the terms of that act.

Buyer is allowed _____ calendar days from acceptance of the offer to make further inquiries at appropriate governmental agencies concerning the use of the subject property under the terms of the Special Studies Zone Act and local building, zoning, fire, health, and safety codes. When such inquiries disclose conditions or information unsatisfactory to the Buyer, which the Seller is unwilling or unable to correct, Buyer may cancel this agreement. BUYER'S FAILURE TO NOTIFY SELLER IN WRITING SHALL CONCLUSIVELY BE CONSIDERED APPROVAL.

Buyer's Initials   **Seller's Initials**

_____ / _____   _____ / _____   **G. ENERGY CONSERVATION RETROFIT:** If local ordinance requires that the property be brought in compliance with minimum energy conservation standards as a condition of sale or transfer, ☐ Buyer, ☐ Seller shall comply with and pay for these requirements. Where permitted by law, Seller may, if obligated hereunder, satisfy the obligation by authorizing escrow to credit Buyer with sufficient funds to cover the cost of such retrofit.

Buyer's Initials   **Seller's Initials**

_____ / _____   _____ / _____   **H. HOME PROTECTION PLAN:** Buyer and Seller have been informed that Home Protection Plans are available. Such plans may provide additional protection and benefit to a Seller or Buyer. The CALIFORNIA ASSOCIATION OF REALTORS® and the Broker(s) in this transaction do not endorse or approve any particular company or program:

a) ☐ A Buyer's coverage Home Protection Plan to be issued by _____
Company, at a cost not to exceed $_____, to be paid by ☐ Buyer, ☐ Seller; or

b) ☐ Buyer and Seller elect not to purchase a Home Protection Plan.

Buyer's Initials   **Seller's Initials**

_____ / _____   _____ / _____   **I. CONDOMINIUM/P.U.D.:** The subject of this transaction is a condominium/planned unit development (P.U.D.) designated as unit _____ and _____ parking space(s) and an undivided interest in community areas, and _____. The current monthly assessment charge by the homeowner's association or other governing body(s) is $_____. As soon as practicable, Seller shall provide Buyer with copies of covenants, conditions and restrictions, articles of incorporation, by-laws, current rules and regulations, most current financial statements, and any other documents as required by law. Seller shall disclose in writing any known pending special assessment, claims, or litigation to Buyer. Buyer shall be allowed _____ calendar days from receipt to review these documents. If such documents disclose conditions or information unsatisfactory to Buyer, Buyer may cancel this agreement. BUYER'S FAILURE TO NOTIFY SELLER IN WRITING SHALL CONCLUSIVELY BE CONSIDERED APPROVAL.

Buyer's Initials   **Seller's Initials**

_____ / _____   _____ / _____   **J. LIQUIDATED DAMAGES: If Buyer fails to complete said purchase as herein provided by reason of any default of Buyer, Seller shall be released from obligation to sell the property to Buyer and may proceed against Buyer upon any claim or remedy which he/she may have in law or equity; provided, however, that by initialling this paragraph Buyer and Seller agree that Seller shall retain the deposit as liquidated damages. If the described property is a dwelling with no more than four units, one of which the Buyer intends to occupy as his/her residence, Seller shall retain as liquidated damages the deposit actually paid, or an amount therefrom, not more than 3% of the purchase price and promptly return any excess to Buyer. Buyer and Seller agree to execute a similar liquidated damages provision, such as CALIFORNIA ASSOCIATION OF REALTORS® Receipt for Increased Deposit (RID-11), for any increased deposits. (Funds deposited in trust accounts or in escrow are not released automatically in the event of a dispute. Release of funds requires written agreement of the parties, judicial decision or arbitration.)**

Buyer and Seller acknowledge receipt of copy of this page, which constitutes Page 3 of _____ Pages.

Buyer's Initials (_____) (_____)   Seller's Initials (_____) (_____)

┌─────────── OFFICE USE ONLY ───────────┐
Reviewed by Broker or Designee _____
Date _____
└──┘

REAL ESTATE PURCHASE CONTRACT AND RECEIPT FOR DEPOSIT (DLF-14 PAGE 3 OF 4)

Subject Property Address

K. ARBITRATION OF DISPUTES: Any dispute or claim in law or equity arising out of this contract or any resulting transaction shall be decided by neutral binding arbitration in accordance with the rules of the American Arbitration Association, and not by court action except as provided by California law for judicial review of arbitration proceedings. Judgment upon the award rendered by the arbitrator(s) may be entered in any court having jurisdiction thereof. The parties shall have the right to discovery in accordance with Code of Civil Procedure § 1283.05. The following matters are excluded from arbitration hereunder: (a) a judicial or non-judicial foreclosure or other action or proceeding to enforce a deed of trust, mortgage, or real property sales contract as defined in Civil Code § 2985, (b) an unlawful detainer action, (c) the filing or enforcement of a mechanic's lien, (d) any matter which is within the jurisdiction of a probate court, or (e) an action for bodily injury or wrongful death, or for latent or patent defects to which Code of Civil Procedure § 337.1 or § 337.15 applies. The filing of a judicial action to enable the recording of a notice of pending action, for order of attachment, receivership, injunction, or other provisional remedies, shall not constitute a waiver of the right to arbitrate under this provision.

Any dispute or claim by or against broker(s) and/or associate licensee(s) participating in this transaction shall be submitted to arbitration consistent with the provision above only if the broker(s) and/or associate licensee(s) making the claim or against whom the claim is made shall have agreed to submit it to arbitration consistent with this provision.

"NOTICE: BY INITIALLING IN THE SPACE BELOW YOU ARE AGREEING TO HAVE ANY DISPUTE ARISING OUT OF THE MATTERS INCLUDED IN THE 'ARBITRATION OF DISPUTES' PROVISION DECIDED BY NEUTRAL ARBITRATION AS PROVIDED BY CALIFORNIA LAW AND YOU ARE GIVING UP ANY RIGHTS YOU MIGHT POSSESS TO HAVE THE DISPUTE LITIGATED IN A COURT OR JURY TRIAL. BY INITIALLING IN THE SPACE BELOW YOU ARE GIVING UP YOUR JUDICIAL RIGHTS TO DISCOVERY AND APPEAL, UNLESS THOSE RIGHTS ARE SPECIFICALLY INCLUDED IN THE 'ARBITRATION OF DISPUTES' PROVISION. IF YOU REFUSE TO SUBMIT TO ARBITRATION AFTER AGREEING TO THIS PROVISION, YOU MAY BE COMPELLED TO ARBITRATE UNDER THE AUTHORITY OF THE CALIFORNIA CODE OF CIVIL PROCEDURE. YOUR AGREEMENT TO THIS ARBITRATION PROVISION IS VOLUNTARY."

"WE HAVE READ AND UNDERSTAND THE FOREGOING AND AGREE TO SUBMIT DISPUTES ARISING OUT OF THE MATTERS INCLUDED IN THE 'ARBITRATION OF DISPUTES' PROVISION TO NEUTRAL ARBITRATION."

Buyer's Initials   Seller's Initials

_____   _____ /

17. **OTHER TERMS AND CONDITIONS:** _____
_____
_____
_____

18. **ATTORNEY'S FEES:** In any action, proceeding or arbitration arising out of this agreement, the prevailing party shall be entitled to reasonable attorney's fees and costs.

19. **ENTIRE CONTRACT:** Time is of the essence. All prior agreements between the parties are incorporated in this agreement which constitutes the entire contract. Its terms are intended by the parties as a final expression of their agreement with respect to such terms as are included herein and may not be contradicted by evidence of any prior agreement or contemporaneous oral agreement. The parties further intend that this agreement constitutes the complete and exclusive statement of its terms and that no extrinsic evidence whatsoever may be introduced in any judicial or arbitration proceeding, if any, involving this agreement.

20. **CAPTIONS:** The captions in this agreement are for convenience of reference only and are not intended as part of this agreement.

21. **AGENCY CONFIRMATION:** The following agency relationships are hereby confirmed for this transaction:

LISTING AGENT: _____ is the agent of (check one)
                        (Print Firm Name)

☐ the Seller exclusively; or ☐ both the Buyer and Seller

SELLING AGENT: _____ (if not the same as Listing Agent) is the agent of (check one)
                        (Print Firm Name)

☐ the Buyer exclusively; or ☐ the Seller exclusively; or ☐ both the Buyer and Seller.

22. **AMENDMENTS:** This agreement may not be amended, modified, altered or changed in any respect whatsoever except by a further agreement in writing executed by Buyer and Seller.

23. **OFFER:** This constitutes an offer to purchase the described property. Unless acceptance is signed by Seller and a signed copy delivered in person, by mail, or facsimile, and received by Buyer at the address below or by _____
who is authorized to receive it, on behalf of Buyer within _____ calendar days of the date hereof, this offer shall be deemed revoked and the deposit shall be returned. Buyer has read and acknowledges receipt of a copy of this offer. This agreement and any supplement, addendum or modification relating hereto, including any photocopy or facsimile thereof, may be executed in two or more counterparts, all of which shall constitute one and the same writing

REAL ESTATE BROKER _____   BUYER _____

By _____   BUYER _____

Address _____   Address _____

Telephone _____   Telephone _____

ACCEPTANCE

The undersigned Seller accepts and agrees to sell the property on the above terms and conditions and agrees to the above confirmation of agency relationships (☐ subject to attached counter offer).

Seller agrees to pay to Broker(s) _____
compensation for services as follows: _____

Payable: (a) On recordation of the deed or other evidence of title, or (b) if completion of sale is prevented by default of Seller, upon Seller's default, or (c) if completion of sale is prevented by default of Buyer, only if and when Seller collects damages from Buyer, by suit or otherwise, and then in an amount not less than one-half of the damages recovered, but not to exceed the above fee, after first deducting title and escrow expenses and the expenses of collection, if any. Seller shall execute and deliver an escrow instruction irrevocably assigning the compensation for service in an amount equal to the compensation agreed to above. In any action, proceeding, or arbitration between Broker(s) and Seller arising out of this agreement, the prevailing party shall be entitled to reasonable attorney's fees and costs. The undersigned has read and acknowledges receipt of a copy of this agreement and authorizes Broker(s) to deliver a signed copy to Buyer.

Date _____ Telephone _____   SELLER _____

Address _____   SELLER _____

Real Estate Broker(s) agree to the foregoing.

Broker _____ By _____ Date _____

Broker _____ By _____ Date _____

Page 4 of _____ Pages.

┌─ OFFICE USE ONLY ─┐
Reviewed by Broker or Designee _____
Date _____

REAL ESTATE PURCHASE CONTRACT AND RECEIPT FOR DEPOSIT (DLF-14 PAGE 4 OF 4)

Form 3.40–2

CALIFORNIA ASSOCIATION OF REALTORS

INTERIM OCCUPANCY AGREEMENT
(Buyer In Possession)
THIS IS INTENDED TO BE A LEGALLY BINDING AGREEMENT — READ IT CAREFULLY.
CALIFORNIA ASSOCIATION OF REALTORS® (CAR) STANDARD FORM

_____ , California _____ , 19____.

_____ , ''LESSOR'' and

_____ , ''LESSEE'' agree:

1. On _____ , 19____, LESSOR as SELLER and LESSEE as BUYER entered into an agreement for the sale and purchase of the real property commonly known as _____ , _____ , California (''Premises'') and the escrow thereof is scheduled to close on or before _____ , 19____.

2. Pending completion of sale and close of escrow, LESSEE is to be given immediate occupancy of the premises in accordance with the terms of this agreement.

3. LESSEE acknowledges an inspection of, and has found the premises in satisfactory condition and ready for occupancy, except as follows: _____

4. LESSEE shall pay to LESSOR for the occupancy of said premises the sum of $ _____ per _____
   day/week/month
   commencing _____ , 19____, to and including _____
   specific date/other
   _____ . Said sum shall be paid _____ in advance.
   weekly/monthly

   Prorations, if any, shall be predicated upon a 30 day month. As additional consideration LESSEE shall pay for all utilities and services based upon occupancy of the premises and the following charges: _____ except _____ which shall be paid by LESSOR.

5. If the purchase and sale agreement between LESSOR and LESSEE is not completed within its designated term, or any written extension thereof through no fault of LESSOR, LESSEE agrees to vacate the premises upon service of a written notice in the form and manner provided by law. Any holding over thereafter shall create a day-to-day tenancy with a fair rental value of $ _____ per day. Except as to daily rent and tenancy, all other covenants and conditions herein contained shall remain in full force and effect.

6. Except as provided by law LESSEE shall keep the premises and yards clean, sanitary, and in good order and repair during the term hereof and shall surrender the same in like condition if the said sale is not completed, reasonable wear and tear excepted. Additionally, LESSEE shall save and hold LESSOR harmless from any and all claims, demands, damages or liabilities arising out of LESSEE's occupancy of the premises caused or permitted by LESSEE, LESSEE'S family, agents, servants, employees, guests and invitees.

7. As additional consideration passing from LESSEE to LESSOR, LESSEE shall obtain and maintain during the term of this agreement public liability insurance naming both LESSOR and LESSEE as co-insureds in the amount of not less than $ _____ for injury to one person; $ _____ for injury to a group; and $ _____ for property damage. If permitted, LESSOR agrees to retain his fire insurance on the premises until close of escrow. Otherwise, LESSEE shall obtain fire insurance on the premises in a sum of not less than that designated as the sales price of the subject property.

8. The premises are to be used as a residence only by LESSEE and his immediate family and no animal, bird or pet except _____ shall be kept on or about the premises without LESSOR'S prior written consent. LESSEE shall not violate any law or ordinance in the use of the premises, nor permit waste or nuisance upon or about the premises and, except as provided by law, LESSEE shall not make any additions, alterations, or repairs to the premises without the prior written consent of LESSOR.

9. $ _____ as security has been deposited. LESSOR may use therefrom such amounts as are reasonably necessary to remedy LESSEE defaults in the payment of rent, to repair damages caused by LESSEE, or to clean the premises if necessary upon the termination of tenancy. If used toward rent or damages during the term of this agreement, LESSEE agrees to reinstate said total security deposit upon 5 days written notice delivered to LESSEE in person or by mail. The balance of the security deposit, if any, shall be mailed to LESSEE'S last known address within 14 days of surrender of premises. Alternatively, and upon completion of sale, said security deposit shall be mailed to LESSEE at the subject premises within 10 days of close of escrow.

10. In the event of any action or proceeding between LESSOR and LESSEE under this agreement, the prevailing party shall be entitled to recover reasonable attorney's fees and costs.

11. The right to occupy the premises as granted LESSEE herein is personal to LESSEE and any attempt to assign, transfer, or hypothecate the same shall be null and void.

12. The undersigned LESSEE acknowledges having read the foregoing and receipt of a copy.

   LESSOR and LESSEE have executed this agreement on the day and year above written.

Lessor _____   Lessee _____

Lessor _____   Lessee _____

OFFICE USE ONLY
Reviewed by Broker or Designee _____
Date _____

FORM IOA-14   M-CG-May-90

RESIDENTIAL LEASE AGREEMENT AFTER SALE

THIS IS INTENDED TO BE A LEGALLY BINDING AGREEMENT—READ IT CAREFULLY.

CALIFORNIA ASSOCIATION OF REALTORS® (CAR) STANDARD FORM

(Possession Retained by Seller)

_____ , California, _____ , 19_____ .

_____ , "LESSOR" and

_____ , "LESSEE"

agree:

1. On _____ , 19_____ , LESSOR as Buyer and LESSEE as Seller entered into an agreement for the sale and purchase of the real property commonly known as _____ , California ("Premises"), wherein escrow is designated to close on or about _____ , 19_____ .

2. LESSOR leases to LESSEE the premises as LESSEE'S personal residence in accordance with the terms of this lease.

3. Occupancy shall commence on the day following close of escrow and terminate _____ thereafter

at which time the premises shall be vacated and possession surrendered to LESSOR.

4. LESSEE shall pay to LESSOR as rent for the said premises the sum of $_____ per _____

commencing _____ , 19_____ to and including _____ . Said specific date/other

sum shall be paid _____ in advance. Prorations, if any, shall be predicated upon a 30 day month. Additionally, weekly/monthly

LESSEE shall pay for all utilities and services based upon occupancy of the premises and the following charges: _____
except, _____ which shall be paid by LESSOR. Any holding over without the express written consent of LESSOR shall create a day-to-day tenancy with a fair rental value of _____ per day. Except as to daily rent and tenancy, all other covenants and conditions herein contained shall remain in full force and effect.

5. As part of the consideration passing from LESSEE to LESSOR, but for which LESSOR would not have entered into this agreement, except as provided by law, LESSEE shall maintain the premises and yards and all real and personal property as conveyed by LESSEE to LESSOR in clean, sanitary, operable condition and repair, reasonable wear and tear excluded, at LESSEE'S sole cost and expense. LESSEE further agrees upon surrendering possession that said premises shall otherwise be in the same condition as required of LESSEE to have delivered them to LESSOR at close of escrow.

6. $_____ as security has been deposited. LESSOR may use therefrom such amounts as are reasonably necessary to remedy LESSEE'S defaults in the payment of rent, to repair damages caused by LESSEE, or clean the premises if necessary upon the termination of tenancy. If used toward rent or damages during the term of this agreement, LESSEE agrees to reinstate said total security deposit upon 5 days written notice delivered to LESSEE in person or by mail. The balance of the security deposit, if any, shall be mailed to LESSEE'S last known address within 14 days of surrender of the premises.

7. As additional consideration passing from LESSEE to LESSOR, LESSEE shall obtain and maintain during the term of this lease, public liability insurance naming both LESSOR and LESSEE as co-insureds in the amount of not less than $_____ for injury to one person; $_____ for any injury to a group; and $_____ for property damage. If permitted, LESSEE agrees to retain his fire insurance on the premises in a sum of not less than designated as the sales price of the subject property.

8. In the event of any action or proceeding between LESSOR and LESSEE under this agreement, the prevailing party shall be entitled to recover reasonable attorney's fees and costs.

9. The undersigned LESSEE acknowledges having read the foregoing and receipt of a copy.

LESSOR and LESSEE have executed this lease on the day and year above written.

LESSOR _____   LESSEE _____

LESSOR _____   LESSEE _____

Form 3.40–4

VA AND FHA AMENDMENTS
CALIFORNIA ASSOCIATION OF REALTORS® STANDARD FORM

This addendum is attached as Page _____ of _____ Pages to the Real Estate Purchase Contract and Receipt for Deposit dated _____ 19 _____ in which _____

_____

is referred to as Buyer and _____

_____ is referred to as Seller.

VA LOAN

It is expressly agreed that, notwithstanding any other provisions of this contract, the purchaser shall not incur any penalty by forfeiture of earnest money or otherwise or be obligated to complete the purchase of the property described herein, if the contract purchase price or cost exceeds the reasonable value of the property established by the Veterans Administration. The purchaser shall, however, have the privilege and option of proceeding with the consummation of this contract without regard to the amount of the reasonable value established by the Veterans Administration.

Receipt of a copy is hereby acknowledged.

DATED: _____ , 19 _____   BUYER: _____

Receipt of a copy is hereby acknowledged.

DATED: _____ , 19 _____   SELLER: _____

_____

FHA LOAN

It is expressly agreed that notwithstanding any other provisions of this contract, the buyer shall not be obligated to complete the purchase of the premises and shall not incur any penalty or loss of his deposit money or otherwise unless the seller has delivered to the buyer a written statement issued by the Federal Housing Commissioner setting forth the appraised value of the property for mortgage insurance purposes of not less than $_____ , which statement the seller shall deliver to the buyer promptly after such appraised value statement is made available to the seller.

The buyer shall, however, have the privilege and option of proceeding with the consummation of this contract without regard to the amount of the appraised valuation made by the Federal Housing Commissioner.

The appraised valuation is arrived at to determine the maximum mortgage the Department of Housing and Urban Development will insure. HUD does not warrant the value or the condition of the property. The purchaser should satisfy himself/herself that the price and condition of the property are acceptable.

Receipt of a copy is hereby acknowledged.

DATED: _____ , 19 _____   BUYER: _____

Receipt of a copy is hereby acknowledged.

DATED: _____ , 19 _____   SELLER: _____

_____

NO REPRESENTATION IS MADE AS TO THE LEGAL VALIDITY OF ANY PROVISION OR THE ADEQUACY OF ANY PROVISION IN ANY SPECIFIC TRANSACTION. A REAL ESTATE BROKER IS THE PERSON QUALIFIED TO ADVISE ON REAL ESTATE. IF YOU DESIRE LEGAL ADVICE CONSULT YOUR ATTORNEY.

To order, contact—California Association of Realtors®
525 S. Virgil Avenue, Los Angeles, California 90020   **VA-FHA-11**
California Association of Realtors®

TT-L5-FG

Form 3.40–5

SPECIAL STUDIES ZONE AND FLOOD HAZARD DISCLOSURE
CALIFORNIA ASSOCIATION OF REALTORS® (CAR) STANDARD FORM

This Addendum is attached as Page _____ of _____ Pages to the Real Estate Purchase Contract and Receipt for Deposit
dated _____ 19_____ in which _____
_____

is referred to as Buyer and _____
_____ is referred to as Seller.

SPECIAL STUDIES ZONE DISCLOSURE
The property which is the subject of the contract is situated in a Special Study Zone as designated under Sections 2621-2625, inclusive, of the California Public Resources Code; and, as such, the construction or development on this property of any structure for human occupancy may be subject to the findings of a geologic report prepared by a geologist registered in the State of California, unless such report is waived by the city or county under the terms of that act. No representations on the subject are made by Seller or Agent, and the Buyer should make his/her own inquiry or investigation.
Note: California Public Resources Code #2621.5 excludes structures in existence prior to May 4, 1975;
California Public Resources Code #2621.7 excludes conversion of existing apartment houses into condominiums;
California Public Resources Code #2621.8 excludes alterations and additions under 50% of value of structure from the Special Studies Zone Act.

Buyer is allowed _____ days from date of Seller's acceptance to make further inquiries at appropriate governmental agencies concerning the use of the subject property under the terms of the Special Study Zone Act and local building, zoning, fire, health and safety codes. When such inquiries disclose conditions or information unsatisfactory to the Buyer, Buyer may cancel this agreement. If notice in writing has not been delivered within such time, this condition shall be deemed waived.

Receipt of a copy is hereby acknowledged.

DATED: _____ , 19_____   BUYER: _____

Receipt of a copy is hereby acknowledged.   _____

DATED: _____ , 19_____   SELLER: _____

_____

FLOOD HAZARD AREA DISCLOSURE
The subject property is situated in a "Special Flood Hazard Area" as set forth on a Federal Emergency Management Agency (FEMA) "Flood Insurance Rate Map" (FIRM) or "Flood Hazard Boundry Map" (FHBM). The law provides that, as a condition of obtaining financing on most structures located in a "Special Flood Hazard Area," lenders require flood insurance where the property or its attachments are security for a loan.

This requirement is mandated by the H.U.D. National Insurance Program, which requirement became effective March 1, 1976. The purpose of the program is to provide flood insurance to property at a reasonable cost.

The extent of coverage and the cost may vary. For further information consult the lender or insurance carrier. No representation or recommendation is made by the Seller and the Brokers in this transaction as to the legal effect or economic consequences of the National Flood Insurance Program and related legislation.

Receipt of a copy is hereby acknowledged.

DATED: _____ , 19_____   BUYER: _____

Receipt of a copy is hereby acknowledged   _____

DATED: _____ , 19_____   SELLER: _____

_____

┌─ OFFICE USE ONLY ─┐
Reviewed by Broker or Designee _____
Date _____
└──────────────────┘

EQUAL HOUSING OPPORTUNITY
SF-Mar-88

Reprinted by permission, California Association of Realtors. Endorsement not implied.

[§3.41] Basic Purchase and Sale Agreement

See Update §3.8 for discussion of home equity sales contracts.

[§3.42] Form: Opening Clause; Parties

The identifying names used in real property exchanges are discussed in detail in Real Property Exchanges §§1.9, 4.10 (Cal CEB 1982).

[§3.43] Form: Warranty of Partnership Authority

For limited partnerships subject to the California Revised Limited Partnership Act (discussed in Update §3.23) the certificate of partnership need not be recorded to be effective; it must be filed with the Secretary of State. Corp C §15621. However, Corp C §15621(d) provides that the certificate may be recorded and the recording creates a conclusive presumption (among other presumptions) in favor of any bona fide purchaser or encumbrancer for value that the general partners named in the certificate are all of the general partners. See Corp C §15010.5.

Purchase Price

[§3.47] Form: Fixed Price and Deposit

The treatise by Miller & Starr, cited in the Book, has been replaced by 1 Miller & Starr, California Real Estate §2.9 (2d ed 1989).

Effect of Taking Subject to Encumbrances

[§3.50] General Considerations

For further discussion of due-on-sale clauses, see Update §5.24.
Former CC §1624(7) has been redesignated as CC §1624(f).
The reference to California Mortgage and Deed of Trust Practice §§2.32–2.45, 3.26, 3.29 (Cal CEB 1979) in the Book should now be to California Mortgage and Deed of Trust Practice §§7.10–7.17, 8.44, 8.48 (2d ed Cal CEB 1990); the reference to California Mortgage and Deed of Trust Practice §§4.53–4.58 (Cal CEB 1979) in the Book should now be to 2 California Real Property Financing §§3.4–3.14 (Cal CEB 1989).

[§3.56] Form: Proration of Taxes, Insurance, and Interest

California Taxes §4.70 (Cal CEB 1978) has been replaced by 1 California Taxes §§1.45–1.49 (2d ed Cal CEB 1988).

POTENTIAL PROBLEMS AND CONTRACTUAL SOLUTIONS

[§3.65] Kinds of Solutions; Warranties

The eighth edition of Witkin, Summary of California Law, is in the process of being replaced by a ninth edition. On warranties as an affirmation, now see Witkin, Summary of California Law, *Sales* §§50–75 (9th ed 1987). On breach of warranty as an excuse for nonperformance, now see 1 Witkin, Summary, *Contracts* §§38, 40.

Problems Raised by Conditions

[§3.69] Mutuality

Friedman, Contracts and Conveyances of Real Property (3d ed 1975), cited in Book §3.69, has been replaced by Friedman, Contracts and Conveyances of Real Property (4th ed 1984).

[§3.78] Marketable Title

The Civil Code has been amended to provide specific procedures to cure defects of title caused by ancient or expired interests in property.

Civil Code §§882.020–882.040 now provide for the expiration of ancient mortgages and deeds of trust. Civil Code §§885.010–885.070 provide for the expiration of powers to enforce conditions subsequent. New CC §§886.010–886.050 provide for the expiration of unperformed contracts for sale of real property, and CC §§880.020–880.370 (on marketable record title) simplify and facilitate the transfer of real property in which interests or defects in title were created in remote times and are no longer valid. See Update §4.36 for discussion of expiration of unexercised options.

The treatise by Miller & Starr, cited in the Book, has been replaced by 1 Miller & Starr, California Real Estate §2.53 (2d ed 1989).

Exceptions to Marketable Title

[§3.83] Real Property Taxes

The law governing the procedure for a county to enforce its tax liens on real property when taxes are unpaid has been changed since publication of the Book. Effective September 11, 1984, many sections of the Revenue and Taxation Code were amended, renumbered, or repealed. Of those sections cited in the Book, Rev & T C §3351 was amended and §3511 was repealed.

The change in that part of the procedure to which Book §3.84 refers is the substitution of "notice of impending default" for "notice of intent to sell to the state," and the deletion of the reference to property sold to the state by operation of law as being "tax-sold property." Now that type of property is referred to as "tax-defaulted property."

The treatise by Miller & Starr, cited in Book §3.83, has been replaced by 3 Miller & Starr, California Real Estate §§8.123–8.143 (2d ed 1989).

[§3.85] Federal Tax Liens

Internal Revenue Code §6166A has been repealed and some of its provisions incorporated into amended IRC §6166.

ROWR Form 2333 no longer exists. However, the district offices of the IRS will issue a certificate of nonattachment of federal tax lien.

[§3.91] Reservations and Exceptions

The treatise by Miller & Starr, cited in Book §3.91, has been replaced by 5 Miller & Starr, California Real Estate §15.18 (2d ed 1989).

[§3.92] Easements

The references to CLTA forms cited in Book §3.92 should now be to the current CLTA Standard Coverage Policy revised in July 1, 1988. Those forms are reprinted in California Title Insurance Practice Update, App B (Cal CEB). The Schedule and section references to the 1973 form in the Book remain valid for the 1988 form.

[§3.93] Effect of Visible Easements

For an example of a real property buyer's being charged with constructive knowledge of a visible easement not included in a title report, see *Alcan Aluminum Corp. v Carlsberg Fin. Corp.* (9th Cir 1982) 689 F2d 815 (utility easement with wires running 80 feet above property visible from various parts of property).

[§3.95] Party Walls

For provisions for party-wall agreements, see 21 West's Legal Forms 2d Chap 36 (1986).

Powell, The Law of Real Property (1968) is updated periodically with looseleaf inserts, the most recent being December 1989.

[§3.97] Uses for Covenants, Conditions, and Restrictions

Prohibiting residency of minors in apartments has been held a violation of the Unruh Civil Rights Act (CC §§51–53) except when the project is designed for and used by senior citizens. See *Marina Point, Ltd. v Wolfson* (1982) 30 C3d 721, 180 CR 496. Civil Code §51.3 was amended effective January 1, 1986, to expand the categories of people covered by the senior citizen exceptions in the Unruh Civil Rights Act. Included by the new amendment is any person 45 years of age or older, or a spouse cohabitant, or person providing primary physical or economic support to a senior citizen (62 years of age or older, or 55 years of age or older residing in a senior citizen housing development), who resides with a senior citizen and has an ownership interest in the dwelling unit.

Note that CC §51.4 exempts senior housing built before February 8, 1982 (the date of the *Marina Point* decision) from certain special design requirements until the year 2000.

The California Supreme Court has also denied a nonprofit condominium owners association the right to exclude families with children from owning condominiums in *O'Connor v Village Green Owners Ass'n* (1983) 33 C3d 790, 191 CR 320.

A covenant restricting residents of a development to those 45 and over was held to be invalid under CC §53 in *Park Redlands Covenant Control Comm. v Simon* (1986) 181 CA3d 87, 226 CR 199. Also at issue in *Park Redlands* was a covenant that limited the maximum number of occupants per residence to three. The court found this restriction violated the owners' right to privacy as contained in the California Constitution because (1) it denied owners the right to choose with whom they lived and to live as a family, (2) it was not the least restrictive alternative to limit population density, and (3) state action was involved because a city had required the restriction in return for allowing construction of homes smaller than the minimum size imposed by its ordinance.

An adults-only restriction in a condominium development's covenants, conditions, and restrictions and the homeowners association's rules was only partially invalidated in *Sunrise Country Club Ass'n v Proud* (1987) 190 CA3d 377, 235 CR 404. The CC&Rs and association rules divided the large development into adult and family sections with separate pools for each section. A party occupying a unit in an adult section adopted two children. The homeowner's association's injunction restraining the minors from living in the unit and using the adult pools was upheld by the court of appeal, which held that division of the development into adult and family sections was not unreasonable or arbitrary age discrimination. However, a prohibition on ownership was held to violate CC §§51–53 because ownership has no necessary relationship to use.

Civil Code §798.76, effective January 1, 1979, provides that the management of a mobile home park may require a purchaser of a mobile home that will remain in the park to comply with any rule or regulation limiting residence to adults only.

In *Schmidt v Superior Court* (1989) 48 C3d 370, 256 CR 750, a mobilehome park rule requiring new residents in the park to be 25 years or older was held by the supreme court not to conflict with CC §798.76 or violate the broad antidiscrimination policy embodied in the Unruh Civil Rights Act (CC §51). The court noted that the rule may be in violation of the Fair Housing Amendments Act of 1988 (Pub L 100–430, 102 Stat 1619), effective March 13, 1989, which added provisions to the federal laws prohibiting discrimination in housing to generally bar discrimination against families with children under 18 (except for certain senior housing). However, the supreme court held that the actions in *Schmidt* occurred before the effective date of the federal law amendments. See also *Huntington Landmark Adult Community Ass'n v Ross* (1989) 213 CA3d 1012, 261 CR 875, relative to the federal law. For further discussion of *Schmidt* and the federal act, see California Condominium and Planned Development Practice Update §3.79 (Cal CEB).

Civ. Code §51 was amended effective January 1, 1988, to include blindness and physical disability as precluded basis of discrimination. However, the section specifically provides that any person renting, leasing, or otherwise providing real property for compensation shall not be required to modify the real property in any way, or to provide a higher degree of care for a blind or disabled person than for any other person.

Former CC §1355, cited in Book §3.97, was repealed. Now see CC §§1353–1354.

Existing Deed of Trust and Note

[§3.100] Importance of Examining Documents

The reference to California Mortgage and Deed of Trust Practice (Cal CEB 1979) in the Book should now be to California Mortgage and Deed of Trust Practice §§7.12–7.17 (2d ed Cal CEB 1990).

Mechanics' Liens

[§3.103] General Considerations

Civil Code §3154, providing the procedure to obtain cancellation of a mechanic's lien, was added to the Mechanics' Lien Law, effective January 1, 1980.

California Mechanics' Liens and Other Remedies (Cal CEB 1972) has been superseded by a second edition published in 1988.

The treatise by Miller & Starr, cited in the Book, has been replaced by 3 Miller & Starr, California Real Estate §7.87 (2d ed 1989).

Leases Affecting the Property

[§3.109] Purchase Subject to Leases

In the transfer of tenant-occupied property that is subject to a local rent control ordinance, the buyer should investigate whether the rents being charged comply with any limitations set out in the applicable ordinance. The buyer may also want to require the seller to warrant and represent that all rents comply with the local ordinance. See Update §3.111.

[§3.111] Form: Buyer's Right To Approve Leases; Seller's Warranty

The last sentence of paragraph (3) of Form 3.111–1 should be changed as follows if the property is subject to a local rent control ordinance:

Seller warrants and represents that, at this time and as of the closing, no other leases of the property are or will be in force; no one else has a right of possession; no rent concessions were given _ _[_state exceptions_**]_ _; no rent charged violates _ _[**_name and number of local rent control ordinance_**]_ _; no other violations of _ _[**_name and number of local rent control ordinance_**]_ _ exist; no other agreements**

were made with the tenant(s) _ _[*or any of them*]_ _; and neither Seller nor any tenant is in default under any lease.

[§3.113] Form: No New Leases

Louison v Yohanan (1981) 117 CA3d 258, 172 CR 602, is an example of a successful suit for damages for breach of a purchase contract clause providing that there would be no changes in existing leases.

[§3.116] Physical Condition of the Property

Operative July 1, 1982, owners or subdividers of units in a condominium, stock cooperative, or community apartment project converted from existing dwellings must provide to prospective buyers at the time of the first sale of the converted unit a written statement listing all substantial defects or malfunctions in the major systems in the unit or common areas of the premises. If the owner or subdivider finds after a reasonable inspection that there are no substantial defects or malfunctions, the written statement must disclaim knowledge of any substantial defects or malfunctions. CC §1134.

[§3.117] Engineering Studies and Reports

A "reasonable" exception to the rule that an upstream landowner who increases the flow into a natural watercourse is not liable to a downstream landowner for damages caused by the increased flow (*Archer v City of Los Angeles* (1941) 19 C2d 19, 119 P2d 1) was interposed by the court in *Ektelon v City of San Diego* (1988) 200 CA3d 804, 246 CR 483. The court held that an upstream landowner no longer has an absolute right to protect his land from floodwaters if the result is to increase the flow into a natural watercourse and thereby damage a downstream landowner. The court further held that the right of the upstream landowner to protect his land will be governed by ordinary principles of negligence. See also *Weaver v Bishop* (1988) 206 CA3d 1351, 254 CR 425, in which an owner on one side of a creek who placed boulders along the creek banks to protect his property from washing away was held to have acted reasonably and was found not to be liable to his neighbors on the other side of the creek. Although a natural watercourse was involved, the court relied on both the "common enemy" doctrine applicable to flood waters (right to build levees even if result is to flood downstream lands) and the surface water rule of *Keys v Romley* (1966) 64 C2d 396, 50 CR 273, (abolishing the strict liability of an owner altering the flow of surface waters which then cause damage to neighboring owners in favor of a rule of reasonableness under which an owner modifying the flow of surface waters can successfully defend a claim for damages by showing that his conduct was reasonable and that of the neighbor was unreasonable), to determine that the defendant's liability depended on the reasonableness of his conduct.

A public flood control entity is liable in inverse condemnation for the failure of a flood control improvement only if the failure can be attributed to unreasonable conduct on the public entity's part. *Belair v Riverside County Flood Control Dist.* (1988) 47 C3d 550, 253 CR 693.

[§3.123] Form: "As Is" Clause; No Warranties Given by Seller

See Update §1.73 for discussion of former CC §1134.5, which required a transferor of real property containing one to four residential units to disclose to the transferee whether structural additions or significant other changes that were made while the transferor owned the property (or that the transferor knew about) were made under an appropriate permit.

Structural Pest Control Inspection

[§3.126] Form: Condition; Structural Pest Control Inspection

Operative January 1, 1987, only individuals will be licensed as structural pest control operators. Bus & P C §8506. Sole proprietorships, partnerships, corporations, and other business organizations that are registered to engage in the practice of structural pest control will be known as "registered companies." Bus & P C §8506.1. Effective January 1, 1987, references in Book §3.126 to structural pest control operators should be to registered companies. Effective January 1, 1987, the following form should be used instead of that set out in Book §3.126:

Form 3.126–1

Buyer's approval of the report issued under Business and Professions Code §8516 of a registered company, dated _ _ _ _ _ _, 19_ _ or later, certifying that the company inspected the property and that no accessible areas of the property are infested by termites, dry rot, fungi, or other wood-destroying pests or organisms. _ _[Seller/ Buyer]_ _ shall pay the cost of such inspections.

If the registered company's report discloses any infestation of or damage to the property caused by wood-destroying pests or organisms, Seller shall cause the necessary corrective work to be done and shall deliver to the escrow holder and Buyer before the close of escrow a certificate or a Notice of Work Completed under Business and Professions Code §8519(b) attested to by the registered company stating that the required corrective work has been completed and that the property is now free of evidence of active infestation or infection. The cost of such corrective work shall be paid from funds accruing to Seller at the close of escrow. If the registered company's report also indicates that preventive work is recommended, Buyer shall have the option of having such work done at the same time as the corrective work by delivering a notice in writing to escrow holder and Seller within _ _[e.g., five]_ _

days after Seller advises Buyer in writing of the recommended preventive work. Buyer shall pay for such preventive work through escrow.

Use and Development of Property

[§3.132] Zoning

The reference in Book §3.132 to Los Angeles Mun Ct R §96.302 should be to Los Angeles Mun C §96.302.

Subdivision

[§3.143] Need for Map and Related Approvals

The Davis-Stirling Common Interest Development Act (CC §§1350–1372), effective January 1, 1986, contains provisions respecting the creation and essential attributes of common interest developments, including community apartment projects, condominium projects, planned developments, and stock cooperatives. See Bus & P C §11018.1. See also California Condominium and Planned Development Practice Update §1.1A (Cal CEB); Rosenberry, *The Davis-Stirling Common Interest Development Act,* 8 CEB Real Prop L Rep 172 (Nov. 1985).

Cities and local agencies may adopt regulations or ordinances concerning matters covered by the Subdivision Map Act (Govt C §§66410–66499.37) if they are not inconsistent with the act. In *Griffin Dev. Co. v City of Oxnard* (1985) 39 C3d 256, 217 CR 1, the supreme court held that the Subdivision Map Act did not preempt Oxnard's condominium conversion ordinance.

[§3.144] Form: Condition; Subject to Map and Related Approvals

Effective March 1, 1982, Govt C §66499.30 was amended to specifically declare that an offer or contract to sell, lease, or finance real property or to construct improvements on real property is not prohibited by the requirement that a final map and parcel map be recorded before taking those actions (Govt C §66499.30(a)–(b)) when the transaction or the beginning of construction is expressly conditioned on the approval and filing of a final subdivision map or parcel map. Govt C §66499.30(e).

Environmental Requirements

[§3.147] California Environmental Quality Act

The provisions of Title 14 of the California Code of Regulations (formerly the California Administrative Code) dealing with CEQA have been extensively renumbered since publication of the Book. The following chart gives the old section or sections as cited in the Book and the corresponding new section or sections:

14 Cal Code Regs

Old Section(s)	New Section(s)
§15060	§15061(a)(3)
§15071(b)	§15269(b)
§§15100–15129	§§15260–15329
§15100.1	§15300.1
§15073	§15268
§§15035.5, 15074	§§15061–15062
§§15033, 15083	§§15070–15075

Other specific exemptions to CEQA have been adopted since publication of the Book. They are found at 14 Cal Code Regs §§15300–15329.

Public agencies are exempt under Pub Res C §21080 from preparing an EIR or a negative declaration for specified actions, including actions taken before January 1, 1982, to implement changes in property taxation resulting from adoption of the Jarvis-Gann Initiative (Proposition 13), Cal Const art XIIIA, on June 6, 1978. Pub Res C §21080(b)(9).

In *Newberry Springs Water Ass'n v County of San Bernardino* (1984) 150 CA3d 740, 749, 198 CR 100, 105, the court noted that *No Oil, Inc. v City of Los Angeles* (1974) 13 C3d 68, 118 CR 34 (cited in Book §3.147), stated that the existence of a serious public controversy may make an EIR desirable but did not make an EIR necessary.

[§3.148] National Environmental Policy Act

The current citation for the National Environmental Policy Act (NEPA) is 42 USC §§4321–4370.

[§3.149] California Coastal Act

The conversion of an apartment building located in the coastal zone into a stock cooperative has been held subject to the permit requirements of the California Coastal Commission. *California Coastal Comm'n v Quanta Inv. Corp.* (1980) 113 CA3d 579, 609, 170 CR 263, 280.

[§3.150] Form: Special Studies Zone

See Update §3.40–1 for the current Special Studies Zone form.

Effective January 1, 1991, for all transactions subject to CC §1102 (specified transactions of real property with one to four dwelling units), the disclosure required by Pub Res C §2621.9 must be made in the real estate transfer disclosure statement set out in CC §1102.6 or the local option real estate transfer disclosure statement set out in CC §1102.6a. Pub Res C §2621.9(b).

[§3.157] Business Operations on Property

Drafting Agreements for the Sale of Businesses (Cal CEB 1971) has been superseded by a second edition published in 1988.

[§3.160] Business Assets and Liabilities

The conclusive presumption of fraud regarding certain personal property transfers has been deleted from CC §3440 effective January 1, 1986. See CC §§3440–3440.1. However, the type of transfer covered by CC §3440 is still void as to the transferor's creditors.

Drafting Agreements for the Sale of Businesses, chap 2 (Cal CEB 1971) has been replaced by Drafting Agreements for the Sale of Businesses §§2.15–2.53 (2d ed Cal CEB 1988).

Business Buy-Out Agreements (Cal CEB 1976) has been replaced by Business Buy-Sell Agreements (Cal CEB 1991).

Brokers

[§3.175] Form: Broker's Commission

Former CC §1624(5) has been redesignated as CC §1624(d).

Remedies

[§3.180] Form: Liquidated Damages

Comment: An agreement for the sale of property in *Bleecher v Conte* (1981) 29 C3d 345, 173 CR 278, provided that the seller's sole remedy for breach was liquidated damages. The court held that this provision did not prevent the buyers from compelling the specific performance of the contract because California no longer requires mutuality of remedy as a prerequisite to obtaining an order for specific performance.

See Update §12.46 on availability of specific performance when there is a liquidated damages provision.

[§3.181] Form: Attorneys' Fees

Comment: An attorneys' fee provision between the buyer and the seller in a purchase-and-sale agreement cannot be enforced by the buyer against an intervening non-bona fide buyer from the seller, against whom the original buyer brings his or her successful specific performance action. The intervening buyer, although the proper defendant in the specific performance action (CC §3395), was not a party to the original purchase-and-sale agreement and had not assumed the obligations of the agreement. *Glynn v Marquette* (1984) 152 CA3d 277, 199 CR 306.

[§3.182] Form: Effect of Waiver of Provision on Remedy

The references to Witkin in the Book should now be to 1 Witkin, Summary of California Law, *Contracts* §767 (9th ed 1987) and 3 California Procedure, *Actions* §131 (3d ed 1985), respectively.

[§3.183] Form: Arbitration

An arbitration clause in a purchase and sale agreement was held to apply and arbitration was compelled in *Izzy v Mesquite Country Club* (1986) 186 CA3d 1309, 231 CR 72, a tort class action. The court held that the alleged tort (failing to disclose the creation of a special assessment district) had its roots in the vendor-purchaser relationship created by the purchase and sale agreement and was within the scope of the arbitration clause.

Operative July 1, 1989, CCP §§1298, 1298.5, 1298.7, and 1298.8 require specified statutory language in certain real property contracts that are entered into on or after that date and that contain binding arbitration clauses. The contracts requiring the statutory language include contracts to convey real property, contracts that contemplate conveying real property in the future, and contracts or agreements between principals and agents in real property sales transactions. Examples of such contracts given in CCP §1298(a) include marketing contracts, deposit receipts, real property sales contracts, leases together with options to purchase, ground leases coupled with improvements, and listing agreements. Powers of sale contained in deeds of trust and mortgages are specifically excluded by CCP §1298(a).

Code of Civil Procedure §1298(b) requires that binding arbitration clauses in covered contracts be clearly titled "ARBITRATION OF DISPUTES." If the contract is printed, this title must be in at least 8-point bold type or in contrasting red in at least 8-point type. If the contract is typed, the title must be set out in capital letters.

In addition to the required title, CCP §1298(c) requires that the following language must appear immediately before the line or space provided for the parties to indicate their assent or nonassent to the binding arbitration clause and immediately following the binding arbitration clause in the same type size and style stated in CCP §1298(b):

NOTICE: BY INITIALING IN THE SPACE BELOW YOU ARE AGREEING TO HAVE ANY DISPUTE ARISING OUT OF THE MATTERS INCLUDED IN THE "ARBITRATION OF DISPUTES" PROVISION DECIDED BY NEUTRAL ARBITRATION AS PROVIDED BY CALIFORNIA LAW AND YOU ARE GIVING UP ANY RIGHTS YOU MIGHT POSSESS TO HAVE THE DISPUTE LITIGATED IN A COURT OR JURY TRIAL. BY INITIALING IN THE SPACE BELOW YOU ARE GIVING UP YOUR JUDICIAL RIGHTS TO DISCOVERY AND APPEAL, UNLESS SUCH RIGHTS ARE SPECIFICALLY INCLUDED IN THE "ARBITRATION OF DISPUTES" PROVISION. IF YOU REFUSE TO SUBMIT TO ARBITRATION AFTER AGREEING TO THIS PROVISION, YOU MAY BE COMPELLED TO ARBITRATE UNDER THE AUTHORITY OF THE CALIFORNIA CODE OF CIVIL PROCE-

DURE. YOUR AGREEMENT TO THIS ARBITRATION PROVISION
IS VOLUNTARY. "WE HAVE READ AND UNDERSTAND THE FORE-
GOING AND AGREE TO SUBMIT DISPUTES ARISING OUT OF THE
MATTERS INCLUDED IN THE 'ARBITRATION OF DISPUTES' PRO-
VISION TO NEUTRAL ARBITRATION."

[§3.183A] Form: Private Judging

**Any controversy or claim arising out of or relating to this agree-
ment or the breach thereof shall be tried by a _ _[*referee under an
order of general reference to try all the issues/judge pro tem*]_ _ to be
chosen by counsel for the parties from a list of retired judges furnished by the presiding judge of the Superior Court for the County
of _ _ _ _ _, California; if counsel are unable to agree, then by a
_ _[*referee/judge pro tem*]_ _ chosen by said presiding judge from
said list. Each party waives the right to trial by jury. The trial should
be conducted and the issues determined under the statutory and
decisional law of California.**

**The _ _[*referee/judge pro tem*]_ _ is to be compensated at a rate
of $_ _ _ _ _ _ per hour. Each party shall pay his or her prorata share
of the fee of the _ _[*referee/judge pro tem*]_ _, together with other
expenses incurred or approved by the _ _[*referee/judge pro tem*]_ _,
not including counsel fees or witness fees or other expenses incurred
by a party for his or her own benefit. The prevailing party shall
not be entitled to reimbursement from the losing party for any such
fees or expenses.**

Comment: An alternative to suit or arbitration is to engage a private
judge—either a referee as authorized under CCP §§638–645.1 or a tempo-
rary judge under Cal Const art VI, §21. See also Cal Rules of Ct 244;
Oster & Wheatley, *"Rent-A-Judge—Private Judging": What It Is and
How It Works,* 4 CEB Civ Litigation Rep 65 (June 1982).

Interpretation of the Agreement

[§3.186] Form: Integration Clause

On admitting extrinsic evidence to interpret ambiguities in contracts,
now see Witkin, California Evidence §§983, 989 (3d ed 1986), which
replace the sections cited in Book §3.186.

[§3.188] Form: Binding on Successors

On contracts surviving the death of the promisor, now see 1 Witkin,
Summary of California Law, *Contracts* §782 (9th ed 1987).

4

Options

ANALYSIS OF OPTIONS

[§4.6] Requisites for Enforceability

Former CC §1624(4) has been redesignated as CC §1624(c).

An option price designated simply as the "fair market value" was held sufficiently specific to render an option to purchase in a lease specifically enforceable. *Goodwest Rubber Corp. v Munoz* (1985) 170 CA3d 919, 216 CR 604. The court relied on a number of out-of-state cases that held price terms such as "fair market value," "reasonable value," or "current market value" to be sufficiently certain to support specific performance of an option to purchase. The court noted that determining fair market value was a common task performed by courts, did not require the future agreement of the buyer and seller, and consequently seemed a proper substitute for a specific purchase price.

Consideration for the Option

[§4.7] Value of Consideration for the Option

The treatise by Miller & Starr, cited in the Book, has been replaced by 1 Miller & Starr, California Real Estate §1.42 (2d ed 1989).

[§4.11] The Rule Against Perpetuities

Effective January 1, 1992, CC §§715.2 and 715.6 have been repealed and their provisions combined and moved to Prob C §21205. See the Uniform Statutory Rule Against Perpetuities at Prob C §§21200–21225. Under Prob C §21205, an interest that vests or terminates within 90 years of its creation will not violate the rule.

When co-owners of real property enter into an agreement giving each preemptive rights such as a right of first refusal, the agreement is personal to the co-owners and cannot be enforced by one party's testamentary trustee. It would violate the rule against perpetutities if the agreement was interpreted to allow a testamentary trustee the benefit of the preemptive right. *Strong v Theis* (1986) 187 CA3d 913, 232 CR 272.

Termination of Options

[§4.17] Death of Optionor Does Not Terminate Option

Operative July 1, 1988, Prob C §850 has been repealed and replaced by Prob C §§9860(a)(1), 9867 without substantive change.

Operative July 1, 1989, Prob C §300 is repealed and replaced by Prob C §§7000–7001 without substantive change.

[§4.22] Remedies

Civil Code §3306 was amended effective January 1, 1984, to delete the requirement that bad faith be shown before the optionee may recover the difference between the price agreed to be paid and the value of the estate at the time of breach and expenses incurred in preparing to enter on the land. That section was also amended to provide for the recovery of consequential damages and interest.

The lessee who succeeds in specifically enforcing an option contained in his or her lease may be entitled to attorneys' fees and court costs in both the trial and appellate courts if the lease provides for those damages. The lessee may also be entitled to interim rent paid from the end of the option period to the date of judgment if the lessor acted in bad faith in failing to honor the option contract. *Erich v Granoff* (1980) 109 CA3d 920, 167 CR 538.

THE OPTION AGREEMENT

[§4.36] Form: Recording Quitclaim Deed on Termination of Option

Comment: Civil Code §1213.5 was repealed effective January 1, 1983, and replaced by CC §§884.010–884.030, which apply to all recorded instruments that create or give constructive notice of options to purchase real property (CC §884.030(a)).

An option now expires of record unless an instrument that gives notice of exercise or extension of the option is recorded within six months after the expiration date of the option according to its terms. CC §884.010(a). However, CC §884.010 did not cause an option that expired according to its terms between January 1, 1982, and January 1, 1984, to expire of record before January 1, 1984. If the option does not provide an expiration date, the six-month period (five years for options recorded before January 1, 1983, with no expiration date; CC §884.030(c)) begins when the instrument creating or giving constructive notice of the option is recorded. CC §884.010(b).

Although CC §884.010 does not prescribe the time within which the option must be exercised or how it must be exercised, an optionee who has exercised his or her option before its expiration should also record a notice of exercise when the actual transfer will or may occur more than six months after the expiration date of the option. CC §884.030(b). See 16 Calif L Rev'n Comm'n Reports 440 (1981), relating to marketable title of real property; CC §884.020. Options that expired under former CC §1213.5 are not revived by new CC §§884.010–884.030. CC §884.030(d).

RECORDING THE OPTION

[§4.42] Reasons for Recording Memorandum of Option

Civil Code §1213.5 has been repealed. See discussion in Update §4.36.

5

Seller Financing

INTRODUCTION

[§5.1] Why Seller Financing?

The disclosure requirements of CC §§2956–2967 are discussed in more detail in Fishkin, *Disclosures in Creative Financing: Disclosures I, II, and III,* 6 CEB Real Prop L Rep 133 (Oct. 1983).

[§5.1A] Seller Financing Disclosures

Effective July 1, 1983, CC §§2956–2967 require that certain specified written disclosures be made to both the buyer and the seller regarding financing provided through an "arranger of credit" by the seller of a one-to-four-unit dwelling. An arranger of credit is broadly defined in CC §2957(a) to include any party to the transaction who is a real estate licensee or attorney or any nonparty who is involved in developing or negotiating credit terms, who participates in completion of credit documents, and who directly or indirectly receives compensation for arranging the financing or from the transaction that the financing facilitates. Exceptions to the definition of arranger of credit are provided for the escrow agent, an attorney who represents one of the parties, and real estate licensees and attorneys who are parties themselves, but only if they are represented by a real estate licensee. Violation of the provisions does not invalidate the credit or security document concerned but subjects the violator to liability for actual damages incurred by the seller or buyer as a result of the violation.

For further discussion of CC §§2956–2967, see Fishkin, *Disclosures in Creative Financing: Disclosures I, II, and III,* 6 CEB Real Prop L Rep 133 (Oct. 1983).

[§5.1B] Form: Seller Financing Disclosure

Form 5.1B

CALIFORNIA ASSOCIATION OF REALTORS

SELLER FINANCING DISCLOSURE STATEMENT
(California Civil Code 2956-2967)
CALIFORNIA ASSOCIATION OF REALTORS' (CAR) STANDARD FORM

This two page disclosure statement from the Purchaser (Buyer) and Vendor (Seller) is prepared by an arranger of credit [defined in Civil Code 2957 (a)] and provided to **both** the Purchaser (Buyer) and Vendor (Seller) in a residential real estate transaction involving four or fewer units whenever the Seller has agreed to extend credit to the Buyer as part of the purchase price.

Buyer: _____

Seller: _____

Arranger of Credit: _____

Real Property: _____

A. Credit Documents: This extension of credit by the Seller is evidenced by ☐ note and deed of trust, ☐ all-inclusive note and deed of trust, ☐ installment land sale contract, ☐ lease/option (when parties intend transfer of equitable title), ☐ other (specify) _____

B. Credit Terms:
1. ☐ See attached copy of credit documents referred to in Section A above for description of credit terms; **or**
2. ☐ The terms of the credit documents referred to in Section A above are: Principal amount $_____ interest at _____% per annum payable at $_____ per _____ (month/year/etc.) with the entire unpaid principal and accrued interest of approximately $_____ due _____ 19_____ (maturity date).

Late Charge: If any payment is not made within _____ days after it is due, a late charge of $_____ or _____% of the installment due may be charged to the Buyer.

Prepayment: If all or part of this loan is paid early, the Buyer ☐ will, ☐ will **not**, have to pay a prepayment penalty as follows: _____
_____

Due on Sale: If any interest in the property securing this obligation is sold or otherwise transferred, the Seller ☐ has, ☐ does **not** have, the option to require immediate payment of the entire unpaid balance and accrued interest.

Other Terms: _____
_____

C. Available information on loans/encumbrances * that will be **senior** to the Seller's extension of credit:

	1st	2nd	3rd
1. Original Balance	$_____	$_____	$_____
2. Current Balance	$_____	$_____	$_____
3. Periodic Payment (e.g. $100/month)	$_____ / _____	$_____ / _____	$_____ / _____
4. Amt. of Balloon Payment	$_____	$_____	$_____
5. Date of Balloon Payment			
6. Maturity Date			
7. Due On Sale ('Yes' or 'No')			
8. Interest Rate (per annum)	_____%	_____%	_____%
9. Fixed or Variable Rate: If Variable Rate:	☐ a copy of note attached ☐ variable provisions are explained on attached separate sheet	☐ a copy of note attached ☐ variable provisions are explained on attached separate sheet	☐ a copy of note attached ☐ variable provisions are explained on attached separate sheet
10. Is Payment Current?			

☐ SEPARATE SHEET WITH INFORMATION REGARDING OTHER SENIOR LOANS/ENCUMBRANCES IS ATTACHED.

* IMPORTANT NOTE: Asterisk ( ) denotes an estimate.

D. Caution: If any of the obligations secured by the property calls for a balloon payment, then Seller and Buyer are aware that refinancing of the balloon payment at maturity may be difficult or impossible depending on the conditions in the mortgage marketplace at that time. There are no assurances that new financing or a loan extension will be available when the balloon payment is due.

E. Deferred Interest:
"Deferred interest" results when the Buyer's periodic payments are less than the amount of interest earned on the obligation, or when the obligation does not require periodic payments. This accrued interest will have to be paid by the Buyer at a later time and may result in the Buyer owing more on the obligation than at origination.
☐ The credit being extended to the Buyer by the Seller does **not** provide for "deferred interest," **or**
☐ The credit being extended to the Buyer by the Seller does provide for "deferred interest."
    The credit documents provide the following regarding deferred interest:
    ☐ All deferred interest shall be due and payable along with the principal at maturity (simple interest); **or**
    ☐ The deferred interest shall be added to the principal _____ (e.g., annually, monthly, etc.) and thereafter shall bear interest at the rate specified in the credit documents (compound interest); **or**
    ☐ Other (specify) _____

F. All-Inclusive Deed of Trust or Installment Land Sale Contract:
☐ This transaction does **not** involve the use of an all-inclusive (or wraparound) deed of trust or an installment land sale contract; **or**
☐ This transaction **does** involve the use of either an all-inclusive (or wraparound) deed of trust or an installment land sale contract which provides as follows:
    1) In the event of an acceleration of any senior encumbrance, the responsibility for payment or for legal defense is:
      ☐ **Not** specified in the credit or security documents; **or**
      ☐ Specified in the credit or security documents as follows:
_____
_____

Buyer and Seller acknowledge receipt of copy of this page, which constitutes Page 1 of 2 Pages.
Buyer's Initials (_____) (_____) Seller's Initials (_____) (_____)

---- OFFICE USE ONLY ----
Reviewed by Broker or Designee _____
Date _____

EQUAL HOUSING OPPORTUNITY

SELLER FINANCING DISCLOSURE STATEMENT (SFD-14 PAGE 1 OF 2)

2) In the event of the prepayment of a senior encumbrance, the responsibilities and rights of Seller and Buyer regarding refinancing, prepayment penalties, and any prepayment discounts are:
☐ **Not** specified in the credit or security documents; **or**
☐ Specified in the credit or security documents as follows:
_____
_____

3) The financing provided that the Buyer will make periodic payments to _____ [e.g., a collection agent (such as a bank or savings and loan); Seller; etc.] and that _____ will be responsible for disbursing payments to the payee(s) on the senior encumbrance(s) and to the Seller.

CAUTION: The parties are advised to consider designating a neutral third party as the collection agent for receiving Buyer's payments and disbursing them to the payee(s) on the senior encumbrance(s) and to the Seller.

G. Buyer's Creditworthiness: Section 580(b) of the California Code of Civil Procedure generally limits a Seller's rights in the event of a default by the Buyer in the financing extended by the Seller, to a foreclosure of the property.
☐ No disclosure concerning the Buyer's creditworthiness has been made to the Seller; **or**
☐ The following representations concerning the Buyer's creditworthiness have been made by the Buyer(s) to the Seller:

1. Occupation: _____	1. Occupation: _____
2. Employer: _____	2. Employer: _____
3. Length of Employment: _____	3. Length of Employment: _____
4. Monthly Gross Income: _____	4. Monthly Gross Income: _____
5. Buyer ☐ has, ☐ has **not**, provided Seller a current credit report issued by: _____	5. Buyer ☐ has, ☐ has **not**, provided Seller a current credit report issued by: _____
6. Buyer ☐ has, ☐ has **not**, provided Seller a completed loan application.	6. Buyer ☐ has, ☐ has **not**, provided Seller a completed loan application.
7. Other (specify): _____	7. Other (specify): _____

H. Insurance:
☐ The parties' escrow holder or insurance carrier has been or will be directed to add a loss payee clause to the property insurance protecting the Seller, **or**
☐ No provision has been made for adding a loss payee clause to the property insurance protecting the Seller. Seller is advised to secure such clauses or acquire a separate insurance policy.

I. Request for Notice:
☐ A Request for Notice of Default under Section 2924(b) of the California Civil Code has been or will be recorded; **or**
☐ No provision for recording a Request for Notice of Default has been made. Seller is advised to consider recording a Request for Notice of Default.

J. Title Insurance:
☐ Title insurance coverage will be provided to **both** Seller and Buyer insuring their respective interests in the property; **or**
☐ No provision for title insurance coverage of **both** Seller and Buyer has been made. Seller and Buyer are advised to consider securing such title insurance coverage.

K. Tax Service:
☐ A tax service has been arranged to report to Seller whether property taxes have been paid on the property. _____ (e.g., Seller, Buyer, etc.) will be responsible for the continued retention and payment of such tax service; **or**
☐ No provision has been made for a tax service. Seller should consider retaining a tax service or otherwise determine that the property taxes are paid.

L. Recording:
☐ The security documents (e.g., deed of trust, installment land contract, etc.) will be recorded with the county recorder where the property is located; **or**
☐ The security documents will **not** be recorded with the county recorder. Seller and Buyer are advised that their respective interests in the property may be jeopardized by intervening liens, judgments or subsequent transfers which **are** recorded.

M. Proceeds to Buyer:
☐ Buyer will **NOT** receive any cash proceeds at the close of the sale transaction; **or**
☐ Buyer will receive approximately $_____ from _____ (indicate source from the sale transaction proceeds of such funds). Buyer represents that the purpose of such disbursement is as follows: _____

N. Notice of Delinquency:
☐ A Request for Notice of Delinquency under Section 2924(e) of the California Civil Code has been or will be made to the Senior lienholder(s); **or**
☐ No provision for making a Request for Notice of Delinquency has been made. Seller should consider making a Request for Notice of Delinquency.

The above information has been provided to: (a) the Buyer, by the arranger of credit and the Seller (with respect to information within the knowledge of the Seller); (b) the Seller, by the arranger of credit and the Buyer (with respect to information within the knowledge of the Buyer).

Arranger of Credit _____
Date _____, 19____ By _____

Buyer and Seller acknowledge that the information each has provided to the arranger of credit for inclusion in this disclosure form is accurate to the best of their knowledge.

Buyer and Seller hereby acknowledge receipt of a completed copy of this disclosure form.

Date _____, 19____ Date _____, 19____

Buyer _____ Seller _____

Buyer _____ Seller _____

OFFICE USE ONLY
Reviewed by Broker or Designee _____
Date _____

Comment: Operative July 1, 1985, CC §2963 requires, in addition to the information listed in the above form, either a statement that a request for notice of delinquency under CC §2924e has been made or, if no request has been made, a statement that the seller should consider making a request for a notice of delinquency.

The required disclosures, which are set forth in CC §2963(a)–(p), must be given to the buyer by both the arranger of credit and the seller (information within the knowledge of the seller), and to the seller by both the arranger of credit and the buyer (information within the knowledge of the buyer). CC §2956.

No disclosure is required to be given the buyer or seller, however, when he or she is entitled to receive a disclosure under other disclosure laws set forth in CC §2958, such as the federal Truth in Lending Act (15 USC §1604).

Lawyer's Role in Financing

[§5.3] Standard of Care

The duty of an attorney to his or her client in a real property sales transaction does not extend to other third parties involved in the transaction. In *St. Paul Title Co. v Meier* (1986) 181 CR3d 948, 226 CR 538, an escrow agent, sued by a buyer for failure to properly implement escrow instructions, cross-complained against the buyer's attorney on the theory that the attorney created confusing escrow instructions. The court of appeal affirmed a summary judgment in favor of the attorney, holding he owed no professional duty to an escrow agent whom he did not represent.

SELLER FINANCING DEVICES

The Installment Land Contract

[§5.5] Periods of Usage; Disadvantages

In *Petersen v Hartell* (1985) 40 C3d 102, 219 CR 170, the supreme court avoided treating an installment land contract as the equivalent of a mortgage or deed of trust. The court allowed a willfully defaulting vendee who made substantial payments on an installment sale contract, used only as a security device, to complete the purchase by paying the entire remaining balance plus damages before the seller was allowed to quiet title. The court held that this right to redeem was absolute in such a situation. However, the majority opinion specifically refused to extend mortgagor or trustor protections under CC §2924 to the installment sale contract vendee as was urged by former Chief Justice Bird in a concurring and dissenting opinion. The court held that such an extension was unnecessary under the facts of the case and thus limited its holding to defaulting vendees who have paid a substantial part of the purchase price. Note that four out of the five justices in support of the majority opinion in the case are no longer on the court.

Effective January 1, 1987, new CC §2920(b) was added, which for purposes of CC §§2924–2924h (nonjudicial foreclosure sales) defines "mortgage" as any security device, including a real property sales contract, that contains a power of sale.

The reference to California Mortgage and Deed of Trust Practice (Cal CEB 1979) in the Book should now be to California Mortgage and Deed of Trust Practice §1.35 (2d ed Cal CEB 1990).

[§5.6] Protective Statutory and Regulatory Provisions

Former 10 Cal Adm C §§2814–2814.8 (now called the California Code of Regulations) have been repealed. Now see 10 Cal Code Regs §2791.9.

[§5.7] Income Tax Reporting by Seller

California has conformed the California income tax law on taxation of installment payments to IRC §§453–453B. See Rev & T C §17551.

Anderson, Tax Factors in Real Estate Operations (6th ed 1980) has been replaced by Manolakas, Tax Factors in Real Estate Operations (7th ed 1990).

[§5.9] Promissory Note Secured by Mortgage or Deed of Trust

The reference to California Mortgage and Deed of Trust Practice (Cal CEB 1979) in the Book should now be to California Mortgage and Deed of Trust Practice (2d ed Cal CEB 1990), and 1, 2 California Real Property Financing (Cal CEB 1988, 1989).

POSTPONING SELLER'S INCOME TAX LIABILITY

[§§5.10–5.14] Installment Method of Reporting Gain; IRC §453

Transfers between spouses or incident to divorce do not result in gain or loss. IRC §453B(g), added by the Tax Reform Act of 1984 (Pub L 98–369, 98 Stat 494).

California has conformed the California income tax law on taxation of installment payments to IRC §§453–453B. See Rev & T C §17551.

The reference to California Mortgage and Deed of Trust Practice (Cal CEB 1979) in Book §5.13 should now be to California Mortgage and Deed of Trust Practice §§7.19–7.25 (2d ed Cal CEB 1990).

[§5.13] Seller's Ability To Limit Prepayments

Both CC §2954.9 and Bus & P C §10242.6 have been amended effective

January 1, 1991, to provide that their prepayment penalty provisions do not apply when the subject residential structure securing the loan "has been damaged to such an extent by a natural disaster for which a state of emergency is declared by the Governor, pursuant to Chapter 7 (commencing with Section 8550) of Division 1 of Title 2 of the Government Code, that the dwelling cannot be occupied and the prepayment is causally related thereto." Bus & P C §10242.6.

[§5.16] Deferred Payment Sales

Revenue Ruling 79–292, cited in Book §5.16, has been clarified by Rev Rul 89–122, 1989–47 Int Rev Bull 6.

[§§5.17–5.22] DEFERRING PAYMENTS; FORM PROVISIONS FOR THE PURCHASE AND SALE AGREEMENT

The references to California Mortgage and Deed of Trust Practice §6.17 (Cal CEB 1979) in Book §§5.19–5.21 should now be to California Mortgage and Deed of Trust Practice §2.17 (2d ed Cal CEB 1990).

The references to California Mortgage and Deed of Trust Practice §§2.22, 2.24, 2.30, 2.32, 2.46–2.49 (Cal CEB 1979) in the Book should now be to 1 California Real Property Financing §§3.9–3.14, 3.35–3.39, 3.42 (Cal CEB 1989), respectively.

[§5.20] Form: Note for Balance; Annual Payments Limited

Civil Code §2954.9 has been amended effective January 1, 1991, to provide that its prepayment penalty provisions do not apply when the subject residential structure securing the loan "has been damaged to such an extent by a natural disaster for which a state of emergency has been declared by the Governor, pursuant to Chapter 7 (commencing with Section 8550) of Division 1 of Title 2 of the Government Code, that the residential structure cannot be occupied and the prepayment is causally related thereto."

[§5.21] Form: Acceleration of Balance on Deferred Payments

Civil Code §2924c was amended effective January 1, 1986, to allow curing of a monetary default and reinstatement of a deed of trust or mortgage at any time during the period beginning with the date of recordation of the notice of default until five business days before the date of trustee's sale set forth in the initial recorded notice of trustee's sale or, if the sale is postponed for more than five business days, until five business days before the date of the postponed sale.

RETAINING EXISTING ENCUMBRANCES

[§5.23] General Considerations

Former CC §1624(7) was redesignated CC §1624(f).

Buyer's Assumption of, or Sale Subject to, Existing Encumbrances

[§5.24] Due-on-Sale Clauses

Due-on-sale clauses in Cal-Vet contracts were held enforceable in *Department of Veterans Affairs v Duerksen* (1982) 138 CA3d 149, 187 CR 832.

The United States Congress entered the due-on-sale enforcement controversy by enacting the Garn-St. Germain Depository Institutions Act of 1982 (Pub L 97–320, 96 Stat 1469) on October 15, 1982 (known as the Garn Act). Garn Act §341 (12 USC §1701j–3) preempts all state law, after October 14, 1982, including judicial decisions limiting or restricting enforcement of due-on-sale clauses in real property loans, and provides that enforcement of those clauses shall be exclusively governed by the terms of the loan contract secured by the real property. Garn Act §341(b)(1) (12 USC §1701j–3(b)(1)).

Garn Act §341(c)(1) (12 USC §1701j–3(c)(1)) created a window period for loans (other than loans originated by a federal savings and loan association or a federal savings bank; Garn Act §341(c)(2)(C) (12 USC §1701j–3(c)(2)(C)) made, taken subject to, or assumed during the period beginning on the date a State adopted a constitutional provision or statute prohibiting the exercise of due-on-sale clauses, or the date on which the highest court of such State has rendered a decision (or if the highest court has not so decided, the date on which the next highest appellate court has rendered a decision resulting in a final judgment if such decision applies State-wide) prohibiting such exercise, and ending on October 15, 1982.

Such "window period" loans were not subject to federal preemption for a three-year period ending October 15, 1982. The Federal Home Loan Bank Board issued final regulations (12 CFR §§591.1–591.6) effective May 13, 1983, implementing Garn Act §341. For a discussion of these regulations and their possible impact on due-on-sale clauses used in California, see Rader, *The Federal Home Loan Bank Board Issues Final Regulations To Implement the Due-on-Sale Provisions of the Garn-St. Germain Act,* 6 CEB Real Prop L Rep 93 (July 1983).

A lender may not impose a prepayment penalty or equivalent fee for, or in connection with, the loan's acceleration by exercising a due-on-sale clause for security on an owner-occupied residence under Garn Act §341. 12 CFR §591.5(b)(2). Depending on the wording of the prepayment penalty clause, the imposition of a prepayment penalty may also be prohibited following a due-on-sale acceleration of a loan entered into before Garn

Act §341 was enacted. See *Tan v California Fed. Sav. & Loan Ass'n* (1983) 140 CA3d 800, 189 CR 775.

After the decision in *Tan,* CC §2954.10 was enacted to prohibit a lender from charging a prepayment fee following acceleration of a loan, secured by residential real property containing four units or fewer, by the exercise of a due-on-sale clause. That provision does not apply if the property is nonresidential real property or residential real property containing more than four units and the obligor has expressly waived the right to repay without penalty or has agreed to pay a prepayment penalty on acceleration. For loans made on or after January 1, 1984, the waiver must be separately signed or initialed by the borrower and "its enforcement shall be supported by evidence of a course of conduct by the obligee of individual weight to the consideration in that transaction for the waiver or agreement." It can be argued that CC §2954.10 is preempted by the Garn Act and its implementing regulations because, except for window-period loans, as stated in 12 CFR §591.5(a), the "due-on-sale practices of Federal associations and other lenders shall be governed exclusively by the Board's regulations."

Even if a lender does possess the right to accelerate a loan under a due-on-sale clause, that right may be waived. *Rubin v Los Angeles Fed. Sav. & Loan Ass'n* (1984) 159 CA3d 292, 205 CR 455 (lender did not proceed to foreclose and accepted payments from new buyer with full knowledge of the transfer and without any reservation of rights).

The reference to California Mortgage and Deed of Trust Practice (Cal CEB 1979) in Book §5.24 should now be to California Mortgage and Deed of Trust Practice §§7.12–7.17 (2d ed Cal CEB 1990).

The Wraparound Deed of Trust and All-Inclusive Note

Purposes and Uses

[§5.27] Higher Effective Interest Rate

The reference to California Mortgage and Deed of Trust Practice (Cal CEB 1979) in Book §5.27 should now be to California Mortgage and Deed of Trust Practice §§8.31–8.32 (2d ed Cal CEB 1990).

[§5.29] Usury Considerations

The treatise by Miller & Starr, cited in Book §5.29, has been replaced by 4 Miller & Starr, California Real Estate §9.20 (2d ed 1989).

[§5.30] Seller's Control Over Security

The treatise by Miller & Starr, cited in Book §5.30, has been replaced by 4 Miller & Starr, California Real Estate §9.20 (2d ed 1989).

Tax Considerations

[§5.31] Installment Reporting

See Update §§5.7, 5.10–5.14 for discussion of California's conformity to the Installment Sales Revision Act of 1980 (Pub L 96–471, 94 Stat 2247).

Anderson, Tax Factors in Real Estate Operations (6th ed 1980) has been replaced by Manolakas, Tax Factors in Real Estate Operations (7th ed 1990).

SELLER'S PARTICIPATION IN BUYER'S FINANCING

Subordination

[§5.39] Buyer's Need; Usual Methods

The exception to the purchase-money antideficiency protection of CCP §580b announced in *Spangler v Memel* (1972) 7 C3d 603, 102 CR 807, is continually being expanded by the courts of appeal. In *Wright v Johnston* (1988) 206 CA3d 333, 253 CR 418, the court did not apply the antideficiency protection of CCP §580b in a case involving a refinancing and subsequent subordination of a purchase-money loan to a large loan obtained from a farm credit association for the purpose of farming the real property that was the security, when the loan proceeds were not in fact used primarily for that purpose.

The sections of the treatise by Miller & Starr, cited in the Book, has been replaced by 3 Miller & Starr, California Real Estate §§8.161, 8.167 (2d ed 1989).

The reference to California Mortgage and Deed of Trust Practice (Cal CEB 1979) in Book §5.39 should now be to California Mortgage and Deed of Trust Practice §§8.50–8.51 (2d ed Cal CEB 1990).

[§5.40] Seller's Need for Protection

The treatise by Miller & Starr, cited in the Book, has been replaced by 3 Miller & Starr, California Real Estate §8.160 (2d ed 1989).

[§5.41] Types of Subordination Agreements

The treatise by Miller & Starr, cited in the Book, has been replaced by Miller & Starr, California Real Estate (2d ed 1989), but §11.175 of the former treatise was not replaced in the new treatise.

Executory Subordination Agreements

[§§5.42–5.43] Enforceability; Required Terms

In *Ray Thomas Enters. v Fox* (1982) 128 CA3d 361, 180 CR 253, the court upheld a subordination provision in an agreement for purchase of a mobile home park even though it did not state the terms of the institutional loan to be taken out by the purchaser. The court distinguished *Handy v Gordon* (1967) 65 C2d 578, 55 CR 769, discussed in Book §§5.42–5.43, because the loan to be obtained was a purchase money loan rather than a construction loan and because there was sufficient equity to protect the holder of the note.

In an action seeking to declare a subordination agreement unenforceable based on the uncertainty of the agreement, *Handy* held that specific performance was not available. *Schneider v Ampliflo Corp.* (1983) 148 CA3d 637, 196 CR 172, distinguished *Handy* and held that under those circumstances foreclosure is available even though specific performance is not.

The treatise by Miller & Starr, cited in Book §5.43, has been replaced by 3 Miller & Starr, California Real Estate §8.164 (2d ed 1989).

Executed Subordination Agreements

Automatic Subordination Provisions

[§5.50] Form: Disbursement Method

California Mechanics' Liens and Other Remedies §6.36 (Cal CEB 1972) has been superseded by California Mechanics' Liens and Other Remedies §§4.37–4.38 (2d ed Cal CEB 1988).

[§5.53] De Facto Subordination

The treatise by Miller & Starr, cited in the Book, has been replaced by Miller & Starr, California Real Estate (2d ed 1989). Section 11.181 of the former treatise has been replaced by §8.167 in the new treatise. Former §11.175 has not been replaced.

Release and Partial Reconveyance

[§5.55] Agreement Required

The Subdivision Map Act is found at Govt C §§66410–66499.37. Government Code §§66499.38–66499.58 cover official maps.

[§5.59] Requirement of Certainty and Fairness

The equitable relief granted to the buyer following the remand order by the appellate court in *Eldridge v Burns* (1978) 76 CA3d 396, 142 CR 845, cited in Book §5.59, was affirmed in a subsequent appeal. *Eldridge v Burns* (1982) 136 CA3d 907, 186 CR 784. The trial court rescinded the sales contract retroactive to the date of the buyer's original demand for release under the release clause and awarded the buyer restitution of the principal paid less the taxes, assessments, accrued interest, and legal expenses the seller incurred in evicting tenants from the property. The seller was not allowed any offset for the three years of the buyer's possession after the original demand for release.

Subdivision Requirements

[§5.60] Subdivision Map Act

The Subdivision Map Act is found at Govt C §§66410–66499.37. Government Code §§66499.38–66499.58 cover official maps.

[§5.63] Form: Partial Release (Lots Not Determined); Limiting Buyer's Discretion

Paragraph (e) of Form 5.63–1 is superseded by the following:

(e) Each portion of the real property released from the lien of this deed of trust shall consist of one or more legal lots or parcels as shown on a recorded parcel or final map. Notwithstanding the description of the release parcels in paragraph (a) above, trustor reserves the right, in order to satisfy this condition, to have beneficiary cause trustee to release less than the entire portion of the real property which trustor would otherwise be entitled to have released by reason of the payment made. Portions of the real property not included in a partial release under this provision but included in computing the principal payment required to obtain a partial release shall not be included in computing the principal payment required to obtain any subsequent release which includes that portion, or any part of it.

[Continue with last paragraph in provision at §5.62]

Comment: Paragraph (e) has been revised to clarify its meaning. The intent of this paragraph is to reserve the right to the trustor to have the beneficiary cause the trustee to release less than all of the property that the trustor would be otherwise entitled to have released. This enables the trustor to specify that land be released only in legally subdivided parcels, even though a greater portion of the real property has actually been paid for.

[§5.64] Form: Partial Release (Lots Not Determined); Adjustment of Release Price

The correct number of the form in Book §5.64 is Form 5.64–1.

6

Institutional Financing

INTRODUCTION

[§6.2] Lawyer's Role

The statutes governing the legal limitations on loans made by state savings and loan associations are now found at Fin C §§7150–7191.

See also 12 CFR §§545.6–545.8–11 for legal limitations on loans made by federal savings and loan associations.

INSTITUTIONAL LENDERS

Savings and Loan Associations

[§6.5] Federal Versus State Associations

The Financial Institutions Reform, Recovery, and Enforcement Act of 1989 (FIRREA; Pub L 101–73, 103 Stat 183), effective August 9, 1989, fundamentally altered the regulatory scheme governing federal and state savings and loan institutions and savings banks. Sixty days after enactment, the Federal Home Loan Bank Board (FHLBB) was abolished by FIRREA. The former chartering and supervisory authority over federal savings and loans of the FHLBB was transferred to the newly created Office of Thrift Supervision (OTS). The Federal Savings and Loan Insurance Corporation (FSLIC) was dissolved by FIRREA as of the effective date of that act, and the Federal Deposit Insurance Corporation (FDIC) became the federal deposit insurer for savings associations, savings banks, and, as had been the case, commercial banks. FIRREA provides, as a general matter, that all rules, regulations, orders, and other determinations of the FSLIC and the FHLBB in effect on August 9, 1989, continue in effect unless or until they are amended, superseded, terminated, or otherwise modified. See Pub L 101–73, §402.

Federal chartered savings and loans do not now have to have the words "federal savings and loan" in their names. See 12 CFR §543.1.

The OTS Office of Thrift Supervision, which now has authority to regulate federal savings institutions under the Home Owner's Loan Act of 1933, 12 USC §1464(a), as amended, has acted to assume plenary and exclusive authority to regulate all aspects of the operation of federal savings institutions by adopting 12 CFR §545.2. This regulation purports to preempt "any state law purporting to address the subject of the operations" of a federal savings institution. The chief counsel of the Office of Thrift supervision has stated that 12 CFR §545.2 preempts state laws requiring interest on mortgage escrow accounts (see CC §2954.8). OTS Chief Counsel Opinion No. 91/CC–08 (Jan. 3, 1991).

See Update §5.24 for discussion of developments concerning due-on-sale clauses.

State savings and loan associations are subject to the Savings and Loan Association Law. Fin C §§5000–10013.

[§6.6] Lending Practices

Federal savings and loan associations have gained greater latitude in the types of mortgage loans they may make; the present regulation authorizing residential mortgage loans is 12 CFR §§545.32–545.34.

Title 12 CFR §545.6–4(c)(5), cited in Book §6.6, was repealed effective August 16, 1982, and Fin C §7153.1 was repealed in 1981.

[§6.7] Life Insurance Companies

Life insurance companies are now exempt from the usury limitations of Cal Const art XV, §1. Ins C §1100.1.

[§6.10] Mortgage Bankers and Mortgage Brokers

The Book notes that very few corporations had sought to qualify as mortgage bankers under Fin C §§18680–18705. The reality of this situation led the legislature to repeal Fin C §§18680–18705 effective January 1, 1988.

[§6.11] The Secondary Mortgage Market

California has added its own secondary mortgage market participant by the creation of the California Home Loan Mortgage Association (CHLMA, or Callie Mae) to guarantee the payment of principal and interest on securities backed by a pool composed of eligible residential mortgages. Fin C §§40000–40158.

The Federal Home Loan Bank Board (FHLBB) was abolished as of August 9, 1989, and its chartering and supervisory authority was transferred to the newly created Office of Thrift Supervision (OTS). All rules, regulations, orders, and other determinations of the FSLIC and the FHLBB in effect on August 9, 1989, continue in effect unless or until they are amended, superseded, terminated, or otherwise modified. See Update §6.5 for discussion.

Title 12 CFR §545.6–4(c) (variable rate loan authority for federal savings and loan associations), cited in Book §6.11, was repealed effective August 16, 1982. The current authorization for all types of residential mortgage loans made by federal savings and loan associations is found at 12 CFR §§545.32–545.34.

TYPES OF LOANS

Miscellaneous Loans

[§6.17] Government Subsidized Loans

Effective January 1, 1989, Health & S C §§33740–33746 were added to authorize redevelopment agencies to issue tax-exempt bonds for the purpose of lending the proceeds to nonprofit organizations exempt from federal income tax under IRC §501(c)(3) for financing acquisition of multi-family rental housing.

The citation in Book §6.17 to Health & S C §§50660–50670 should now be to Health & S C §§50660–50671.5.

[§6.19] Mobile Home Loans

The mobile home loan regulation governing federal savings and loan associations is now found solely at 12 CFR §545.45 instead of at 12 CFR §§545.7–545.7–8, as cited in Book §6.19.

OBTAINING THE LOAN

Credit Standards

[§6.21] Individual Borrowers

The Housing Financial Discrimination Act of 1977 may be referred to and cited as the Holden Act. Health & S C §35800.

[§6.23] Work History

The Federal Home Loan Bank Board (FHLBB) was abolished as of August 9, 1989, and its chartering and supervisory authority was transferred to the newly created Office of Thrift Supervision (OTS). See Update §6.5 for discussion.

[§6.25] Fair Credit Reporting Act

Title 12 CFR §202.9 has been amended to add provisions governing business credit applications. See 12 CFR §202.9(a)(3).

Residential Loans

[§6.27] Cosignors or Guarantors

The reference to California Mortgage and Deed of Trust Practice (Cal

CEB 1979) in the Book should now be to California Mortgage and Deed of Trust Practice §§8.10–8.19 (2d ed Cal CEB 1990).

[§6.28] Partnership Borrowers

Treasury Regulation §1.752–1 has been removed. Now see Temp Reg §1.752–1T(a)(2).

Property Standards

[§6.30] Residential Property (Loan-to-Value Ratio)

The standard loan-to-value ratio for loans on single-family, owner-occupied residences made by federal savings and loan associations is now 100 percent (12 CFR §545.32(d)), but most lenders still prefer loans having an 80-percent loan-to-value ratio and offer their best terms on those loans. The current maximum permissible amount of a loan that can be sold by a lender to the Federal Home Loan Mortgage Corporation (FHLMC, or Freddie Mac) is $191,250 for a one-unit, owner-occupied residence. This figure is adjusted annually, effective January 1, as provided in 12 USC §1454(a)(2).

The $60,000 limit on 95-percent loan-to-value ratio loans has been revoked. There is no current limit. 12 CFR §545.32(d).

Title 10 Cal Adm C §235 has been renumbered and is now found at 10 Cal Code Regs §109.100.

[§6.37] Redlining

The Housing Financial Discrimination Act of 1977 may be referred to and cited as the Holden Act. Health & S C §35800.

The introductory section of Subchapter 4 of the Regulations of the Business, Transportation, and Housing Agency (21 Cal Code Regs §§7100–7117) has been repealed effective July 3, 1985. The current citation to the regulations made under the Housing Financial Discrimination Act of 1977 is 21 Cal Code Regs §§7101–7122.

Negotiating Loan Terms

Negotiability of Other Loan Provisions

[§6.42] Prepayment

The Federal Home Loan Bank Board (FHLBB) was abolished as of August 9, 1989, and its chartering and supervisory authority was transferred to the newly created Office of Thrift Supervision (OTS). All rules, regulations, orders, and other determinations of the FHLBB in effect on August 9, 1989, continue in effect unless or until they are amended, superseded, terminated, or otherwise modified. See Update §6.5 for discussion.

The reference to California Mortgage and Deed of Trust Practice (Cal CEB 1979) in the Book should now be to California Mortgage and Deed of Trust Practice §§7.19–7.25 (2d ed Cal CEB 1990).

[§6.43] Due-on-Sale Clauses

The Federal Home Loan Bank Board (FHLBB) was abolished as of August 9, 1989, and its chartering and supervisory authority was transferred to the newly created Office of Thrift Supervision (OTS). All rules, regulations, orders, and other determinations of the FHLBB in effect on August 9, 1989, continue in effect unless or until they are amended, superseded, terminated, or otherwise modified. See Update §6.5 for discussion.

See Update §5.24 for discussion of developments concerning due-on-sale clauses.

[§§6.45–6.46] Hazard Insurance Requirements; Statutory Restrictions

Civil Code §2924.7, effective January 1, 1989, provides that a lender's right to accelerate the maturity date of any loan secured by a mortgage or deed of trust on real property for failure of the borrower to pay any taxes, rents, assessments, or insurance premiums on the property, as provided in the deed of trust or mortgage, and the lender's right to receive and control the disbursement of the proceeds of any insurance policy respecting the property, as provided in the deed of trust or mortgage, are enforceable whether or not the lender's security interest has been impaired. However, the legislature has declared that CC §2924.7 was not intended to abrogate the holding in *Schoolcraft v Ross* (1978) 81 CA3d 75, 146 CR 57 (discussed in Book §6.46), insofar as it provides that a lender may not prohibit the use of insurance proceeds for the restoration of the security property without a showing that the lender's security interest in the property has been impaired. Thus under CC §2924.7 a lender apparently still may not apply insurance proceeds to reduce the loan balance when the security is not impaired and the loan is not in default; but if the mortgage or deed of trust so provides, a lender apparently may hold the insurance proceeds and disburse them as repairs to the property are made, similar to the way lenders disburse construction loan funds.

The ruling in *Schoolcraft v Ross, supra,* that a lender must let insurance proceeds be used to repair the real property security if the security is not impaired, does not apply when a borrower is in default on his loan. In *Ford v Manufacturers Hanover Mortgage Corp.* (9th Cir 1987) 831 F2d 1520, a borrower was not allowed to force his lender to use insurance proceeds to repair the property, because the borrower was in default before the loss for which the proceeds were paid. Thus, the lender had the right to demand the entire loan due and payable and to foreclose. Moreover, if the borrower had been able to force the use of the proceeds for repairs, the contractual rights of the lender would have been defeated because in effect the borrower could have used the insurance proceeds to cure the default or at least could have postponed foreclosure while the property was being repaired.

Operative July 6, 1988, CC §2955.5 prevents a lender from requiring a borrower to maintain hazard insurance in excess of the replacement value of the improvements on the property.

[§§6.47–6.52] Alternative Mortgage Instruments

The Federal Home Loan Bank Board (FHLBB) was abolished as of August 9, 1989, and its chartering and supervisory authority was transferred to the newly created Office of Thrift Supervision (OTS). All rules, regulations, orders, and other determinations of the FHLBB in effect on August 9, 1989, continue in effect unless or until they are amended, superseded, terminated, or otherwise modified. See Update §6.5 for discussion.

The freedom of real property lenders to create and originate diverse forms of mortgage loans and the acceptance of such loans in the secondary mortgage market has rendered much of the material in the Book concerning limitations on such loans obsolete.

The FHLBB, which regulated federal savings and loan associations before it was abolished in 1989, broadened the ability of those lenders to use new types of mortgage instruments. Title 12 CFR §545.33(e), which replaces former 12 CFR §§545.6–4, 545.6–4a, and 545.6–4b, allows federally chartered savings and loans to offer adjustable rate loans subject only to limited restrictions: The index used to adjust the interest rate must be readily verifiable by the borrower and beyond the control of the lender, and the lender must give mandated disclosures and follow certain procedural rules for giving notice and making adjustments. Subject to these requirements the lender is otherwise free to develop a mortgage loan that provides for changes in the monthly payment, the principal balance (negative amortization), and the loan term (but no longer than 40 years). There are no restrictions on the maximum interest rate change either at one adjustment or over the life of the loan, or on the frequency of adjustments.

Civil Code §1916.7 provides for an adjustable-payment, adjustable-interest-rate loan secured by residential real property. The loan authorized by CC §1916.7 is far more restrictive than those authorized for federal savings and loan associations by 12 CFR §545.6–2. For example, under CC §1916.7 the lender may choose between only two interest rate indexes to determine rate changes. These indexes are (a) the contract interest rate on the purchase of previously occupied homes in the most recent monthly national average mortgage rate index for all major lenders published periodically by the FHLBB and (b) the weighted average cost of funds for California Associations of the 11th District Savings and Loan Association as published periodically by the Federal Home Loan Bank of San Francisco. CC §1916.7(b)(5).

In addition, CC §1916.7(b)(2) restricts rate and payment changes to only two per year at least six months apart and limits the amount of any monthly payment increase to 7.5 percent per year.

Civil Code §1916.8 provides for a renegotiable rate loan secured by residential real property more restrictive than a similar loan subject to 12 CFR §545.33(e). As with loans under CC §1916.7, only the two interest rate indexes mentioned above may be used (CC §1916.8(b)(1)), and the interest rate changes allowed are limited to a maximum of one-half percentage point per year, with a maximum increase or decrease of five percentage points over the life of the loan. CC §1916.8(b)(2).

To lessen the competitive disadvantage to state licensed savings and loan associations, the legislature has adopted CC §§1918–1920, which provide that the Secretary of the Business, Transportation, and Housing Agency, or the Secretary's designee, may, by rule or regulation, permit all lenders to make loans secured by residential real property that are not subject to the limitations regarding changes in interest rates imposed by CC §§1916.5–1916.10 and Fin C §7150.1 (repealed, effective December 31, 1983). CC §1919(c). Any such regulated loans must satisfy the requirements stated in CC §1920, including the type size to be used, mandated disclosure requirements, and a prohibition against a prepayment charge. Any regulation adopted by the Secretary expires on January 1 of the fourth year following the end of the calendar year in which the regulation was promulgated. CC §1919(d). Effective December 31, 1983, CC §1916.12 provides a procedure under which the Secretary of the Business, Transportation, and Housing Agency, or the Secretary's designee, may extend to state-regulated financial institutions the same authority that federally regulated financial institutions have to make loans.

New CC §§1917.010–1917.075 provide for a shared appreciation loan that may be made on behalf of a pension fund subject to the Employee Retirement Income Security Act of 1974 (Pub L 93–406, 88 Stat 829), to finance the purchase of a one-to-four-unit family dwelling, of which at least one unit is owner occupied. These shared appreciation loans may have a term of at least 7 but no more than 30 years, but they must be amortized over 30 years regardless of the term. CC §1917.031(a)–(b). The interest rate on these loans must be fixed for the term of the loan and set at a rate one third below a specified rate established at a Federal National Mortgage Association (FNMA, or Fannie Mae) auction. CC §§1917.020(h), 1917.031(d). In addition to this stated interest rate, the borrower is also liable for contingent deferred interest in the amount of one third of the net appreciated value of the real property at the time of sale or other event designated in CC §1917.031(e). A right to prepay the loan is granted to the borrower (CC §1917.032), and the lender must refinance the loan at maturity if it is not paid off or if the property was not sold or transferred before maturity. CC §1917.033. Provisions are also made for annual appraisals of the real property (CC §§1917.040–1917.044) and the effect that subsequent capital improvements have on determination of the contingent deferred interest (CC §1917.050). Certain notices and disclosures are required by CC §§1917.070–1917.075. Civil Code §1917.063 provides that this shared appreciation loan is not the only type that may be made and that any shared appreciation loan authorized by any other provision of law, or that is not otherwise unlawful, can be made.

Civil Code §§1917.110–1917.175 state a type of general shared appreciation loan not limited to pension funds as are the provisions of CC §§1917.010–1917.075. The primary differences between the two are that the general shared appreciation loan may be amortized over a period of not less than 30 nor more than 40 years (CC §1917.131(b)), and the stated interest rate and the contingent deferred interest that may be charged are partly dependent on the relation between the two and the loan-to-value ratio of the loan. See CC §1917.131(d)–(e).

Former 10 Cal Adm C §178–178.6 (regulations governing experimental alternative mortgage instruments) have been repealed and a number of other 10 Cal Adm C sections have been renumbered as follows:

Old Section(s)	New Section(s)
§240	§107.500
§240.1	§107.100
§240.2	§107.501
§240.3	§107.502
§240.4	§107.503
§240.5	§107.504
§240.6	§107.505

[§6.48] Variable Interest Rate Loans

The assumability feature of a variable interest loan may again be an advantage. See Update §5.24 for discussion of developments concerning due-on-sale clauses.

Civil Code §1916.5 was amended in 1989 to specify that it does not apply to "supervised financial organizations," which include regulated banks, savings associations, savings banks, credit unions, and most other institutional lenders making loans secured by one-to-four-unit residences. CC §1916.5(a), (d)(1).

The Loan Application

Documenting the Multifamily or Commercial Loan

[§6.55] Assignment of Rents

The reference to California Mortgage and Deed of Trust Practice (Cal CEB 1979) in the Book should now be to California Mortgage and Deed of Trust Practice §5.10 (2d ed Cal CEB 1990).

[§6.58] Refinancing Loans; Documentation

The section of Regulation Z to the federal Truth-in-Lending Act, which governs waiver of the right to rescind a credit transaction in the event of a borrower's personal financial emergency, is now found at 12 CFR §226.15(e).

7

Deeds

REQUISITES OF DEEDS

Types of Deeds

[§7.5] Warranty Deed

The treatise by Miller & Starr, cited in the Book, has been replaced by 2 Miller & Starr, California Real Estate §6.11 (2d ed 1989).

COMPONENTS ANALYZED

Body of Deed

[§7.13] Consideration

California has adopted the Uniform Fraudulent Transfer Act, effective January 1, 1987, for transfers made or obligations incurred on or after that date only, and repealed the former Uniform Fraudulent Conveyance Act. However, the old act still applies to transfers made or obligations incurred during the existence of the act. The new Uniform Fraudulent Transfer Act is found at CC §§3439–3439.12, replacing the old act (former CC §§3439–3439.12). The changes do not affect the reference in the Book to general law involving fraudulent transfers.

Grantor Recitals

[§7.18] Form: Trustee

Because of changes in the Probate Code that substantially reduce the need for court supervision of executors, administrators, and testamentary trustees, Prob C §§786 and 1222 dealing with the recordation of certified copies of orders confirming sale of estate real property were repealed, effective July 1, 1988. To the extent an estate fiduciary uses the court-supervised confirmation of sale procedures to sell real property, Prob C §1292, effective July 1, 1988, provides that a certified copy of the order confirming the sale be recorded in the office of the county recorder of each county in which the land, or any part of it, lies. Operative July 1, 1989, Prob C §1292 is repealed and replaced by Prob C §7263 without substantial change.

[§7.21] Other Grantor Clauses

See Update §7.18 on the repeal of former Prob C §786. On the sale of real property by an administrator or executor and the form of executor's deed, now see 1 California Decedent Estate Practice §§13.14–13.60 (Cal

CEB 1986), which replaces California Decedent Estate Administration, cited in Book §7.21.

Grantee

[§7.26] Estate, Nature of Ownership, and Proportion of Interest

California Will Drafting (Cal CEB 1965) has been superseded by California Will Drafting (3d ed Cal CEB 1992).

Grantee Recitals

[§7.27] Form: Joint Tenancy

Comment: Probate Code §§1170–1175 were repealed and reenacted as Prob C §§200–204 and 210, effective January 1, 1985.

[§7.29] Form: Community Property

Comment: See Update §3.30 on changes in the presumptions affecting title of property owned by a husband and wife. The suggestion in Book §7.29 that the parties express in the deed their intention to hold property as community property is still a good suggestion.

State of California   )
County of   ) **ss.**
) **Dated**

On _ _ _ _ _ _, **before me** _ _[*insert name and title of the officer*]_ _, **personally appeared** _ _ _ _ _ _, **personally known to me (or proved to me on the basis of satisfactory evidence) to be the person(s) whose name(s)** _ _[*is/are*]_ _ **subscribed to the within instrument and acknowledged to me that** _ _[*he/she/they*]_ _ **executed the same in** _ _[*his/her/their*]_ _ **authorized capacity(ies), and that by** _ _[*his/her/their*]_ _ **signature(s) on the instrument the person(s), or the entity on behalf of which the person(s) acted, executed the instrument.**

WITNESS my hand and official seal.

Signature _____   **(Seal)**

[§7.30] Form: Changing Title From Joint Tenancy to Community Property

The following form may be used as an independent agreement that the property will be treated as community property.

Form 7.30–2

INDIVIDUAL GRANT DEED
(Excluded from reappraisal under Proposition 13)
INTERSPOUSAL TRANSFER

RECORDING REQUESTED BY

WHEN RECORDED MAIL TO ▼

MAIL TAX STATEMENTS TO ▼

This space for Recorder's use

The undersigned grantor(s) declare(s):   Documentary transfer tax is $
☐ computed on full value of property conveyed, or ☐ computed on full value less value of liens and encumbrances remaining at time of sale.
☐ Unincorporated area ☐ City of   , and
This is an Interspousal Transfer under §63 of the Revenue and Taxation Code. Grantee(s) has (have) checked the applicable exclusion:
☐ From joint tenancy to community property;
☐ From one spouse to both spouses;
☐ From one spouse to the other spouse;
☐ From both spouses to one spouse;
☐ Other:
and for a valuable consideration, receipt of which is acknowledged.

hereby grant(s) to

the following described real property in the County of   , State of California.

Dated

STATE OF CALIFORNIA   } ss.
County of
On   , before me,
a Notary Public in and for said State, personally appeared

known to me

to be the person(s) whose name(s) is (are) subscribed to the within Instrument and acknowledged that
executed the same

WITNESS my hand and official seal.

Mail tax statements as directed above.

FOR RECORDING PURPOSES, *print Assessor's Identification Number*

Comment: Note that this form does not reflect the change in form of acknowledgment made by the addition of CC §1189, effective January 1, 1991. See Update §3.26. If the person recording this form claims exemption from the documentary transfer tax, some counties will require that the document include a statement of authority for the exemption. See Update §7.66A.

Special Recitals

[§7.35] Form: Recital of Separate Property; Spouse to Spouse

See Update §3.17 covering a recodification of the statutory law on trusts.

Effective January 1, 1992, CC §5103 was amended to subject spouses to the same rights and duties of nonmarital business partners as provided in Corp C §§15019–15022.

[§7.37] Form: Deed in Lieu of Foreclosure

Comment: See Update §3.8 for discussion of home equity sales contracts.

The reference to California Mortgage and Deed of Trust Practice (Cal CEB 1979) in the Book should now be to 2 California Real Property Financing §§1.25–1.27 (Cal CEB 1989).

Compliance With Obligation Recitals

[§7.43] Form: Conveyance on Distribution of Trust

Former CC §§869, 869a, and 870 on trusts have been repealed. See Update §3.17 covering a recodification of the statutory law on trusts.

Execution

[§7.50] Definition and Requirements

Spouses holding homesteaded property can unilaterally alter the form of ownership from joint tenancy to tenancy in common without affecting the homestead. *Estate of Grigsby* (1982) 134 CA3d 611, 618, 184 CR 886, 890 (spouse severed joint tenancy by transfer to straw man, who then transferred property back). See Update §3.9 regarding changes in homestead law, including repeal of CC §1242.

One joint tenant may terminate the joint tenancy by deeding his or her interest to himself or herself. *Estate of Carpenter* (1983) 140 CA3d 709, 189 CR 651.

[§7.52] Form: Attorney-in-Fact

Comment: For a brief discussion of the new durable power of attorney that is not revoked by death or incapacity, see Update §3.18.

[§7.55] Form: Executors and Administrators

See Update §7.18 on the repeal of former Prob C §§786 and 1222. For the form of executor's deed, now see 1 California Decedent Estate Practice §13.60 (Cal CEB 1986), which replaces California Decedent Estate Administration, cited in Book §7.55.

Acknowledgment

[§7.59] Legal Requirements

Civil Code §1242, cited in Book §7.59, was repealed effective July 1, 1983. Starting July 1, 1983, statutes governing homesteads became effective as discussed in Update §3.9; however, no provision comparable to former CC §1242 is included in the new homestead law, so acknowledgment is no longer essential to the validity of a deed conveying the homestead of a married person.

The statutory forms of certificates of acknowledgment found in former CC §§1189, 1190, 1190a, 1190.1, 1191 and 1192 have been combined into a single statutory form of certificate of acknowledgment in which the capacity of the person signing the documents is indicated below the signature. See CC §§1189–1190. Acknowledgments conforming to previous law and executed before January 1, 1993, have the same force and effect as if the former Civil Code sections had not been repealed.

See Update §11.94, regarding changes in forms of certificates of acknowledgment.

VALIDITY OF DEEDS

[§7.66A] Forms: Deeds Under Proposition 13

Forms 7.66A–1—7.66A–5 are deeds useful in making transfers that are exempt from reappraisal under Cal Const art XIIIA. They are presented by courtesy of the law offices of Irving Kellogg, a law corporation; they were designed by Catherine Marsalla, legal assistant, and incorporate the ideas of Irving Kellogg developed from information from the County Assessor of Los Angeles County, the County Recorder of Los Angeles County, and representatives of some title companies.

See the chart in the Appendix for information on what transfers are exempt from reappraisal.

Note that, if a transfer is claimed to be exempt from payment of a documentary transfer tax, the Los Angeles County Recorder's office requires that a statement be added to the forms in this section indicating the authority for any exemption from the duty to pay documentary transfer taxes. These exemptions are included in Rev & T C §§11921–11927 and in former Treas Reg §47.4361. See Los Angeles County Ord. No. 9443 and a pamphlet entitled "Notice of Exempt Transactions Under the Documentary Transfer Tax," available from the County of Los Angeles Registrar Recorder, 227 N. Broadway, Los Angeles 90012, (213) 974–6611; mailing address P.O. Box 115, Los Angeles, CA 90053–0115. See further discussion in Update §11.96.

Persons claiming an exemption from payment of the documentary transfer tax who wish to record the following forms in counties other than Los Angeles should first ascertain from that county's recorder what additional statements, if any, must be on the deed.

Form 7.66A–1

INDIVIDUAL GRANT DEED
(Excluded from reappraisal under Proposition 13)
TRUST TRANSFER

RECORDING REQUESTED BY

WHEN RECORDED MAIL TO ▼

MAIL TAX STATEMENTS TO ▼

This space for Recorder's use

The undersigned grantor(s) declare(s):   Documentary transfer tax is $
☐ computed on full value of property conveyed, or ☐ computed on full value less value of liens and encumbrances remaining at time of sale.
☐ Unincorporated area: ☐ City of   , and
This is a Trust Transfer under §62 of the Revenue and Taxation Code. Grantee(s) has (have) checked the applicable exclusion:
☐ To a revocable trust;
☐ To a short-term trust not exceeding 12 years with trustor holding the reversion;
☐ To a trust where the trustor or the trustor's spouse is the sole beneficiary;
☐ Change of trustee holding title;
☐ From trust to trustor or trustor's spouse where prior transfer to trust was excluded from reappraisal
and for a valuable consideration, receipt of which is acknowledged.

hereby grant(s) to

the following described real property in the County of   , State of California.

Dated

STATE OF CALIFORNIA   } ss.
County of
On   , before me,
a Notary Public in and for said State, personally appeared

known to me

to be the person(s) whose name(s) is (are) subscribed to the
within Instrument and acknowledged that
executed the same.

WITNESS my hand and official seal.

Signature   This area for official notarial seal

Mail tax statements as directed above.

Comment: Note that this form does not reflect the change in form of acknowledgment made by the addition of CC §1189, effective January 1, 1991. See Update §3.26. Also note that trust transfers other than those for which boxes are provided in this form may also be excluded from reappraisal. See Rev & T C §62.

Form 7.66A–2

INDIVIDUAL GRANT DEED
(Excluded from reappraisal under Proposition 13)
JOINT TENANCY TRANSFER

RECORDING REQUESTED BY

WHEN RECORDED MAIL TO ▼

PARCEL

MAIL TAX STATEMENTS TO ▼

PAGE

This space for Recorder's use

MAP BOOK

print Assessor's Identification Number

FOR RECORDING PURPOSES.

The undersigned grantor(s) declare(s):   Documentary transfer tax is $

☐ computed on full value of property conveyed, or ☐ computed on full value less value of liens and encumbrances remaining at time of sale.

☐ Unincorporated area: ☐ City of   , and

This is a Joint Tenancy Transfer under §62 or 65 of the Revenue and Taxation Code. Grantee(s) has (have) checked the applicable exclusion:

☐ Grantor-transferor is named as one of the transferee joint tenants;

☐ An original grantor-transferor's interest vests in whole or in part in a remaining original grantor-transferor;

☐ Person(s) added as joint tenant(s) in a transfer previously excluded under §62 grants back to the original grantor-transferor;

☐ Other: (See Code §65)

and for a valuable consideration, receipt of which is acknowledged,

hereby grant(s) to

the following described real property in the County of   , State of California.

Dated

STATE OF CALIFORNIA

County of   } ss.

On   , before me,

a Notary Public in and for said State, personally appeared

known to me

to be the person(s) whose name(s) is (are) subscribed to the within Instrument and acknowledged that executed the same.

WITNESS my hand and official seal.

Signature

Mail tax statements as directed above.

Comment: Note that this form does not reflect the change in form of acknowledgment made by the addition of CC §1189, effective January 1, 1991. See Update §3.26. Also note that joint tenancy transfers other than those for which boxes are provided in this form may also be excluded from reappraisal. See Rev & T C §62.

Form 7.66A–3

CORPORATION GRANT DEED
(Excluded from reappraisal under Proposition 13)
CORPORATION TRANSFER

RECORDING REQUESTED BY

WHEN RECORDED MAIL TO ▼

MAIL TAX STATEMENTS TO ▼

This space for Recorder's use

The undersigned grantor(s) declare(s):   Documentary transfer tax is $
☐ computed on full value of property conveyed, or ☐ computed on full value less value of liens and encumbrances remaining at time of sale.
☐ Unincorporated area: ☐ City of   , and
This is a transfer to or from a legal entity under §§62 and 64 of the Revenue and Taxation Code, Grantee(s) has (have) checked the applicable exclusion:
☐ Proportional ownership interests before and after transfer remain the same (organization or dissolution of entity).
☐ Transfers where grantor-corporation and grantee-corporation are affiliated by 100% stock ownership.
☐ Other:

and for a valuable consideration, receipt of which is acknowledged,

hereby grant(s) to

the following described real property in the County of   , State of California

In Witness Whereof, said corporation has caused its corporate name and seal to be affixed hereto and this instrument to be executed by its   President and   Secretary thereunto duly authorized.

STATE OF CALIFORNIA
County of   } ss   Dated
On   before me, the undersigned, a Notary Public in and for said State, personally appeared
                                            , known to me
to be the   President, and   By
                                            , known to me
to be   Secretary of the Corporation that   By
executed the within Instrument, known to me to be the persons
who executed the within Instrument on behalf of the
Corporation therein named, and acknowledged to me that such
Corporation executed the within Instrument pursuant to its
by-laws or by a resolution of its board of directors.

WITNESS my hand and official seal.

Signature

Mail tax statements as directed above.

FOR RECORDING PURPOSES, print Assessor's Identification Number

Comment: Note that this form does not reflect the change in form of acknowledgment made by the addition of CC §1189, effective January 1, 1991. See Update §3.26. Also note that corporate transfers other than those for which boxes are provided in this form may also be excluded from reappraisal. See Rev & T C §62.

Form 7.66A–4

PARTNERSHIP GRANT DEED
(Excluded from reappraisal under Proposition 13)
PARTNERSHIP TRANSFER

RECORDING REQUESTED BY

WHEN RECORDED MAIL TO ▼

MAIL TAX STATEMENTS TO ▼

This space for Recorder's use

The undersigned grantor(s) declare(s): Documentary transfer tax is $
☐ computed on full value of property conveyed, or ☐ computed on full value less value of liens and encumbrances remaining at time of sale.
☐ Unincorporated area: ☐ City of , and
This is a transfer to or from a legal entity under §§62 and 64 of the Revenue and Taxation Code, Grantee(s) has (have) checked the applicable exclusion:
☐ Proportional ownership interests before and after transfer remain the same (organization or dissolution of entity).
☐ Other:

and for a valuable consideration, receipt of which is acknowledged,

hereby grant(s) to

the following described real property in the County of , State of California.

Name of Partnership

Dated BY
Partner
Dated BY
Partner

STATE OF CALIFORNIA,
County of
} ss.

On
before me, the undersigned, a Notary Public in and for said County and State, personally appeared
and known to me

to be the partner(s) of the partnership that executed the within instrument, and acknowledged to me that such partnership executed the same.

WITNESS my hand and official seal.

Signature This area for official notarial seal

Mail tax statements as directed above.

For recording purposes, print Assessor's Identification Number

Comment: Note that this form does not reflect the change in form of acknowledgment made by the addition of CC §1189, effective January 1, 1991. See Update §3.26. See Rev & T C §11925, exempting certain partnership transfers from payment of the documentary transfer tax. Note that other partnership transfers may be excluded from reappraisal in Rev & T C §62.

Form 7.66A–5

INDIVIDUAL GRANT DEED
(Excluded from reappraisal under Proposition 13)
TRANSFER TO A PARTNERSHIP OR CORPORATION

RECORDING REQUESTED BY

WHEN RECORDED MAIL TO ▼

PARCEL

MAIL TAX STATEMENTS TO ▼

PAGE

MAP BOOK

FOR RECORDING PURPOSES, *print Assessor's Identification Number*

This space for Recorder's use

The undersigned grantor(s) declare(s):   Documentary transfer tax is $
☐ computed on full value of property conveyed, or ☐ computed on full value less value of liens and encumbrances remaining at time of sale.
☐ Unincorporated area: ☐ City of   , and
This is a transfer to a partnership or a corporation under §64 of the Revenue and Taxation Code. Grantee(s) has (have) checked the applicable exclusion:
☐ Proportional ownership interests before and after transfer remain the same (organization of entity):
☐ Other:

and for a valuable consideration, receipt of which is acknowledged,

hereby grant(s) to

the following described real property in the County of   , State of California.

Dated

STATE OF CALIFORNIA   } ss.
County of
On   , before me,
a Notary Public in and for said State, personally appeared

known to me

to be the person(s) whose name(s) is (are) subscribed to the
within Instrument and acknowledged that
executed the same.

WITNESS my hand and official seal.

Signature   This area for official notarial seal

Mail tax statements as directed above.

Comment: Note that this form does not reflect the change in form of acknowledgment made by the addition of CC §1189, effective January 1, 1991. See Update §3.26.

8

Descriptions of Property

INTRODUCTION

[§8.1] Nature and Purpose of Descriptions

The reference to Witkin in the Book should now be to 4 Witkin, Summary of California Law, *Real Property* §§153–159 (9th ed 1987).

FINDING CORRECT DESCRIPTIONS

[§§8.8–8.25] Surveys and Engineering Studies

Civil engineers who become registered after January 1, 1982, may not do land surveys until they have passed the examination required by Bus & P C §8741(b) (former Bus & P C §8740.2). Bus & P C §8731.

For articles discussing surveys, see York, *Surveys in Real Property Transactions—Part I,* 5 CEB Real Prop L Rep 121 (Oct. 1982), *Part II,* 5 CEB Real Prop L Rep 145 (Nov. 1982), and additional comments in Cummins, *Comment on Surveys in Real Property Transactions,* 6 CEB Real Prop L Rep 57 (Apr. 1983).

The publication by Wattles, cited in Book §8.13, has been replaced by Wattles, Writing Legal Descriptions in Conjunction With Survey Boundary Control (1979). Brown & Eldridge, Evidence and Procedures for Boundary Location 430 (1962), cited in Book §§3.13 and 8.21, has been replaced by Brown & Eldridge, Evidence and Procedures for Boundary Location (2d ed 1981). Bureau of Land Management, Manual of Instruction for the Survey of Public Lands of the United States (1973), cited in Book §8.13, was revised in 1983. Bowman, Real Estate Law in California (5th ed 1978), cited in Book §8.18, has been replaced by Bowman & Milligan, Real Estate Law in California (8th ed 1992).

The California Coordinate System mentioned in the Book has been renamed the California Coordinate System of 1927, effective January 1, 1987, and is now found at Pub Res C §§8801–8819.

READING DESCRIPTIONS

Determining Sufficiency of Description

[§8.10] Requirement of Certainty

Former CC §1624(4) has been redesignated as CC §1624(c).

Types of Discriptions

[§8.18] Courses and Distances

Real Estate Law in California, cited in Book §8.18, is now in its 8th edition, by Bowman & Milligan.

Matters Altering or Affecting Descriptions; Easements

Problems With Easements

[§8.26] Benefit or Burden

The reference to Witkin in the Book should now be to 4 Witkin, Summary of California Law, *Real Property* §§434–480 (9th ed 1987).

[§8.27] Off-Record Easements

The common ownership requirement for creation of an easement of necessity can be met even if the ownership of one parcel is only an equitable title (purchaser under an installment land sale contract) at the time of the conveyance, according to the court in *Roemer v Pappas* (1988) 203 CA3d 201, 249 CR 743. The court held that the purchaser under an installment land sale contract is generally deemed the owner of the real property notwithstanding the retention of legal title by the seller. This "ownership" was enough to establish the common ownership test when the purchaser eventually obtained legal title by performing under the installment land sale contract.

In *Noronha v Stewart* (1988) 199 CA3d 485, 245 CR 94, the court held that, although a license to build a wall on an adjoining owner's property created by an oral promise lacked the formal requirements necessary to create an easement, it was nevertheless irrevocable because the wall had already been built at the time the subsequent owner of the property on which the wall was built brought suit against his neighbor demanding that the wall be torn down. The court allowed the wall to remain, giving the neighbor the equivalent of an easement. The original owner of the property on which the wall was built held only equitable title at the time the license was granted but later acquired legal title. The court held that the doctrine of "after-acquired title" applied to overcome the technicality that the original owner did not have a sufficient interest in the property to grant the license at the time that it was granted.

[§8.28] Termination of Easements

For a case following *Glatts v Henson* (1948) 31 C2d 368, 188 P2d 745, cited in Book §8.28(f), see *Masin v La Marche* (1982) 136 CA3d 687, 186 CR 619, in which a servient tenement owner's blockade of, and storage of materials on, an access easement were held to have extinguished the easement by adverse possession.

[§8.30] Appurtenant or In Gross

The reference to Witkin in the Book should now be to 4 Witkin, Summary of California Law, *Real Property* §436 (9th ed 1987).

[§8.32] Uncertain Duration

For a later case on problems created by granting of railroad rights-of-way, see *Machado v South Pac. Transp. Co.* (1991) 233 CA3d 347, 284 CR 560 (distinguishing and disagreeing with *Johnson v Ocean Shore R.R.* (1971) 16 CA3d 429, 94 CR 68).

[§8.38] Adverse Possession, Prescription, and Implied Dedication

Prescriptive easements are easier to obtain than title by adverse possession because the payment of real property taxes is not a prerequisite unless the easement was separately assessed. *Gilardi v Hallam* (1981) 30 C3d 317, 322, 178 CR 624, 626. See *Warsaw v Chicago Metallic Ceilings, Inc.* (1984) 35 C3d 564, 199 CR 773, for a discussion upholding the acquisition of a prescriptive easement.

An example of an implied dedication is found in *Brumbaugh v County of Imperial* (1982) 134 CA3d 556, 562, 184 CR 11, 14, in which the court differentiated between dedication implied in fact ("by the affirmative acts or acquiescence of the property owner") and dedication implied in law ("by the continuous adverse public use of the property throughout the prescriptive period without substantial interference by the owner").

[§8.39] Abandonment and Vacation

The references to Witkin in the Book should now be to 4 Witkin, Summary of California Law, *Real Property* §§474–476, and §§664–665 (9th ed 1987).

[§8.40] Effect of Water on Land

Title Insurance & Trust Company, Title Handbook for Title Men (22d ed 1980) has been replaced by the 32d edition published in 1990.

[§8.41] Inverse Condemnation

An inverse condemnation action can be used to attack a rent control ordinance that does not provide a just and reasonable return on property and that, when applied, constitutes a taking. See *Kirkpatrick v City of Oceanside* (1991) 232 CA3d 267, 283 CR 191.

[§8.42] Doctrine of Agreed Boundaries

One court has disagreed with the holding in *Kraus v Griswold* (1965) 232 CA2d 698, 706, 43 CR 139, 145, that the boundary is definite when it can be made certain from the deed by survey. In *Armitage v Decker* (1990) 218 CA3d 887, 267 CR 399, the court stated that since the critical question is the parties' intent to create a boundary to settle their subjective uncertainty of the true line, the great weight of authority adheres to the rule that the possibility of accurately surveying the true line is immaterial.

ELIMINATING DEFECTS IN DESCRIPTIONS

Solutions to Typical Problems

[§8.45] Failure To Close Metes and Bounds Description

Chadbourne, Grossman & Van Alstyne, California Pleading (1961) has been replaced by Chadbourne, Grossman & Van Alstyne, California Pleading (2d ed 1981).

3 Witkin, California Procedure, *Pleading* §§522–534, 661–673 (2d ed 1971) have been replaced by 5 Witkin, California Procedure, *Pleading* §§605–622, 755–767 (3d ed 1985), respectively.

[§8.46] Incomplete or Confusing Descriptions

The reference to California Decedent Estate Administration (Cal CEB 1971) should now be to 1 California Decedent Estate Practice §§6.23–6.27 (Cal CEB 1986).

The reference to Witkin in the Book should now be to 7 Witkin, California Procedure, *Judgment* §§68–72 (3d ed 1985).

[§8.49] Fraudulent or Erroneous Surveys

Bureau of Land Management, Manual of Instructions for the Survey of Public Lands of the United States (1973) was revised in 1983.

[§8.64] Describing Personal Property

For sample descriptions of personal property suitable for creating security interests, now see Secured Transactions in California Commercial Law Practice §§2.21–2.24 (Cal CEB 1986), which replaces 3 California Commercial Law (Cal CEB 1966).

Drafting Agreements for the Sale of Businesses, chap 4 (Cal CEB 1971) has been replaced by Drafting Agreements for the Sale of Businesses, chap 5 (2d ed Cal CEB 1988).

9

Covenants of Title

COVENANTS AND WARRANTIES

[§9.1] Need for Title Covenants

The implied warranty held to apply in the sale of newly constructed housing by the Supreme Court in *Pollard v Saxe & Yolles Dev Co.* (1974) 12 C3d 374, 115 CR 648, cited in the Book §9.1, was not extended to the sale of existing housing by the court of appeal in *Siders v Schloo* (1987) 188 CA3d 1217, 233 CR 906.

Covenants and Warranties Distinguished

[§9.3] Warranties

The reference to Witkin in the Book should now be to 3 Witkin, Summary of California Law, *Sales* §54 (9th ed 1987).

Avoiding Effect of Title Covenants

[§9.22] "Restrained" Grant Deed

See Update §4.36 for a discussion of the repeal of CC §1213.5.

10

Risk of Loss-Property Insurance

[§10.12] TRANSFER OF SELLER'S PROPERTY INSURANCE TO BUYER

Insurance Code §2070 was amended effective January 1, 1983, to allow any insurance policy (whether providing coverage against the peril of fire only, or fire in combination with coverage against other perils) to be substituted for the California Standard Form Fire Insurance Policy if its coverage against fire loss is substantially equal to or more favorable to the insured than that of the standard form policy.

COUNSELING HOLDERS OF SECURED INTERESTS

[§10.17] Protecting the Secured Lender

See Update §§6.45–6.46 on the lender's right to control disbursement of insurance proceeds.

See CC §2955.5, discussed in Update §§6.45–6.46, limiting amount of hazard insurance a lender can require.

The reference to Witkin in the Book should now be to 3 Witkin, Summary of California Law, *Security Transactions in Real Property* §160 (9th ed 1987).

The reference to California Mortgage and Deed of Trust Practice (Cal CEB 1979) in the Book should now be to Chapter 4 of California Mortgage and Deed of Trust Practice (2d ed Cal CEB 1990).

11

Escrow and Closing the Sale

ELEMENTS OF ESCROW

Parties to Escrow

Escrow Holder

[§11.10] Relationship to Buyer and Seller

The treatise by Miller & Starr, cited in the Book, has been replaced by Miller & Starr, California Real Estate (2d ed 1989). Section 11.50 of the former treatise has been replaced by volume 3, §8.61 of the new, and §12.103 of the old has been replaced by volume 2, §5.23 of the new.

[§11.11] Who Can Act as Escrow Holder

The regulations covering the activities of independent escrow companies are now found at 10 Cal Code Regs §§1709–1769.

The Financial Code sections governing escrow law are now found at Fin C §§17000–17702.

Financial Code §17011 was repealed effective October 2, 1985, and replaced by Fin C §§17700–17701, which have increased the penalties for any willful violations of the provisions in Fin C §§17000–17702 or regulations issued under those sections to imprisonment in state prison for one year or more or in a county jail for not more than one year, and a fine of not more than $10,000, or both. Financial Code §17702 was added, effective January 1, 1989, concerning willful statements of material facts or omissions of material facts required to be stated in any application, notice, or report filed with the Real Estate Commissioner under Fin C §§17000–17702, or regulations issued under those sections.

Operative September 28, 1989, Fin C §17409.1 was added to require that licensed escrow companies maintain separate escrow trust accounts for each licensed location and to prohibit transfers between escrow accounts except by the writing of a check from one escrow to the other, and by depositing the check for the account of, and writing a receipt for, the escrow to which the files are being transferred.

CONSEQUENCES OF ESCROW

Escrow Holder's Duties

[§11.20] Fiduciary Responsibilities

Since an escrow holder is a fiduciary, a party to the escrow has less of a duty of diligence to discover a fraud that may toll the limitations period than would be true if the escrow holder was not a fiduciary. *Lee v Escrow Consultants, Inc.* (1989) 210 CA3d 915, 259 CR 117. Although the issue in *Lee* concerned a statute of limitations, the court also discussed the nature of an escrow holder's duty. The escrow holder's conduct to which the plaintiff objected was the disbursement of escrowed funds to the seller before the transfer of title to the plaintiff-buyer. The escrow holder made the premature disbursement on the receipt of a written amendment to the escrow instructions on which the plaintiff's signature was allegedly forged. The escrow holder argued that, because escrow holders do not owe a duty to go beyond the escrow instructions and notify the parties of suspicious facts or circumstances (*Lee v Title Ins. & Trust Co.* (1968) 264 CA2d 160, 70 CR 378), it had no duty to investigate the validity of the amendment which, on its face, appeared proper. The court distinguished *Lee,* however, holding that the original escrow instructions provided that changes to the escrow instructions had to be "given in a writing by all parties," and that the escrow holder, therefore, had a fiduciary duty to verify the signatures on a purported amendment to the instructions.

Lee seems to require escrow holders to verify the parties' signatures or adopt some other protective measures to avoid acting on instructions with forged signatures.

An escrow holder has no duty to deposit funds held in escrow in an interest-bearing account, absent an instruction to do so. *Hannon v Western Title Ins. Co.* (1989) 211 CA3d 1122, 260 CR 21.

[§11.22] Inconsistent Demands; Interpleader

For an example of a situation in which an escrow holder, complying with instructions of the seller not to pay the broker's commission, was held not liable to a broker, see *Contemporary Inv. v Safeco Title Ins.* (1983) 145 CA3d 999, 193 CR 822 (in absence of a notice to escrow holder of assignment, escrow holder must strictly comply with instructions of principal, both before and after close of escrow).

[§11.23] Liability

The escrow holder in *Zang v Northwestern Title Co.* (1982) 135 CA3d 159, 185 CR 176, attempted to avoid liability for failing to comply with an oral escrow instruction by alleging that Fin C §§17403.2 and 17403.3 require escrow instructions to be in writing. The court, denoting this a question of first impression, held that the two sections (dealing with an escrow holder's acceptance of instructions with blanks to be filled in and its duty to deliver a copy of escrow instructions to the parties executing them) did not abrogate the principles of contract and agency law that allow for binding oral agreements, so that the escrow holders were not exempt from liability for negligence in carrying out oral instructions. 135 CA3d at 167, 185 CR at 180.

An escrow holder was held not liable to a creditor of a real estate broker who was to receive a commission on the close of escrow when the creditor attempted, before the close of escrow, to garnish the portion of the escrow funds due the broker. *First Central Coast Bank v Cuesta Title Guar. Co.* (1983) 143 CA3d 12, 191 CR 433. The court held that because the broker's commission was contingent on the closing of escrow, there was nothing for the creditor to garnish before escrow closed. On the date of the garnishment, the escrow holder properly answered the garnishment by saying it owed no money to the broker. The escrow did close later, and the escrow holder properly paid the broker because on that date there was no outstanding garnishment.

It is possible that CCP §§708.210–708.290, which authorize a judgment creditor to bring an action against a third person (such as an escrow holder) who has possession or control of property in which the judgment debtor has an interest, could be used by the creditor in this situation. Service of summons on the third party creates a lien on the interest. CCP §708.250. The language of §§708.210–708.290 neither includes nor exludes application to contingent interests.

Although punitive damages can be recovered from an escrow holder for its negligent performance of its duties as a fiduciary, mere breach of the escrow holder's fiduciary duty does not support an award of punitive damages. *Flyer's Body Shop Profit Sharing Plan v Ticor Title Ins. Co.* (1986) 185 CA3d 1149, 230 CR 276. The court held that malice, fraud, or oppression must exist before punitive damages are appropriate. See Update §12.34 on recent changes in the burden of proof necessary to recover punitive damages.

The statement in the Book that a two-year statute of limitations applies to a cause of action for negligent performance of fiduciary duties is correct only if the escrow instructions are oral. If the instructions are written, the applicable statute of limitations is four years even if the cause of action alleges negligent performance of an implied obligation. *Bruckman v Parliament Escrow Corp.* (1987) 190 CA3d 1051, 235 CR 813.

ESCROW PROCEDURE

[§11.32] Selection of Escrow Holder

To require the use of an escrow holder in which a developer has a financial interest is not only a violation of CC §2995 but also may be a violation of the antitrust laws. See *MacManus v A.E. Realty Partners* (1983) 146 CA3d 275, 194 CR 567.

Buyer's Separate Escrow Instructions

[§11.42] Form: Introductory Clause

Insurance Code §12413, which allowed escrow holders to distinguish between checks drawn on California financial institutions and those drawn on out-of-state institutions has been repealed. Now, title insurance companies, controlled escrow companies, and underwritten title companies cannot distinguish between in-state and out-of-state checks (checks drawn on an office of a financial institution) used to fund escrows. No such regulated company may disburse funds from an escrow until the check (including a cashier's check) representing the deposit into escrow has become available for withdrawal as a matter of right, or the financial institution in which the funds have been deposited informs the escrow holder that final settlement has occurred on the deposited item. Ins C §12413.1.

The ability to obtain the return of funds deposited into escrow on the failure of escrow to close was aided by the enactment of CC §1057.3, effective January 1, 1991. Civil Code §1057.3 requires any party to execute documents required by the escrow holder within 30 days following another party's demand to release any funds deposited by the other party if there is no good faith dispute as to the right to the funds. A party who fails to comply with the requirements of the statute will be liable for damages in an amount equal to three times the amount of funds wrongfully withheld in escrow, but in no event less than $100 or more than $1000, as well as reasonable attorney fees incurred by the aggrieved party.

The reference to California Mortgage and Deed of Trust Practice (Cal CEB 1979) in the Book should now be to chaps 7 and 8 of California Mortgage and Deed of Trust Practice (2d ed Cal CEB 1990).

Other Conditions Precedent

Pest Control

[§11.46] Form: Pest Control Report as Condition; No Work Required

Operative January 1, 1987, only individuals will be licensed as structural pest control operators. Bus & P C §8506. Sole proprietorships, partnerships, corporations, and other business organizations that are registered to engage in the practice of structural pest control will be known as "registered companies." Bus & P C §8506.1. References in Book §3.126 to structural pest control operators should be to registered companies. The following form should be used instead of that set out in Book §11.46:

Form 11.46–1

[Add, if appropriate, as a numbered item to list of conditions precedent in Form 11.44–2]

You have received a written report _ _[*approved by buyer*]_ _ by a registered company selected by _ _[*buyer/seller*]_ _ covering the _ _[*describe improvements, e.g., house and garage*]_ _ situated on the property showing them to be free from infestation of wood-destroying pests or organisms, and that no corrective work is required. _ _[*Buyer/ Seller*]_ _ shall pay the cost of the written report.

[§11.47] Form: Pest Control Report as Condition; Work Required

Effective January 1, 1987, the form set out below should be used instead of the form in Book §11.47. See Update §11.46 for discussion.

Form 11.47–1

[Add, if appropriate, as a numbered item to list of conditions precedent in Form 11.44–2]

All corrective, but not preventive, work required to be performed under the terms of a structural pest control report dated _ _ _ _, 19_ _, furnished by _ _[*name of registered company*]_ _ and approved by buyer shall have been performed before the close of escrow as evidenced by a completion report approved by buyer, or you shall hold in escrow from the funds otherwise due and payable to seller the cost of performing such work as stated in the report. Any funds so withheld are to be paid to _ _[*name of registered company*]_ _ when you have received a clearance certification and notice of work completed in accordance with Business and Professions Code section

8519(b) and you have been informed in writing by buyer that the work has been completed to buyer's satisfaction.

[§11.49] Form: Provision for Assumption of or Taking Subject to Existing Deed of Trust

Civil Code §2943 has been amended, effective January 1, 1989. The amendment provides, among other things, that the beneficiary may charge a fee of $60 or less for furnishing the beneficiary statement.

Prorations

[§11.51] Form: Introduction and Proration of Taxes

California Taxes §§4.70–4.74 (Cal CEB 1971) have been replaced by 1 California Taxes §§1.145–1.149 (Cal CEB 1978).

[§11.54] Form: Proration of Rents

The notice by a landlord to a tenant following transfer of the landlord's interest in the leased real property referred to in Book §11.54 now need only be mailed by first-class mail, postage prepaid, instead of by certified mail as stated in the Book. CC §1950.5(f).

Seller's Separate Escrow Instructions

[§11.66] Form: Introductory Clause

The reference to California Mortgage and Deed of Trust Practice (Cal CEB 1979) in the Book should now be to chaps 7 and 8 of California Mortgage and Deed of Trust Practice (2d ed Cal CEB 1990).

[§11.69] Form: Payoff of Existing Encumbrance

The reference to California Mortgage and Deed of Trust Practice (Cal CEB 1979) in the Book should now be to California Mortgage and Deed of Trust Practice §7.41 (2d ed Cal CEB 1990).

[§11.71] Form: Payment of Closing Costs

Comment: See Update §7.66A on exemptions from documentary transfer tax.

Operative January 1, 1987, only individuals will be licensed as structural pest control operators. Bus & P C §8506. Sole proprietorships, partnerships, corporations, and other business organizations that are registered to engage in the practice of structural pest control will be known as "registered companies." Bus & P C §8506.1. The reference in Book §11.71, item 7, to structural pest control operator should be to a registered company.

The additional taxes charged by the cities of Albany and Oakland have been changed. Albany now charges $4.40 per $1000 of net value, and Oakland $10.00 per $1000 of total sales price.

[§11.76] Form: Lender's Printed Form Escrow Instructions

The form printed in Book §11.76, including Addenda A and B, has been replaced by the following:

 SAN FRANCISCO FEDERAL

DATE:
YOUR REPORT:
OUR LOAN: DATED:
TRUSTOR: GROSS LOAN AMT: $
PROPERTY:

1. ENCLOSED DOCUMENTS:
THE FOLLOWING ENCLOSED DOCUMENTS ARE NOT TO BE REMOVED FROM YOUR OFFICE.
OUR LOAN COMMITMENT EXPIRES ON   . IF YOU ARE UNABLE TO RECORD BY THIS DATE, IMMEDIATELY CONTACT
BORROWERS ARE TO COMPLETE AND/OR DATE (AS INDICATED) AND EXECUTE ALL DOCUMENTS EXACTLY AS TYPED. OUR WRITTEN APPROVAL IS REQUIRED FOR ANY ALTERATIONS AND/OR ADDITIONS. CONTACT BORROWERS AT :

__ Confidential Envelope; **return enclosures with funding package** .
__ Note (copy to Borrower - return original).
__ Deed of Trust, Addendum/Supplement/Rider attached (copy to Borrower).
__ Regulation Z Disclosure Statement (original to Borrower - return copy with live signature); You must deliver the Regulation Z Disclosure Statement to our borrowers at the time they execute the loan documents and obtain the written receipt of our borrowers for such Disclosure Statement on a copy thereof.
__ Itemization of Amount Financed (original to Borrower - return copy with live signature).
__ Notice to Customer of Right to Cancel (original and one copy to Borrower - return copy with live signatures); The conditions precedent set forth in **Addendum B** attached hereto which relates to Truth-in-Lending Law and regulations shall be fully performed prior to closing. THE DATE OF CONSUMMATION OF THIS LOAN TRANSACTION SHALL BE THE DATE THE LOAN DOCUMENTS ARE SIGNED BY THE BORROWER(S) AND THE REGULATION Z DISCLOSURE STATEMENT, IF APPLICABLE, IS DELIVERED TO THE BORROWER(S).
__ Unconditional Loan Guaranty.
__ Pest Control/General Withhold Instructions (copies to Borrower and your file - return original).
   PEST CONTROL : We hold a copy of a pest control inspection report dated   No.   from
                                    . See the enclosed Pest Control Withhold Instructions. Advise us prior to recordation if other than the named inspection report is accepted by our trustor(s).
__ Agreement to Make Payments to Tax Liability Account for completion.
__ Affidavit of Purchaser and Vendor. Must be dated, executed and acknowledged by purchaser and vendor no later than the date on which any disbursement of the loan is made. All signatures must be original. (copy to Borrower - return original and 2 copies).
__ Premium Payment Authorization.
__ Statement of Fees and Charges for completion, date and execution (copy to Borrower - return original).
__ Certificate of One Borrower. Borrower must attest to completeness of Exhibit B and execute (copy to Borrower - return original).
__ Request for Notice of Loan Delinquency (record original, send copy to Beneficiary of senior deed of trust); Complete the recording information for our junior deed of trust, collect $40 and remit with the copy of the Request for Notice of Loan Delinquency to Beneficiary of senior deed of trust by certified mail, return receipt requested. Affix our loan number and address the return receipt to: San Francisco Federal Savings and Loan Association, P.O. Box 3009, Concord, CA 94522-3009, Attn: Quality Loan Review.
__ Request for Notice of Default to be recorded.
__ First Payment Letter (original to Borrower).
__ Notice Requirement of Civil Code Section 2937(d) (copy to Borrower - return original).
__ Road Maintenance Acknowledgement.
__ Affidavit of Co-Borrowers (copy to Borrower - return original).
__

| **THESE DOCUMENTS EXPIRE ON:** |
EXECUTED LOAN DOCUMENTS TOGETHER WITH **CERTIFIED COPIES OF THE GRANT DEED** (IF A SALE), REQUEST FOR NOTICE OF LOAN DELINQUENCY AND REQUEST FOR NOTICE OF DEFAULT (IF INCLUDED), AND DEED OF TRUST WITH ATTACHMENTS AND REQUESTS FOR FUNDS MUST BE RECEIVED AT LEAST 24 HOURS PRIOR TO RELEASE OF LOAN FUNDS BY SAN FRANCISCO FEDERAL SAVINGS AND LOAN ASSOCIATION, CENTRAL FUNDING OFFICE AT 2151 SALVIO STREET, SUITE 360, CONCORD, CA 94520.

2. TERMS OF FINANCING:
Trustor shall deposit cash to escrow in payment of the selling price (not less than) $ **plus closing costs** payable through escrow, less the sum of (1) the net loan proceeds to be funded by Lender (item 4 below) and (2) the amount of any (first or junior) loan permitted by these instructions not to exceed $,for a term of
years and a payment of $ per month. PROVIDE US WITH A DUPLICATE COPY OF THE NOTE COVERING ANY JUNIOR FINANCING PERMITTED. There is to be no other financing permitted except as specifically set forth herein.

3. DEDUCTIONS FROM LOAN PROCEEDS:

As we will charge interest from the date of our disbursement of loan proceeds, please call for the loan funds stated below ONLY when receipt of the funds will permit our loan to be then recorded. Your request for disbursement constitutes your assurance that you are able to record under the provisions of these instructions.

The following amounts will be deducted from the loan proceeds and only the net loan proceeds will be paid into escrow:

A.	Interest at $	per day from the date of our check to			
B.	Assn. Net Loan Fee	$	** L.	Misc. Fee	
C.	Credit Report	$	M.	Tax Impounds* (	months) $
D.	Document Fee	$	N.	MI Premium	$
E.	Tax Service	$	O.	MI Impounds (2 months)	$
F.	Processing Fee	$	P.	Payoff Demand Loan No.	$ (will follow)
G.	Appraisal Fee	$	Q.	Pest Control Withhold	$
H.	Warehouse Fee	$	R.	Withhold (Item 7)	$
I.	Underwriting Fee	$	S.	Buydown Funds	$
J.	Mortgage Rating Fee	$	T.	Other	$
K.	PERS Buydown Fee	$			

* Tax Liability Acct. Agreement, if enclosed, must be checked in the "Yes" box if impounds are to be deducted.

** Total Assn. Loan Fee of $ less $ prepaid.

LPL18 (Rev. 2/92) 021392   PAGE 1 OF 2

BROKER'S CHECK:

____ OUR CHECK FOR MORTGAGE BROKER FEES WILL BE DELIVERED TO PAYEE UPON RECORDATION OF OUR DEED OF TRUST. YOU ARE TO CALL THE LOAN OFFICE INDICATED UNDER ITEM 1 WITH THE DATE OF RECORDING AND SERIAL NO.

4. FUNDING REQUIREMENTS:

Each of the following conditions precedent must be met prior to disbursement of any of the net loan proceeds:

A.   YOU ARE TO COMPLY WITH ALL HAZARD AND FLOOD INSURANCE REQUIREMENTS AS SHOWN IN ADDENDUM "A" ATTACHED HERETO AND MADE A PART HEREOF BY REFERENCE.

____ Flood Insurance is required prior to disbursement of our loan proceeds. See attached Addendum "A" Requirements Regarding Hazard Insurance

B.   **If your escrow closes on or after October 1st,** pay first installment of county and city taxes that are due and payable November 1st; **If your escrow closes on or after February 1st,** pay second installment of county and city taxes that are due and payable February 1st; decrease our tax impound deduction - Item 3M, if any, by six-month portion or five-month portion respectively of that total.

C.   ALL DELINQUENT TAXES, BONDS, ASSESSMENTS, HOMEOWNERS' ASSOCIATION DUES THAT ARE LIENS ON THE SUBJECT PROPERTY MUST BE PAID IN FULL OR TO DATE PRIOR TO CLOSING. JUDGEMENTS MUST BE SATISFIED AND CLEARED OF RECORD.

5. ALTA POLICY OF TITLE INSURANCE:

You are to insure this Association, the beneficiary under said Deed of Trust, as the holder of a valid (first/junior) deed of trust lien encumbering the entire fee interest in the real property described herein and showing title thereto vested in our Trustors, named above and in the Deed of Trust. Except as may be permitted by our specific written amendment to these instruction, said title is to be free from all liens and encumbrances, except only those shown below on your preliminary report bearing a vesting date and number as set forth above.

You shall be able, by recording the Deed of Trust enclosed herewith, to issue an ALTA form of the Title Insurance Policy in favor of association ____ **in the amount of 110% of our Note** ____ **in the amount of our Note** with **CLTA ENDORSEMENTS 100, 116** (116.2, if a condominium) **, 110.8 or 110.9, & 8.1** The 116 Endorsement Property address must agree EXACTLY as it appears on our Deed of Trust with NO DEVIATIONS. If the property is known by two addresses both must be stated on the endorsement. For a property without an address, a description of its exact location is mandatory. Example: West Side of Lobos Street, the fifth house from First Avenue, Carmel, Ca 93921, a single family residence.

_____ Pay first installment all taxes due and payable. _____
_____ The   installment of taxes has been paid by this Association and is presently in transit.
_____ Pay bond payments and/or assessments to date; ALTA Policy to so state. Exception(s) No: _____
_____ Following any Condition, Covenants and Restriction, please recite that there are no express words of forfeiture. Where reverter or re-entry clauses appear in the CC & R's, issue CLTA Endorsement **100.12 or 100.18.** Exception(s) No. _____
_____ All easements must be fully described as to purpose and location. If unable to locate on map or define, issue CLTA Endorsement **103.1 or 103.3** for exception(s) numbered: _____
_____ We will take subject to exceptions: _____
_____ The Plat Map attached to your ALTA policy must have complete Tract/Map name. Delineate lot, show property dimensions in full decimals, fully identify street, show distance to and fully identify nearest cross street, and provide directional arrow.

6. SPECIAL INSTRUCTIONS: SEE ATTACHED ADDENDUM "C"

7. CLOSING INSTRUCTIONS:

When each and every one of said conditions has been fully performed you are authorized to record our Deed of Trust. Closing this transaction constitutes your certification that you have or will comply with all conditions stated above and your agreement that the completed HUD I Settlement Statement (as required by the most current RESPA Regulations) or Buyer's and Seller's Closing Statements will be forwarded immediately. **The ALTA policy must be delivered no later than 5 business days** after recordation of our Deed of Trust to P.O. Box 3009, Concord, CA 94520-3009, Attn: Quality Loan Review Department.

These instructions are expressly made revocable and may be withdrawn, amended or supplemented at any time and from time to time by letter, or wire, or telephone message confirmed by letter or wire, and the enclosures may be withdrawn at any time prior to the recordation of the enclosed Deed of Trust.

We are to be at no expense in connection with the transaction.

Very truly yours,

SAN FRANCISCO FEDERAL SAVINGS AND LOAN ASSOCIATION

By _____

Loan Funding Officer
Phone (415) 686-5700, EXT _____
2151 Salvio Street, Suite 360, Concord, CA 94520

DOCUMENTS MAY BE INTER-BRANCHED TO THE CENTRAL FUNDING DEPARTMENT, CONCORD, FROM THE FOLLOWING LOCATIONS:

88 Kearny St., 8th Fl
SAN FRANCISCO, CA 94108
PHONE: (415) 955-2840

39138 Fremont Boulevard
FREMONT, CA 94538
PHONE: (510) 794-6995

1400 Guerneville Rd., Ste. 4
SANTA ROSA, CA 95401
PHONE: (707) 544-0252

4880 Stevens Creek Blvd., Ste. 204
SAN JOSE, CA 95129
PHONE: (408) 246-8200

Carmel Rancho Center
P.O. Box 221010
CARMEL, CA 93922
PHONE: (408) 624-8250

344 20th Street, Suite 360
OAKLAND, CA 94612
PHONE: (510) 839-2300

1220 41st Avenue
CAPITOLA, CA 95010
PHONE: (408) 476-3311

599 Higuera St., Ste. E
SAN LUIS OBISPO, CA 93401
PHONE: (805) 541-4646

3 Parkcenter Drive, Ste. 101
SACRAMENTO, CA 95825
PHONE: (916) 923-4500

88 Kearny Street
Major Loan Dept
SAN FRANCISCO, CA 94108
PHONE: (415) 955-5851

1660 Olympic Blvd.
WALNUT CREEK, CA 94596
PHONE: (510) 937-7605

LPL 18 (Rev. 01/92) 020792

SAN FRANCISCO FEDERAL SAVINGS AND LOAN ASSOCIATION
REQUIREMENTS REGARDING HAZARD INSURANCE
1-4 / Condo PUD
ADDENDUM A

Acceptable Insurers Any company authorized by the Insurance Commissioner to transact business in the State of California having a minimum rating in Best's Key Rating Guide of B:III. California Fair Plan & Lloyds of London are acceptable (although not rated in Best Key Rating Guide).

Acceptable Fire, Homeowner's or other package type coverage, except for Condominium and PUD coverage

1. **First Loans:** The Evidence of Insurance or Agents Declaration Page issued by an insurance carrier which shows all relevant information as listed below:

    a) Named Insured and Mortgagee.
    b) Property Address.
    c) Insurance type, amount, and effective date of coverage.
    d) Deductible amount.
    e) Any endorsements or optional coverage obtained and made part of the Original Policy.
    f) Insurer's agreement to provide at least 10 days' notice to the mortgagee before any reduction in coverage or cancellation of the policy.
    g) Signature of an authorized representative of the insurer.

    The Evidence or Agents Declaration page must show coverage equal to the principal balance of the first loan or to the full replacement value of the improvements with guaranteed replacement cost endorsement.

2. **Junior Loans:** A copy of the existing Evidence or Agents Declaration Page of Insurance issued by an insurance carrier which shows all relevant information and is signed by the insurance carrier. The coverage amount must be equal to the principal balance of the first and second loans or to the full replacement value of the improvements with guaranteed replacement cost endorsement.

3. **Refinances:** A copy of the Evidence or Agents Declaration page signed by the insurance agent with original 438 BFU.

Notice is hereby given that we have no obligation, either stated or implied, to notify you regarding renewal or cancellation, this is the obligation of your insurance agent or company.

Delivery: Acceptable insurance coverage must be delivered along with this form signed by the borrowers to:

The Title Company prior to close of escrow with a receipt for one year's premium prepaid on new or assumed loans.

Policy Requirements: All policies containing property coverage must contain a Lender's Loss Payable Endorsement (438BFU) in favor of San Francisco Federal Savings & Loan Association, its successor and/or assigns, with San Francisco Federal's address as shown: P.O.Box 3009 Concord, CA 94522-3009.

Deductible: The maximum deductible for 1-4 unit dwellings is $1,000.00 or 1% of the coverage amount whichever is less. This amount covers flood and fire on 1-4 units.

PLANNED UNIT DEVELOPMENT AND CONDOMINIUMS: An Acord 27 or Evidence of Insurance in the name of the Homeowner's Association must be delivered to the Title company prior to close of escrow and must meet the following criteria: **(ACORD 25 IS NOT ACCEPTABLE)**

1) The named insured must be the Homeowners' Association and must also show Unit Owner/Borrower. 2) Insurance company must have a rating of B:III or higher in Best's Key Rating Guide. 3) Deductible cannot exceed $10,000 or 1% of the policy face value, whichever is less. 4) The amount of insurance must be 100% of the insurable value of the common areas. 5) The policy form must contain "All Risk" coverage and must provide that claims are paid on a replacement cost basis. 6) Maximum deductible for flood insurance is $5,000.00 or 1% of the applicable amount of Insurance, whichever is less.

FLOOD INSURANCE: All loans on property identified in a Special Flood Hazard Area, as defined by the Department of Housing and Urban Development must maintain Flood Insurance in accordance with the Flood Disaster Protection Act of 1973. Borrower must submit one year prepaid premium and flood application to the Title Company. It will be the borrower's responsibility to pay the renewal premiums in a timely manner to prevent lapse of coverage. Coverage must be the maximum available or loan amount whichever is less.

FAILURE TO PROVIDE COVERAGE: In the event it becomes necessary for San Francisco Federal to obtain coverage resulting from failure of our borrower to provide such coverage in accordance with the terms of these requirements, such coverage may only be in an amount necessary to protect our interest as herein before stated. No liability shall accrue to San Francisco Federal for omission of any other previous special coverage as may have been contained in the lapsed or non-renewed policy. San Francisco Federal shall, however, have no stated duty to obtain such replacement coverage.

REPAYMENT OF ADVANCED PREMIUMS: San Francisco Federal shall recover any costs incurred for obtaining necessary coverage as previously described herein from the borrower by either (a) Demanding immediate repayment of costs or (b) Establishing a mandatory impound account for recovery and payment of future payments.

Failure to pay such cost upon demand constitutes a default under the terms of the Deed of Trust securing this indebtedness.

These requirements in no way amend or supersede any provisions of the Deed of Trust securing your loan and are subject to all the terms and conditions of such Deed of Trust.

Certification, Interim Certificates, Acord 25 Evidence/Binders **ARE NOT ACCEPTABLE** either at inception or at time of renewal. Please contact your agent in sufficient time to insure that an original policy is issued <u>PRIOR</u> to loan closing. Acord 27, is acceptable in condo or Pud's <u>only.</u>

FUNDING OF YOUR LOAN WILL BE DELAYED IF ALL INSURANCE REQUIREMENTS ARE NOT MET.

YOU ARE ADVISED THAT ADEQUATE INSURANCE MUST BE MAINTAINED IN FORCE THROUGHOUT THE LIFE OF THE LOAN.

LP78(Rev 3/89)   1-Borrower (original)   1-Lender   1-Insurance Agent

ADDENDUM B (TRUTH IN LENDING)

Prior to closing this loan escrow, the following conditions precedent shall be fully performed:

1.   You must deliver the Regulation Z Disclosure Statement and the Itemization of the Amount Financed to our borrowers at the time they execute the loan documents and obtain the written receipt of our borrowers for both of said documents on a copy thereof.

2.   You shall insert the date of execution of the loan documents and delivery of the Disclosure Statements in the first item of the Notice of Right to Cancel and insert the date of the third business day following such date of execution and delivery in the fourth line from the end of said Notice of Right to Cancel.

3.   You must deliver to each borrower two copies of the Notice of Right to Cancel at the time our borrowers execute the loan documents and acknowledge receipt of the Disclosure Statement. On the third copy provided of such Notice of Right to Cancel you must obtain the written receipt and date signed from our borrowers.

4.   You must immediately return to this Association:

     A. Receipted Disclosure Statement,

     B. Receipted Itemization of the Amount Financed and

     C. Receipted Notice of Right to Cancel.

5.   You may request that our loan funds be issued not earlier than the fourth business day following the date the Disclosure Statement is executed and/or the Notice of Right to Cancel is given to our Borrower(s) whichever is later.

6.   Under no circumstances will loan funds be transmitted by this Association until the items called for under paragraph 4 above have been received by our Central Funding Department and the three day waiting period described in paragraph 5 above has elapsed.

LP-89 (Rev. 11/85)

CLOSING THE SALE

Real Estate Settlement Procedures Act

[§11.89] Incidental Provisions

Real Estate Settlement Procedures Act §10 (12 USC §2609) provides that in certain circumstances lenders may not compel borrowers to deposit excess funds in an escrow account. There is a split in the circuit courts, however, on whether §2609 may be enforced by a private right of action. See *Allison v Liberty Sav.* (7th Cir 1982) 695 F2d 1086 (no private right of action); *Vega v First Fed. Sav. & Loan Ass'n* (6th Cir 1980) 622 F2d 918, 925 n8 (private right of action available).

Recordation

[§11.91] Types of Documents Entitled to Recordation

An "instrument" that is entitled to be recorded finally has been given a statutory definition by Govt C §27279, effective January 1, 1989. An "instrument" is defined as "a written paper signed by a person or persons transferring the title to, or giving a lien on real property, or giving a right to a debt or duty." The new statute apparently was intended to codify the holding in *Hoag v Howard* (1880) 55 C 564, cited in Book §11.91. The statute specifically provides that Govt C §27279 is declaratory of existing law and that it is not intended to expand or diminish the scope of documents presently found by recorders to be eligible for recordation. Stats 1988, ch 400, §2.

Civil Code §1262, cited in Book §11.91, was repealed effective July 1, 1983, and superseded in part by CCP §704.920. See generally Update §3.9 on revision of homestead laws.

The treatise by Miller & Starr, cited in the Book, has been replaced by 3 Miller & Starr, California Real Estate §8.5 (2d ed 1989).

Recording Procedures

[§11.94] Acknowledgment of Instruments

Civil Code §1185, concerning acknowledgment of instruments, has been amended to continue the former prohibition on acknowledgment of an instrument unless the officer taking it either "personally knows" (as defined in new CC §1185(b)) the individual executing the document or has satisfactory evidence that the person making the acknowledgment is the individual who is described in and who executed the instrument. CC §1185(a). The definition of "satisfactory evidence" has been expanded to include not only the oath or affirmation of a credible witness personally known to the acknowledging officer, but also certain documentary evidence as well, such as a California driver's license. CC §1185(c).

The statutory forms of certificates of acknowledgment found in former CC §§1189, 1190, 1190a, 1190.1, 1191 and 1192 have been combined into a single statutory form of certificate of acknowledgment in which the capacity of the person signing the documents is indicated below the signature. See CC §§1189–1190. Acknowledgments conforming to previous law and executed before January 1, 1993, have the same force and effect as if the former Civil Code sections had not been repealed.

Effective January 1, 1989, the definition of satisfactory evidence was further amended to include the oath or affirmation of two credible witnesses whose identities are proved to the acknowledging officers that each of several specified facts concerning the person signing the document is true. CC §1185(c)(2).

See Update §7.59 on repeal of CC §1242, and Update §11.91 on repeal and replacement of CC §1262.

[§11.96] Recorder's Procedure

No documentary transfer tax need be paid to record certain instruments, including instruments given to secure a debt (Rev & T C §11921), instruments to which the United States, a state or territory, or a political subdivision is a party (Rev & T C §11922), instruments concerning bankruptcy, receivership, or change of identity (Rev & T C §11923), instruments under orders of the Securities and Exchange Commission (Rev & T C §11924), instruments implementing certain partnership transfers (Rev & T C §11925), instruments taken in lieu of foreclosure (Rev & T C §11926), and instruments transferring certain property between spouses as part of marital dissolution, separation, or nullity proceedings (Rev & T C §11927).

See Update §7.66A for discussion of Los Angeles County Recorder's Office procedures when a transfer is claimed to be exempt from documentary transfer taxes.

When a county recorder caused a delay in the recordation of a submitted document by incorrectly demanding additional fees before recording the document, the court in *Carpenters Health & Welfare Trust Fund v Shafer* (1983) 146 CA3d 504, 194 CR 266, held that the party submitting the document could obtain a writ of mandate to have the county recorder retroactively record the document as of the date it was first submitted. The later recording date would have deprived the party of the right to foreclose on its claim of lien.

If a county recorder fails to properly index a document under the correct name, there is no constructive notice of the recorded document. Thus, later purchasers may be bona fide purchasers for value without notice if they pay substantial value for the property and lack actual notice of the recorded document. *Hochstein v Romero* (1990) 219 CA3d 447, 268 CR 202.

Effectiveness of Recording

[§11.97] Legal Effectiveness Versus Constructive Notice

Civil Code §§1264 and 1268, cited in Book §11.97, have been repealed and superseded by CCP §704.920. See further discussion of changes in the homestead law in Update §3.9.

The possession of real property can be sufficient constructive notice to defeat a claim that a party is a bona fide purchaser or encumbrancer. Compare *Claremont Terrace Homeowners' Ass'n v U.S.* (1983) 146 CA3d 398, 194 CR 216 (unrecorded, unexercised option held to have priority over recorded tax lien, when lienor had constructive notice of option because optionee was in possesion of the property), with *Kane v Huntley Fin.* (1983) 146 CA3d 1092, 194 CR 880 (recorded deed of trust executed by divorced spouse given priority over previous oral agreement between spouses allocating property to other spouse as her separate property, because apparent possession was consistent with record title showing that property was held in joint tenancy).

[§11.99] Form: Uniform Settlement Statement

The form in Book §11.99 has been replaced by the following form:

FORM APPROVED OMB No. 2502-0265

A. SETTLEMENT STATEMENT

B. TYPE OF LOAN

1. ☐ FHA   2. ☐ FmHA   3. ☐ Conv. Unins.
4. ☐ VA   5. ☐ Conv. Ins.

6. File Number	7. Loan Number	8. Mortgage Insurance Case Number

C. NOTE: *This form is furnished to give you a statement of actual settlement costs. Amounts paid to and by the settlement agent are shown. Items marked "(p.o.c.)" were paid outside the closing; they are shown here for informational purposes and are not included in the totals.*

D. NAME AND ADDRESS OF BORROWER	E. NAME AND ADDRESS OF SELLER	F. NAME AND ADDRESS OF LENDER

G. PROPERTY LOCATION	H. SETTLEMENT AGENT	
	PLACE OF SETTLEMENT	I. SETTLEMENT DATE

J. SUMMARY OF BORROWER'S TRANSACTION	
100. GROSS AMOUNT DUE FROM BORROWER:	
101. Contract sales price	
102. Personal property	
103. Settlement charges to borrower (line 1400)	
104.	
105.	
Adjustments for items paid by seller in advance.	
106. City/town taxes	to
107. County taxes	to
108. Assessments	to
109.	

K. SUMMARY OF SELLER'S TRANSACTION	
400. GROSS AMOUNT DUE TO SELLER:	
401. Contract sales price	
402. Personal property	
403.	
404.	
405.	
Adjustments for items paid by seller in advance.	
406. City/town taxes	to
407. County taxes	to
408. Assessments	to
409.	

110.	
111.	
112.	
120.	GROSS AMOUNT DUE FROM BORROWER:
200.	AMOUNTS PAID BY OR IN BEHALF OF BORROWER:
201.	Deposit or earnest money
202.	Principal amount of new loan(s)
203.	Existing loan(s) taken subject to
204.	
205.	
206.	
207.	
208.	
209.	
	Adjustments for items unpaid by seller.
210.	City/town taxes to
211.	County taxes to
212.	Assessments to
213.	
214.	
215.	
216.	
217.	
218.	
219.	
220.	TOTAL PAID BY/FOR BORROWER:
300.	CASH AT SETTLEMENT FROM/TO BORROWER:
301.	Gross amount due from borrower (line 120)
302.	Less amounts paid by/for borrowers (line 220) ( )
303.	CASH (☐ FROM) (☐ TO) BORROWER:

410.	
411.	
412.	
420.	GROSS AMOUNT DUE TO SELLER:
500.	REDUCTIONS IN AMOUNT DUE TO SELLER:
501.	Excess deposit *(see instructions)*
502.	Settlement charges to seller *(line 1400)*
503.	Existing loan(s) taken subject to
504.	Payoff of first mortgage loan
505.	Payoff of second mortgage loan
506.	
507.	
508.	
509.	
	Adjustments for items unpaid by seller.
510.	City/town taxes to
511.	County taxes to
512.	Assessments to
513.	
514.	
515.	
516.	
517.	
518.	
519.	
520.	TOTAL REDUCTION AMOUNT DUE SELLER:
600.	CASH AT SETTLEMENT TO/FROM SELLER:
601.	Gross amount due to seller (line 420)
602.	Less reductions in amount due seller (line 520) ( )
603.	CASH (☐ TO) (☐ FROM) SELLER:

HUD-1 (Rev. 8/87)
RESPA, HB 4305.2

L. SETTLEMENT CHARGES

	PAID FROM BORROWER'S FUNDS AT SETTLEMENT	PAID FROM SELLER'S FUNDS AT SETTLEMENT
700. TOTAL SALES/BROKER'S COMMISSION based on price $ @ %		
Division of Commission (line 700) as follows:		
701. $ to		
702. $ to		
703. Commission paid at Settlement		
704.		
800. ITEMS PAYABLE IN CONNECTION WITH LOAN		
801. Loan Origination Fee %		
802. Loan Discount %		
803. Appraisal Fee to		
804. Credit Report to		
805. Lender's Inspection Fee		
806. Mortgage Insurance Application Fee to		
807. Assumption Fee		
808.		
809.		
810.		
811.		
900. ITEMS REQUIRED BY LENDER TO BE PAID IN ADVANCE		
901. Interest from to @ $ day		
902. Mortgage Insurance Premium for months to		
903. Hazard Insurance Premium for years to		
904. years to		
905.		
1000. RESERVES DEPOSITED WITH LENDER		
1001. Hazard Insurance months @ $ per month		
1002. Mortgage Insurance months @ $ per month		
1003. City property taxes months @ $ per month		
1004. County property taxes months @ $ per month		
1005. Annual assessments months @ $ per month		
1006. months @ $ per month		
1007. months @ $ per month		
1008. months @ $ per month		

1100. TITLE CHARGES

1101. Settlement or closing fee	to
1102. Abstract or title search	to
1103. Title examination	to
1104. Title insurance binder	to
1105. Document preparation	to
1106. Notary fees	to
1107. Attorney's fees	to
(includes above items numbers:)	
1108. Title insurance	to
(includes above items numbers:)	
1109. Lender's coverage	$
1110. Owner's coverage	$
1111.	
1112.	
1113.	

1200. GOVERNMENT RECORDING AND TRANSFER CHARGES

1201. Recording fees.	Deed $	: Mortgage $	: Release $
1202. City county tax stamps:	Deed $	: Mortgage $	
1203. State tax stamps:	Deed $	: Mortgage $	
1204.			
1205.			

1300. ADDITIONAL SETTLEMENT CHARGES

1301. Survey	to
1302. Pest inspection	to
1303.	
1304.	
1305.	

1400. TOTAL SETTLEMENT CHARGES (enter on lines 103. Section J and 502. Section K)

FORM 5000 (Rev 6 88)

[§11.100] Change in Ownership Statement

The penalty under Rev & T C §480 is limited to a maximum of $2500 if the failure to file the statement was not willful.

[§11.101] Preliminary Change of Ownership Report

Effective January 1, 1991, Rev & T C §480.3 was amended to provide that transferees of real property "shall complete and may file with the recorder" a "preliminary change in ownership report" concurrent with the recordation of any document effecting a change of ownership. Rev & T C §480.3(a). If such a document is presented to the recorder for recordation without the concurrent filing of a preliminary change of ownership report, the recorder may charge an additional recording fee of $20. Rev & T C §480.3(b). Revenue and Taxation Code §480.4 contains a prescribed form for the preliminary change of ownership and is set out at Update §11.102.

[§11.102] Form: Preliminary Change of Ownership Report

Form 11.102–1

PRELIMINARY CHANGE OF OWNERSHIP REPORT
(To be completed by transferee (buyer) prior to transfer of subject property in accordance with Section 480.3 of the Revenue & Taxation Code.)

FOR RECORDER: , Page D, Date Document No.	
SELLER: BUYER: A.P. #(s): LEGAL DESCRIPTION: ADDRESS (if improved): MAIL TAX INFORMATION TO: Name:_____ Address:_____	FOR ASSESSOR'S USE ONLY:

NOTICE: A lien for property taxes applies to your property on March 1 of each year for the taxes owing in the following fiscal year, July 1 through June 30. One-half of these taxes is due November 1, and one-half is due February 1. The first installment becomes delinquent on December 10, and the second installment becomes delinquent on April 10. One tax bill is mailed before November 1 to the owner of record. If this transfer occurs after March 1 and on or before December 31, you may be responsible for the second installment of taxes due February 1.
The property which you acquired may be subject to a supplemental tax assessment in an amount to be determined by the (name of county) County Assessor. For further information on your supplemental roll tax obligation, please call the (name of county) County Assessor at (phone number).

1. Transfer Information:
   A. Was this transfer solely between husband & wife, addition of a spouse, death of a spouse, divorce settlement, etc.?   a. ( ) YES   b. ( ) NO
   B. Was this transaction only a correction of the name(s) of the person(s) holding title to the property?   a. ( ) YES   b. ( ) NO
   C. Was this document recorded to create, terminate, or reconvey a lender's interest in the property?   a. ( ) YES   b. ( ) NO
   D. Was this document recorded to substitute a trustee under a deed of trust, mortgage, or other similar document?   a. ( ) YES   b. ( ) NO
   E. Did this transfer result in the creation of a joint tenancy in which the seller (transferor) remains as one of the joint tenants?   a. ( ) YES   b. ( ) NO
   F. Return of property to person who created the joint tenancy?   a. ( ) YES   b. ( ) NO
   G. Is this transfer of property:
      a. to a trust for the benefit of the grantor?   a. ( ) YES   b. ( ) NO
      b. to a revocable trust   a. ( ) YES   b. ( ) NO
      c. to a trust from which the property reverts to the grantor within 12 years?   a. ( ) YES   b. ( ) NO
   H. If this property is the subject of a lease, is the lease for a term of less than 35 years including written options?   a. ( ) YES   b. ( ) NO
   I. If the conveying document constitutes an exclusion from a change in ownership as defined in Section 62 of the Revenue & Taxation Code for any reason other than those listed above, set forth the specific exclusion claimed:_____

---

* IF YOU HAVE ANSWERED "NO" TO QUESTIONS A THROUGH H, INCLUSIVE, AND HAVE NOT CLAIMED ANY OTHER EXCLUSIONS UNDER I, PLEASE COMPLETE BALANCE OR FORM. OTHERWISE SIGN AND DATE.

Preliminary Change of Ownership Report   Page Two

2. Type of property transferred:
   a. ( ) Single-family residence
   b. ( ) Multiple-family residence (no. of units:_____)
   c. ( ) Co-op
   d. ( ) Condo
   e. ( ) Mobilehome
   f. ( ) Unimproved lot
   g. ( ) Commercial/Industrial
   h. ( ) Other (description:_____)

3. Intended as principal residence?   a. ( ) YES   b. ( ) NO
4. Transfer is by:
   a. ( ) Deed; b.(Contract of sale;
   c. ( ) Other—explain: _____
5. Is less than 100% of property being transferred?   a. ( ) YES   b. ( ) NO
6. a. ( ) Date of transfer or; b. ( ) If an inheritance, date of
   death _____
7. Is or will, the property produce(ing) income?   a. ( ) YES   b. ( ) NO
8. If answer to Question 4 is yes, is income pursuant to:
   a. ( ) Lease; b. ( ) Contract; c. ( ) Mineral rights;
   d. ( ) Other—explain: _____
9. Did the transfer of this property involve the trade or exchange of a. ( ) YES   b. ( ) NO
   other real property?
10. a. Total Purchase Price or Acquisition Price, If Exchanged: $_____
    b. Cash Downpayment or Value of Trade (excluding closing $_____
      costs):
    c. 1st Deed of Trust $_____
      at _____% interest for _____
      years.
      New Loan ( ); FHA ( ); Cal–Vet ( ); VA ( ); Bank ( );
      Finance Co. ( ); Savings & Loan ( ); Loan Carried By
      Seller ( ); All inclusive ( ); Balloon Payment: Yes ( ) No
      ( ).
    d. 2nd Deed of Trust $_____
      at _____% interest for _____
      years.
      New Loan ( ); Assumed Existing Loan Balance ( ); Loan
      Carried By Seller ( ); Balloon Payment: Yes ( ) No ( ).
    e. Was other type of financing involved not covered in (c) or a. ( ) YES   b. ( ) NO
      (d), above?
    f. Improvement Bond: Yes ( ) No ( ); Outstanding Balance $_____
11. Was any personal property involved in   a. ( ) YES   b. ( ) NO
   purchase other than a mobilehome on real   c. AMOUNT _____
   property?
Preliminary Change of Ownership Report   Page Three

I certify that the foregoing is true, correct, and complete to the best of my knowledge and belief.

Signed _____Date: _____
    (New Owner/Corporate Officer)
Address if other than above _____
Phone No. Where You Are Available From 8:00 am–5:00 pm: ( ) _____
    (note): The Assessor may contact you for further information.)

Comment: This form is set out in Rev& T C §480.4 and becomes operative July 1, 1991. A version of the statute that remains in effect only until July 1, 1991, contains a form that is operative until that date.

12

Remedies

INTRODUCTION

[§12.1] Scope of Chapter

The treatise by Miller & Starr, cited in the Book, has been replaced by 1 Miller & Starr, California Real Estate, chap 1 (2d ed 1989).

The reference to California Mortgage and Deed of Trust Practice (Cal CEB 1979) in the Book should now be to chaps 2–4 of California Mortgage and Deed of Trust Practice (2d ed Cal CEB 1990).

[§12.2] Purchase Agreement and Installment Land Contract Distinguished

The statement in Book §12.2 that the buyer under an installment land contract is entitled to protections applicable to mortgages and deeds of trust is probably overbroad. For a discussion of the seller's remedies for the buyer's default under an installment land contract, see Graham, *The Installment Land Contract in California: Is It Really a Mortgage?* 4 CEB Real Prop L Rep 117 (Oct. 1981).

In *Petersen v Hartell* (1985) 40 C3d 102, 219 CR 170, the supreme court avoided treating an installment land contract as the equivalent of a mortgage or deed of trust. The court allowed a willfully defaulting vendee who made substantial payments on an installment sale contract used only as a security device to complete the purchase by paying the entire remaining balance plus damages before the seller was allowed to quiet title. The court held this right to redeem was absolute in such a situation. However, the majority opinion specifically refused to extend mortgagor or trustor protections under CC §2924 to the installment sale contract vendee, as was urged by former Chief Justice Bird in a concurring and dissenting opinion. The court held that such an extension was unnecessary under the facts of the case and thus limited its holding to defaulting vendees who have paid a substantial part of the purchase price. Note that four out of the five justices in support of the majority decision in the case are no longer on the court.

Effective January 1, 1987, CC §2920(b) was added, which for purposes of CC §§2924–2924h (nonjudicial foreclosure sales) defines "mortgage" as any security device, including a real property sales contract, that contains a power of sale.

The reference to California Mortgage and Deed of Trust Practice (Cal CEB 1979) in the Book should now be to California Mortgage and Deed of Trust Practice §1.35 (2d ed Cal CEB 1990).

ESTABLISHING BREACH

[§12.8] Time for Performance

A willfully defaulting buyer under an installment land contract may, depending on the equities, be permitted by a trial court to reinstate the contract by paying the balance due in full along with any damages incurred by the seller. In any event, a willfully defaulting buyer is entitled to restitution of any principal payments exceeding the seller's damages. *Bartley v Karas* (1983) 150 CA3d 336, 197 CR 749.

[§12.11] Anticipatory Breach or Repudiation

Daum Dev. Corp. v Yuba Plaza Inc. (1970) 11 CA3d 65, 89 CR 458, cited in Book §12.11, was disapproved on other grounds in *Ninety Five Ten v Crain* (1991) 231 CA3d 36, 282 CR 141.

DAMAGES

Seller's Breach

[§§12.13–12.14] General Damages; CC §3306; Bad Faith

Civil Code §3306 was amended effective January 1, 1984, to delete the requirement that bad faith be shown before the optionee may recover the difference between the price agreed to be paid and the value of the estate at the time of breach and expenses incurred in preparing to enter on the land.

The section now reads:

The detriment caused by the breach of an agreement to convey an estate in real property, is deemed to be the price paid, and the expenses properly incurred in examining the title and preparing the necessary papers, the difference between the price agreed to be paid and the value of the estate agreed to be conveyed at the time of the breach, the expenses properly incurred in preparing to enter upon the land, consequential damages according to proof, and interest.

[§12.17] Attorneys' Fees

The reciprocal right to attorneys' fees granted to a prevailing contracting party by CC §1717 may be extended to a noncontracting party if the nonparty would be practically, although not legally, compelled to pay a contracting party's attorneys' fees, in an action in which the contracting party prevailed. *Saucedo v Mercury Sav. & Loan Ass'n* (1980) 111 CA3d 309, 168 CR 552 (buyer taking subject to a loan awarded attorneys' fees in action against lender to enjoin enforcement of due-on-sale clause because, as a practical matter, buyer would have had to tender attorneys' fees in addition to loan amounts to protect the buyer's equity if the buyer had lost). While criticizing part of the *Saucedo* court's reasoning, the court in *Jones v Drain* (1983) 149 CA3d 484, 196 CR 827, agreed with its conclusion that a noncontracting party may be entitled to attorneys' fees allowable under the contract. But see *Glynn v Marquette* (1984) 152 CA3d 277, 199 CR 306 (an action for specific performance to compel a third party purchaser to convey real property to the original prospective buyer did not authorize attorneys' fees as part of the specific performance).

In *Steve Schmidt & Co. v Berry* (1986) 183 CA3d 1299, 228 CR 689, a cooperating broker who was not a signatory to the listing agreement, which contained an attorneys' fee provision, was awarded attorneys' fees under CC §1717 after successfully suing the seller for a commission due under the listing agreement.

For further discussion of attorneys' fees, see California Attorney's Fees Award Practice (Cal CEB 1982).

Buyer's Breach

[§12.19] General Damages; CC §3307

Civil Code §3307 was amended effective January 1, 1984, to provide for the recovery of consequential damages and interest by the seller on the buyer's breach. A buyer will be entitled to a credit against consequential damages, however, for an increased sale price obtained by the seller after a quick resale. *Smith v Mady* (1983) 146 CA3d 129, 194 CR 42.

For a recent example of what constitutes consequential damages in a specific fact situation, see *Askari v R & R Land Co.* (1986) 179 CA3d 1101, 225 CR 285.

Civil Code §3306 no longer distinguishes between good faith and bad faith defaults. See Update §§12.13–12.14.

[§12.22] Effect of Market

In *Spurgeon v Drumheller* (1985) 174 CA3d 659, 220 CR 195, the court applied the principle in *Freedman v The Rector* (1951) 37 C2d 16, 230 P2d 629, discussed in Book §12.22, to a situation in which the buyer had breached his contract to buy the seller's residence and the seller had removed it from the market at the time of trial. The property had appreciated since the buyer's breach, and the court held that the seller had consequently lost the right to recover benefit-of-the-bargain damages. A seller who does not make reasonably diligent efforts to resell the property breaches his or her duty to mitigate damages.

Disposition of Deposit

Liquidated Damages Provisions

[§12.30] Agreements Executed on or After July 1, 1978

If a liquidated damages provision is not initialed as required by CC §1677, it is voidable (but not void) at the option of the buyer only. *Guthman v Moss* (1984) 150 CA3d 501, 198 CR 54. For a case applying CC §1677, see *Hong v Somerset Assocs.* (1984) 161 CA3d 111, 207 CR 597 ($25,000 liquidated damages reasonable in sale of apartment building for $1,325,000).

Fraud

[§12.33] Fraud by Fiduciary

For further discussion of damages for fraud, see California Tort Damages (Cal CEB 1988).

[§12.34] Punitive Damages; CC §3294

Civil Code §3294 was amended effective January 1, 1988, to provide that oppression, fraud, or malice must be proven by clear and convincing evidence. The amendment also changed the definition of malice so that the defendant's conduct must be despicable and done with a willful and conscious disregard of the rights or safety of others. The definition of oppression was changed to mean despicable conduct that subjects a person to cruel and unjust hardship in conscious disregard of that person's rights. The amendments apply to all actions in which the initial trial did not begin before January 1, 1988.

[§12.35] Attorneys' Fees

The defendant in a tort action may not recover attorneys' fees on a cross-complaint based on an agreement including an attorneys' fees provision if the cross-complaint does not attempt to hold the cross-defendant liable under the contract. *Plemon v Nelson* (1983) 148 CA3d 720, 196 CR 190 (cross-complaint was defensive, not offensive, and sought to limit tort liability).

For further discussion of attorneys' fees, see California Attorney's Fees Award Practice (Cal CEB 1982).

SPECIFIC PERFORMANCE

Seller's Breach

[§12.39] General Considerations for Buyer

The buyer and the buyer's attorney should be aware of how the Bankruptcy Code provision allowing for the rejection of executory contracts (11 USC §365) may affect a suit for specific performance. In a bankruptcy case from the Northern District of California, *In re Alexander* (9th Cir 1982) 670 F2d 885, the court held that a contract for the purchase and sale of real property remained executory under the Bankruptcy Code even after the buyers' tender of performance, because other material obligations remained to be performed, including deposit by the institutional lender of its loan funds in escrow and the seller's relinquishment of possession and conveyance of title to the buyers. This holding allowed the seller, who filed for bankruptcy on the first day of trial of the buyers' specific performance action, to reject her contract with the buyers under 11 USC §365 and defeat the specific performance action.

The court in *Alexander* did not refer to California law, under which an institutional lender's commitment to deposit loan funds in escrow on request, rather than the actual deposit of the lender's funds into escrow, constitutes part of the buyer's tender of the purchase price for the purpose of measuring the buyer's performance. See *Hutton v Gliksberg* (1982) 128 CA3d 240, 247, 180 CR 141, 144.

An amendment to CC §3387 provides that the presumption that breach of an agreement to transfer real property cannot be adequately relieved by pecuniary compensation is conclusive if the real property is a single-family dwelling, but that it is only a presumption affecting the burden of proof in all other cases.

Legal Requirements

[§12.42] Performance of Conditions Precedent

The burden of proof with respect to whether a condition precedent to a sales agreement would have existed but for the breach by the seller may properly be shifted to the seller in appropriate circumstances. In *Jacobs v Tenneco West, Inc.* (1986) 186 CA3d 1413, 231 CR 351, the buyer was attempting to specifically enforce a sales agreement that provided the sale was subject to the approval of the seller's board of directors. The seller never submitted the agreement to its board for approval and refused to sell the subject property. In an earlier decision (*Jacobs v Freeman* (1980) 104 CA3d 177, 163 CR 680), the court had determined that the seller had an implied obligation to submit the agreement to its board and that the board would approve or disapprove in good faith. The present appeal dealt with who had the burden of proof with respect to the approval or disapproval of the board. The court held the seller had the burden of proof because its failure to submit the agreement to the board prevented the condition precedent of board approval. In effect the seller was arguing that, even if it had submitted the agreement to its board, the board would have disapproved it. This argument is really an excuse for its nonperformance, which is an affirmative defense on which the seller clearly has the burden of proof.

[§12.43] Certainty of Act To Be Performed

Custom may be relied on to determine the certainty of incidental matters (such as opening an escrow, furnishing deeds and title insurance policies, and prorating taxes) involved in a purchase and sale of real property. *Hutton v Gliksberg* (1982) 128 CA3d 240, 180 CR 141. Extrinsic evidence may also be used to render the material contract provisions sufficiently definite for enforcement. *Hennefer v Butcher* (1986) 182 CA3d 492, 227 CR 318.

The subordination provision in the agreement of sale in *Ray Thomas Enters. v Fox* (1982) 128 CA3d 361, 180 CR 253, was held to be sufficiently certain to warrant granting the buyers specific performance even though it did not specify the rate of interest of the first deed of trust to which the seller was agreeing to subordinate his deed of trust. The court distinguished those cases, holding that the interest rate must be stated, on the ground that they all concerned deeds of trust subordinated to construction loans in which there may be no equity in the property above the amount of the construction loan to provide security for the seller until the property is fully developed. Under the facts in *Ray Thomas Enters.*, the subordination agreement was held not to pose any dangers or security problems to the sellers.

[§12.43A] Recordation

As a prerequisite to any action to enforce the terms of real property sales contracts as defined in CC §2985 (installment land sales contracts) or conditional sales contracts for mobile homes subject to property taxation and governed by Health & S C §§18000–18153, either of which were entered into after January 1, 1986, CCP §1062.10 now requires that the agreement be recorded or the change-in-ownership statement required by Rev & T C §480 be filed. If the agreement is not acknowledged and in recordable form, the filing of the change-in-ownership statement may be used by the party maintaining a specific performance action. The legislation enacting CCP §1062.10 also states that it is declaratory of existing law.

[§12.45] Nature of Buyer's Relief

The incidental compensation a buyer may collect under a decree of specific performance includes any increased financing cost resulting from the seller's failure to perform. *Hutton v Gliksberg* (1982) 128 CA3d 240, 180 CR 141. The court in *Hutton* upheld the trial court's lump-sum damage award for the present value of the difference in total payments over a 30-year period between the payments due on a loan for which the buyer had obtained a commitment at the time of breach and the payments that would have been due under a loan of the same amount at the prevailing interest rate at the time of judgment. The court rejected defendant's argument that if plaintiffs sold the property in less than 30 years they would gain a windfall profit, by noting that property encumbered by a high-interest-rate loan will bring a lower future sale price than the same property encumbered by a loan at a lower interest rate. That holding implies that the future purchaser takes subject to the existing loan or assumes the existing loan, and that the existing loan cannot be accelerated because of the sale. If the loan can be accelerated or the purchaser pays all cash or refinances, the future sale price should not depend on the interest rate of the existing loan and plaintiffs will have gained a windfall. See 5 CEB Real Prop L Rep 78 (June 1982) for further discussion of *Hutton*.

The award of damages for the interest rate differential for the entire 30-year loan term in *Hutton* was criticized in *Stratton v Tejani* (1982) 139 CA3d 204, 187 CR 231. The court in *Stratton* remanded to the trial court with instructions to determine the anticipated period of the buyers' ownership of the property, if possible, and then award the differential amount for only that period rather than automatically awarding it for 30 years.

Code of Civil Procedure §688.1, cited in Book §12.45, was repealed and replaced by new CCP §§708.410–708.480. See also CCP §§695.030(b)(2) and 699.720(a)(3) (causes of action subject to enforcement and execution).

[§12.46] Mutuality of Remedies Not Required

The California Supreme Court has held that CC §3386 rejected the requirements of mutuality of remedy with respect to specific performance, so that a buyer may be entitled to specific performance even though the seller has limited his or her own remedy to liquidated damages. *Bleecher v Conte* (1981) 29 C3d 345, 173 CR 278.

See also *Converse v Fong* (1984) 159 CA3d 86, 205 CR 242.

The treatise by Miller & Starr, cited in the Book, has been replaced by 1 Miller & Starr, California Real Estate §1.43 (2d ed 1989).

Buyer's Breach

[§12.51] Waiver of Conditions

In *Sabo v Fasano* (1984) 154 CA3d 502, 201 CR 270, a buyer's communicated intent to proceed with a sale transaction after the seller's late acceptance of the buyer's offer was held to be a waiver of the time limit, entitling the buyer to specific performance.

[§12.53] Enforcement Problems

Code of Civil Procedure §702 was repealed effective July 1, 1983, as part of the comprehensive revision of the enforcement of judgments law. There is now no right of redemption from execution sales. See CCP §701.680(a) and the Senate Legislative Committee Comment to CCP §701:

COMMENT: The statutory right of redemption provided by former Sections 701–707 is not continued for execution sales. See Section 701.680 and the Comment thereto. However, notice of sale of an interest in real property, other than a leasehold estate with an unexpired term of less than two years, is delayed for 120 days after notice of levy is given. See Section 701.545. A limited right of redemption is available after a foreclosure sale when a deficiency judgment is allowed. See Section 726(e), 729.010–729.090, and the Comments thereto.

See also Dyer, *Judicial Foreclosure After the Revised Enforcement of Judgments Act*, 6 CEB Real Prop L Rep 53 (Mar. 1983), modified at 6 CEB Real Prop L Rep 98 (July 1983).

There is, however, a 120-day waiting period after notice of levy is served on the judgment debtor before notice of sale of an interest in real property (other than a leasehold estate with an unexpired term of less than two years at the time of levy) may be given. CCP §701.545. That period will give the judgment debtor an opportunity to redeem the property or to seek potential purchasers. See the Assembly Legislative Committee Comment to CCP §701.545:

COMMENT: Section 701.545 delays the giving of notice of a sale of real property for at least 120 days after the notice of levy is served on the judgment debtor. This 120-day delay is provided to give the judgment debtor an opportunity to redeem the property from the judgment creditor's lien before the sale or to seek potential purchasers. The statutory right of redemption from execution sales of real property provided by former Sections 700a–707 is repealed. See Section 701.680 and the Comment thereto (sales absolute). See also Section 729.010 (redemption from certain foreclosure sales).

The treatise by Miller & Starr, cited in the Book, has been replaced by Miller & Starr, California Real Estate (2d ed 1989), but §5.27 of the former treatise was not replaced.

RESCISSION

Grounds

Special Statutory Grounds

[§12.65] Home Solicitation Contracts

Effective January 1, 1992, CC §1289.6(b) was added to provide that a buyer may cancel a home solicitation contract or offer to purchase a personal emergency response unit until midnight of the seventh business day after the buyer signs the contract or offer.

[§12.65A] Time Share Projects

The prospective buyer of a time share estate or of use in a time share project has the right to rescind the contract or agreement to purchase until midnight of the third calendar day after he or she executes the offer to purchase. Bus & P C §11024. The owner of the new division must supply the prospective buyer with a rescission form prescribed by the Real Estate Commissioner's regulations. Bus & P C §11024(b).

Actions for Relief

[§12.72] Damages Recoverable

The treatise by Miller & Starr, cited in the Book, has been replaced by Miller & Starr, California Real Estate (2d ed 1989), but §5.3 of the former treatise was not replaced.

LIS PENDENS

[§12.86] Effect

California Civil Procedure Before Trial (Cal CEB 1977) has been replaced by a third edition published in 1990. For discussion of the right to record a lis pendens and the procedure for doing so, see California Lis Pendens Practice, chap 2 (Cal CEB 1983).

[§12.87] Creation

An action to impose a constructive trust on real property purchased with fraudulently obtained funds was held to be an action affecting title or possession of real property for the purpose of filing a lis pendens in *Coppinger v Superior Court* (1982) 134 CA3d 883, 185 CR 24. See further discussion of *Coppinger* in 5 CEB Real Prop L Rep 156 (Nov. 1982).

In *Deane v Superior Court* (1985) 164 CA3d 292, 210 CR 406, a real estate broker claimed a constructive trust arose as a result of an agreement to pay a commission or, under certain conditions (which never occurred), transfer a lot to a sales agent of the broker. As part of the action, the broker recorded a lis pendens on the property involved. The court of appeal mandated the trial court to sustain the defendants' demurrer with leave to amend and to order the lis pendens expunged under CCP §409.1 (the trial court had ordered the lis pendens expunged under CCP §409.2, which required a bond). The court of appeal found that, at best, the defendants merely owed plaintiff a debt and that a constructive trust may not be imposed and a lis pendens recorded to secure an ordinary business debt. The court of appeal found *Coppinger, supra,* did not apply because fraud was not alleged.

In *Burger v Superior Court* (1984) 151 CA3d 1013, 199 CR 227, a third party used fraudulently obtained funds to make improvements to the owner's property, which were considerably less than the overall value of the property. The court held that this was not enough for the defrauded party to impose a constructive trust on the property.

The holding in *Coppinger* was rejected in *Urez Corp. v Superior Court* (1987) 190 CA3d 1141, 235 CR 837, after a full analysis of *Coppinger* and the cases that followed it, including *Deane* and *Burger.* The *Urez* court held that when the fraud action essentially seeks monetary damages and the plaintiff does not claim any ownership or possessory interest in the subject property but merely a "beneficial" interest for the purpose of securing payment of money, alleging entitlement to a constructive trust does not plead an action affecting title or possession of the subject property, and consequently a lis pendens is not proper.

The court in *La Paglia v Superior Court* (1989) 215 CA3d 1322, 264 CR 63, also expressly rejected the holding in *Coppinger.* Both *La Paglia* and *Coppinger* were decided by the Fourth District Court of Appeal. *Urez Corp.* was decided by the Second District Court of Appeal. Consequently, there are now conflicting decisions both in a single district and between two different districts on the issue of whether an action to impose a constructive trust on real property is an action affecting title or possession of real property for the purpose of filing a lis pendens.

Former CCP §409 was renumbered CCP §409(a) and CCP §409(b)–(c) was enacted. Code of Civil Procedure §409(b) provides for service of notice of the lis pendens and filing with the court, and CCP §409(c) provides that the lis pendens is invalid unless the notice has been properly served and a proof of service recorded with the lis pendens.

Code of Civil Procedure §409(a) provides authorization to record a lis pendens only to a plaintiff at the time of filing of a complaint or to a defendant at the time of filing a cross-complaint or at any time thereafter. In *Arrow Sand & Gravel, Inc. v Superior Court* (1985) 38 C3d 884, 215 CR 288, the supreme court held that a defendant who appeals a summary judgment in a judicial foreclosure action and who did not file a cross-complaint is not entitled to record a notice of lis pendens. The court upheld the constitutionality of CCP §409, finding that defendant's interest in the title to the property was adequately protected by CCP §§916 and 917.4, which permit a stay on appeal.

Code of Civil Procedure §409.9 was added, effective January 1, 1990, to require a real property owner who has entered into a contract to transfer any interest in that real property and who receives a notice of pendency of an action concerning that real property, to notify all prospective transferees of the notice, by personal delivery or certified mail, return receipt requested, within three days after receipt of the notice. This notice requirement is in addition to the notice requirement of CCP §409(c), which requires the person causing the notice of pendency of an action to be recorded to first mail a copy of the notice by registered or certified mail, return receipt requested, to all known addresses of adverse parties and all owners of record.

The treatise by Miller & Starr, cited in the Book, has been replaced by 3 Miller & Starr, California Real Estate §8.123 (2d ed 1989).

[§12.88] Expungement

Once a lis pendens has been expunged, any notice, whether constructive or actual, to a nonparty transferee of the pendency of an action affecting real property is entirely eliminated. *Knapp Dev. & Design v Pal-Mal Props. Ltd.* (1987) 195 CA3d 786, 240 CR 920. The plaintiff in *Knapp* had judgment entered against it in a mechanics' lien foreclosure action and an order expunging its lis pendens was recorded. Plaintiff appealed from the judgment and the judgment was reversed. However, before plaintiff was able to obtain an order allowing recordation of a new lis pendens, the property was sold to a third party. The court held that, whether or not the third party had actual knowledge of the pending action, the purchaser was statutorily without notice because the lis pendens had been expunged and the purchaser had taken title as a bona fide purchaser free and clear of the mechanics' lien.

After a lis pendens has been expunged, it cannot be refiled without court approval. *Ranchito Ownership Co. v Superior Court* (1982) 130 CA3d 764, 182 CR 54.

[§12.89] Improper Purpose and Bad Faith; CCP §409.1

The burden on a party filing a lis pendens to show that the underlying action was begun for a proper purpose and in good faith (to avoid expungement under CCP §409.1) requires only the establishment of a prima facie case. The court need not hold a mini-trial to determine whether the underlying action will succeed at trial. *Malcolm v Superior Court* (1981) 29 C3d 518, 174 CR 694. The policy articulated in *Malcolm* against requiring a minitrial, however, is not as important in a postjudgment proceeding. The court in *Peery v Superior Court* (1981) 29 C3d 837, 845, 176 CR 533, 538, held that to avoid expungement after judgment the losing party "must demonstrate that he will raise a substantial issue for review [on appeal]—that is, an issue the proper resolution of which could both affect the disposition of the real property at issue and be the subject of legitimate debate on appeal." The court further held that the trial court may consider the appellant's chance of success on appeal in deciding whether to credit independent evidence of appellant's bad faith offered by respondent. For further discussion of *Peery,* see 4 CEB Real Prop L Rep 143 (Nov. 1981).

Counsel intending to make an expungement motion under CCP §409.1 should also consider making an alternative expungement motion under CCP §409.2 that allows expungement even if the lis pendens is proper, if the party who has recorded the lis pendens is not interested in the property for its unique qualities, but rather is interested in it solely for its monetary value. In that situation, the court may expunge the lis pendens on condition that the owner of the property give an indemnification undertaking to the one who has recorded the lis pendens. For example, in *Erb v Superior Court* (1988) 205 CA3d 1156, 252 CR 881, the expungement motion was brought under CCP §409.1 and the trial court found the plaintiff had met his burden of proving proper purpose and good faith prosecution but nevertheless granted expungement conditioned on the defendant giving the plaintiff an indemnification undertaking. The court of appeal vacated the expungement order, ruling that CCP §409.1 does not authorize granting expungement by requiring an undertaking of the moving party when the proper purpose and good faith issues have been determined in favor of the party opposing the motion. The relief granted by the trial court would have been proper under CCP §409.2 if the court had made a finding that the party recording the lis pendens could be adequately protected by the undertaking. Such a finding was probably implicit in the relief the trial court had tried to grant under CCP §409.1.

[§12.91] Procedure

The period for giving notice before a hearing has been lengthened from 10 to 15 calendar days by an amendment to CCP §1005. See CCP §1005(b). All papers in opposition must be filed with the court and served on each party at least 5 court days before the hearing, and reply papers at least 2 court days before the hearing.

Effective January 1, 1991, CCP §409.1 no longer requires that a motion for expungement be made on 20 days' notice. It now requires that the notice of motion to expunge must be served in the same manner and within the times prescribed by CCP §1005(a). Code of Civil Procedure §1005(a) provides that specified motions (including a motion to expunge under CCP §409.1; see CCP §1005(a)(11)) must be served as prescribed by CCP §1005(b).

Technical defects in following the statutory procedures concerning the filing and recordation of lis pendens may be cause for expungement of the lis pendens. In *McKnight v Superior Court* (1985) 170 CA3d 291, 215 CR 909, a lis pendens was ordered expunged under CCP §409.1 for failure to file a copy of the notice of lis pendens and proof of service with the court or to record the proof of service. The court pointed out, however, that the plaintiff could correct the technical violations and file a second lis pendens. In *Biddle v Superior Court* (1985) 170 CA3d 135, 215 CR 848, the trial court's expungement of a lis pendens for failure to mail the notice of lis pendens properly (to a business address by first class mail instead of to a residence with return receipt requested) was vacated by the court of appeal. The court held that the defendants had actual notice and thus the purposes of the notice provisions had been satisfied. By bringing two prior motions to expunge without raising the technical defects and waiting more than a year before asserting the technical defects in a third motion, the defendants had waived their right to expungement based on those defects. Note that the notice must now be sent by registered or certified mail rather than first class mail. CCP §409(c).

[§12.91A] Withdrawal of Lis Pendens

A party (or the party's successor in interest) may withdraw a lis pendens by recording an acknowledged notice of withdrawal. After the withdrawal is recorded, neither the lis pendens nor any information derived from the lis pendens constitutes notice of matters contained in the lis pendens. CCP §409.55.

[§12.92] Liability for Recording Lis Pendens

The statement in Book §12.92 that "a party filing a lis pendens cannot be liable for slander of title" must now be viewed with caution in light of *Shurpin v Elmhirst* (1983) 148 CA3d 105, 195 CR 743. In *Shurpin* the plaintiff in a nuisance action recorded a lis pendens against the defendant's property, and the defendant was allowed to cross-complain for slander of title. The court found that the recordation of the lis pendens by plaintiff was not authorized by law because the nuisance action did not affect title to, or right of possession of, the defendant's property and could not be afforded the absolute privilege under CC §47.

DEFENSES COMMON TO ALL ACTIONS

Invalid or Nonexistent Agreement

[§12.103] Statute of Frauds

Former CC §1624(4) has been redesignated as CC §1624(c).

The treatise by Miller & Starr, cited in the Book, has been replaced by 1 Miller & Starr, California Real Estate 1.48–1.78 (2d ed 1989).

[§12.104] Statute of Limitations

The second paragraph in Book §12.104 is in error and should be replaced by the following:

The limitation period for a rescission action is four years for an action based on a written contract (CCP §337(3)) and two years for an action based on an oral contract (CCP §339(3)). The period under each statute begins to run when the facts entitling the aggrieved party to rescind occurred. But, if the ground for rescission is fraud or mistake, the period begins to run from the date the aggrieved party discovers the facts constituting fraud or mistake. CCP §§337(3), 339(3).

Appendix: Transfers Triggering Reappraisal

Type of Transfer	Action Required	Remarks—Rev & TC and 18 Cal C Reg
Condominiums and Cooperatives		
1. Transfer of a unit in a complex with common areas or facilities (*i.e.*, housing co-op, condominium, community apartment project, shopping center, etc.).	Reappraisal of the unit transferred and of appurtenant common area	Increased values are not to be prorated by the owner to the other units. Rev & T C §§61(h), 65.1, 18 Cal C Reg §462(a).
2. Transfer of stock in a housing co-op with possessory right in a specific unit.	Reappraisal	Reappraise the unit transferred and any common area appurtenant. Rev & T C §61(h), 18 Cal C Reg §§462(a) and 462(j)(1). See Rev & T C §62(i) and 18 Cal C Reg §462(j)(2) for exclusions. Increased values are not to be prorated by the owner to the other units. Rev & T C §65(c).
Corporations		
3. Corporation *A* transfers property to unrelated Corporation *B*.	Reappraisal	Transfer is from one entity to another. Rev & T C §64, 18 Cal C Reg §462(j)(1).
4. Transfers among affiliated groups (and nontaxable corporate reorganization under IRC §368).	No Reappraisal	(See definition of "affiliated.") Rev & T C §64(b), 18 Cal C Reg §462(j)(2).
5. Person or "legal entity" obtains control of corporation.	Reappraisal	Control: Purchase sufficient stock to give more than 50 percent of voting stock. Rev & T C §§64(c), 25105, 18 Cal C Reg §462(j)(4).
5.1. Purchase or transfer of stock—no control.	No Reappraisal	18 Cal C Reg §462(j)(3).
6. One corporation obtaining control of affiliated corporation.	No Reappraisal	(See definition of "affiliated.") Rev & T C §64(b), 18 Cal C Reg §462(j)(2).

Type of Transfer	Action Required	Remarks—Rev & TC and 18 Cal C Reg
Interspousal		
7. Transfer of property between spouses.	No Reappraisal	Change in ownership shall not include any interspousal transfers. Rev & T C §63, 18 Cal C Reg §462(l).
8. Transfer between ex-spouses in connection with a decree of dissolution of a marriage.	No Reappraisal	Excluded even though parties are ex-spouses. Rev & T C §63(c), 18 Cal C Reg §462(l)(3).
9. Property is transferred to a trustee for the beneficial use of the spouse of the transferor.	No Reappraisal	Excluded even though transfer is to a trustee and not spouse. Rev & T C §63(a), 18 Cal C Reg §462(l)(1).
Joint Tenancy		
10. A and B acquire property as joint tenants.	Reappraisal	Transfer of fee title. Rev & T C §§60, 61(d), 18 Cal C Reg §462(a),(c)(1).
11. Person A owning property in severalty adds person B as a joint tenant.	No Reappraisal	Person A is transferor and joint tenant after the creation of the joint tenancy. Rev & T C §§62(f), 65(b), 18 Cal C Reg §462(c)(2).
a. A transfers his interest to C (B and C become tenants in common).	Reappraise 100 percent	Termination of an original transferor's[1] interest in a joint tenancy may be excluded under Rev & T C §65(c), 18 Cal C Reg §462(c)(1). Held by original transferor[1] before creation of joint tenancy. Rev & T C §65.
b. B tranfers his interest back to A. (Ignore a above).	No Reappraisal	Termination of an interest of other than an original transferor[1] in a joint tenancy excluded under Rev & T C §62(f), 18 Cal C Reg §462(c)(2). The interest reverts to an original transferor,[1] so no reappraisal is warranted. Rev & T C §65(b), 18 Cal C Reg §462(c)(2)(B).

Scenario	Reappraisal	Citation
12. A and B own property as joint tenants. They purchased it together from another individual. B dies.	Reappraisal of interest transferred 50 percent	Termination of a joint tenancy interest. Rev & T C §§61(d), 65(a), 65.1, 18 Cal C Reg §462(a), (o)(1)(A)(ii). 18 Cal C Reg §462(c) has no bearing because the joint tenancy is not one excluded from reappraisal under Rev & T C §62(f), 18 Cal C Reg §462(c)(2).
13. A and B as joint tenants sell to H and W (husband and wife) as joint tenants.	Reappraisal	Not solely between spouses. Rev & T C §§60, 61(d).
a. H dies.	No Reappraisal	Interspousal exclusion. Rev & T C §§63(b), 63(d), 18 Cal C Reg §462(c)(2)(F).
14. H and W own property as joint tenants and grant to H, W, S, and D as joint tenants.	No Reappraisal	H and W are transferors and joint tenants. Rev & T C §62(f), 18 Cal C Reg §462(c)(2)(A).
a. H dies.	No Reappraisal	W still an original transferor.[1]
b. W dies—property goes to S and D.	Reappraisal	100 percent—termination of original transferor's interest. Rev & T C §65(c).
c. S and D grant back to H and W (ignore a and b above).	No Reappraisal	Property reverts to original transferors. Rev & T C §65(d), 18 Cal C Reg §462(c)(2)(C)(i).
15. A and B own property as joint tenants grant to A, B, C, and D all as joint tenants.	No Reappraisal	A and B are transferors and joint tenants after transfer. Rev & T C §62(f), 18 Cal C Reg §462(c)(2).
a. A dies.	No Reappraisal	Vests by operation of law in B, who is original transferor and still joint tenant. Rev & T C §65(c), 18 Cal C Reg §462(c)(2).

---

[1] Spouses of original transferors are considered original transferors for purposes of Cal C Reg §§65(b) and 62(f). There is a rebuttable presumption that a joint tenant before March 2, 1975, is an original transferor. Rev & T C §65(e). See Rev & T C §65 for further provisions concerning original transferors.

Type of Transfer	Action Required	Remarks—Rev & TC and 18 Cal C Reg
b. *A, B, C,* and *D* grant to *B, C,* and *D* (ignore a above).	No Reappraisal	An original transferor still holds an interest. Rev & T C §65(c), 18 Cal C Reg §462(c)(2)(B).
c. *B, C,* and *D* grant to *B* (after either a or b).	No Reappraisal	The interests of *C* and *D* were other than original transferor's interests, and reverted to original transferor *B*. Rev & T C §65(d), 18 Rev & T C §462(c)(2)(C)(i).
16. *A* grants property to *A* and *B* as joint tenants.	No Reappraisal	*A* is transferor and joint tenant after transfer. Rev & T C §62(f), 18 Cal C Reg §462(c)(2)(A).
a. *A* and *B* as joint tenants grant *A* and *B* as equal tenants in common.	No Reappraisal	*A* and *B* were and are equal co-owners. Rev & T C §§62(a), 65(c), 18 Cal C Reg §462(b)(2), (c)(2)(D)(ii).

Leases[2]

Type of Transfer	Action Required	Remarks—Rev & TC and 18 Cal C Reg
17. Creation of a leasehold interest in taxable real property for a term of 35 years or more.	Reappraisal	Reappraisal of full fee (leasehold and leased fee); term includes renewal option. Rev & T C §61(c)(1), 18 Cal C Reg §462(f)(1).
18. Leasehold interest that had an *original* term of 35 years or more transfers or reverts to lessor.	Reappraisal	Reappraisal of fee; term includes renewal options. Rev & T C §61(c)(1), 18 Cal C Reg §462(f)(4).
19. Transfer of a lessee's leasehold interest with a *remaining* term of 35 years or more.	Reappraisal	Reappraisal of fee; term includes renewal options. Rev & T C §61(c)(1), 18 Cal C Reg §462(f)(1)(A)(ii), (4).
20. Transfer (other than termination) by lessee of a leasehold interest with a *remaining* term of less than 35 years.	No Reappraisal	Term includes renewal options. Rev & T C §61(c)(1), 18 Cal C Reg §462(f)(2)(A)(ii), (f)(4).
21. Transfer of a lessor's interest in real property subject to a lease with a *remaining* term of less than 35 years.	Reappraisal	Reappraisal of fee; term includes renewal options. Rev & T C §61(c)(2), 18 Cal C Reg §462(f)(1)(B)(i), (4).

22. Transfer of a lessor's interest in real property subject to a lease with a *remaining* term of 35 years or more.	No Reappraisal	Includes transfer to lessee; term includes renewal options. Rev & T C §62(g), 18 Cal C Reg §462(f)(2)(B), (4).

Life Estates

23. Person *A* grants title to person *B* reserving a life estate.	No Reappraisal	*A* retains present interest and beneficial use. Rev & T C §62(e), 18 Cal C Reg §462(d)(1).
a. *A* dies.	Reappraisal	Right of possession vests in B. Rev & T C §§61(f), 62(e), 18 Cal C Reg §462(d)(1). Except when *B* is spouse of *A*. Rev & T C §63(b), 18 Cal C Reg §462(d)(1), 462(l)(2).
24. Person *A* grants title to person *B* for life with remainder to *C*.	Reappraisal when life estate granted	Transfer of present interest and beneficial use. Rev & T C §60, 18 Cal C Reg §462(d)(1). Except if *B* is spouse of *A*. Rev & T C §63, 18 Cal C Reg §462(l).
a. *B* dies—*C* takes property.	Reappraisal	Termination of precedent interest. Rev & T C §§62(f), 62(e), 18 Cal C Reg §462(d)(1). Right to possession vests in C. Rev & T C §60. Except if *C* is spouse of *B*. Rev & T C §63(b), 18 Cal C Reg §§462(d)(1), 462(l).

Mineral Rights

25. Creation, renewal, sublease, assignment, or other transfer of right to produce or extract oil, gas, or other minerals.	Reappraisal of right transferred	Property other than mineral rights not reappraised. Rev & T C §61(a), 18 Cal C Reg §§468, 469.

---

[2]Homes on leased land that are eligible for homeowner's exemption are conclusively presumed to have a renewal option for at least 35 years. Rev & T C §62(g).

Type of Transfer	Action Required	Remarks—Rev & TC and 18 Cal C Reg
Mobilehome Park		
25.1. Transfer of mobilehome park to certain entities formed by tenants to purchase park.	No Reappraisal	Rev & T C §62.1–62.2.
Partnerships		
26. Transfer of real property from a partnership to a partner.	Reappraisal	Rev & T C §61(i), 18 Cal C Reg §462(j)(5)(A). Rev & T C §62(a)(2), 18 Cal C Reg §462(j)(2)(B) do not apply when there is a change in proportional interests in real property.
27. Transfer of real property from a partnership of A and B to A and B as tenants in common.	No Reappraisal	Rev & T C §62(a)(2), 18 Cal C Reg §462(b)(2), (j)(2)(B). If solely a change in method of holding title, resulting in interests in property being held in same proportion.
28. A and B are partners in the A and B partnership *which is a continuing partnership.* C is added as a partner.	No Reappraisal	Rev & T C §64(a), 18 Cal C Reg §462(j)(5)(B).
29. Changing the name of the A and B partnership above to the A, B, C partnership.	No Reappraisal	18 Cal C Reg §462(a)(2).
30. X and Y are partners in the X and Y partnership. Z is added as a partner *and the addition creates a new entity.*	Reappraisal	Transfer is from one entity to another. Rev & T C §61(i), 18 Cal C Reg §462(j)(1), (5)(A).
Possessory Interest		
31. Creation, renewal, sublease, or assignment of a taxable possessory interest in tax-exempt real property.	Reappraisal	Ownership change occurs regardless of length of term. Rev & T C §61(b), 18 Cal C Reg §462(e).
Tenancy in Common		
32. Two or more people acquire property as tenants in common.	Reappraisal	Transfer is of fee title. Rev & T C §§60, 61(e), 18 Cal C Reg §462(b)(1).

33. A person holding title as a tenant in common transfers his interest to one of the other tenants in common.	Reappraisal of the interest transferred	Rev & T C §61(e), 18 Cal C Reg §462(b)(1). Except when interspousal exclusion applies or when interest transferred is less than 5 percent and less than $20,000. Rev & T C §§61(e), 63, 65.1, 18 Cal C Reg §§462(b)(2)(C)–(D), 462(l).
34. A, B, C, and D hold title as tenants in common with 25 percent interest each. D sells his interest to T.	Reappraisal of interest transferred	T now has an undivided ¼ interest in common with A, B, and C. Rev & T C §§61(e), 65.1, 18 Cal C Reg §462(b).

Transfer of Fee Title Generally

35. Transfer of fee title to land and/or improvements from one person to another.	Reappraisal of the interest transferred	Rev & T C §60, 18 Cal C Reg §462(a). Except as otherwise excluded in this table or if a total of less than 5 percent and less than $10,000 undivided interest transfers during an assessment year. Rev & T C §65.1, 18 Cal C Reg §§462(b)(2)(C), 462(c)(2)(H).
35.1. Transfer of fee title to certain disabled children and wards.	No Reappraisal	Rev & T C §62(n); applies only if disabled for at least five years previously; property was principal residence for five years previously; adjusted gross income of child or ward, and parents and spouse is no more than $20,000.

Trusts

Irrevocable Trusts

36. Transfer of property from person A to person C as trustee naming persons A and B as beneficiaries.	Reappraisal to the extent that B is a beneficiary	Rev & T C §62(d)(1), 18 Cal C Reg §462(i)(2)(A). Reappraise per Rev & T C §61(g), 18 Cal C Reg §§462(i)(3), 462(i)(4).

Type of Transfer	Action Required	Remarks—Rev & TC and 18 Cal C Reg
37. Transfer of property from person A to a trust for the benefit of person B for a term of 12 years reversion to A.	No reappraisal at creation or termination	The beneficial interest of other must *exceed* 12 years to be a change in ownership. Rev & T C §62(d), 18 Cal C Reg §§462(i)(2)(C), 462(i)(4)(C).
38. Transfer of property from person A to person C as trustee naming person B as sole beneficiary.	Reappraisal of interest transferred to B	Rev & T C §§60, 61(g), 18 Cal C Reg §462(i)(1). Except when B is spouse of A. Rev & T C §63(a), 18 Cal C Reg §§462(i)(2)(D), 462(i)(4)(D), 462(l)(1).
39. Person A as beneficiary of a trust owning real property assigns his beneficial interest to person B.	Reappraisal if a present beneficial interest transfers	Rev & T C §60, 18 Cal C Reg §462(a). Except when beneficial interest does not exceed 12 years and property reverts to trustor or when B is spouse of A. Rev & T C §§62(d), 63, 18 Cal C Reg §§462(i)(2)(C), 462(l).
	No reappraisal if a future beneficial interest transfers	Rev & T C §60, 18 Cal C Reg §462(a)(2). Reappraise when B receives a present interest, unless interspousal. Rev & T C §63, 18 Cal C Reg §462(l).
40. Transfer of property from person A to a person A as trustee naming person A as sole beneficiary.	No Reappraisal	There is no transfer of a present interest or beneficial use. This does not qualify as a trust under California law. Rev & T C §60, 18 Cal C Reg §462(a)(2).
41. Transfer of property from person A to person B, as trustee, naming persons A and C as income beneficiaries; remainder to D.	Reappraisal to the extent that C and D are present beneficiaries	A is not sole beneficiary of the trust. Rev & T C §62(d)(1), 18 Cal C Reg §462(i)(2)(A). No appraisal to extent C or D is A's spouse. Rev & T C §63, 18 Cal C Reg §§462(i)(2)(D), (l)(1).

a. *A* dies.	Reappraisal of *A*'s interest	Rev & T C §61(f), 18 Cal C Reg §462(i)(3). Exception if *A*'s interest passes to *A*'s spouse. Rev & T C §63(b), 18 Cal C Reg §462(*l*)(2).
b. *A* and *C* die—property to *D*.	Reappraisal	Rev & T C §61(f), 18 Cal C Reg §462(i)(3). Exception if *D* is *A*'s spouse. Rev & T C §63, 18 Cal C Reg §§462(i)(2)(D), (*l*).
42. Transfer of property from *A* and *B* as joint tenants to *A* and *B* as trustees and life beneficiaries of the property; remainder to *C*.		
a. *A* and *B* die.	No Reappraisal	No transfer of a present interest or beneficial use. Rev & T C §62(d)(1), 18 Cal C Reg §462(i)(2)(A).
	Reappraisal	Termination of precedent interest. Right of possession vests in *C*. Rev & T C §61(f), 18 Cal C Reg §462(i)(3).

Revocable Trusts

43. Transfer of property to a revocable trust. (Transferor and trustor are same party.)	No Reappraisal	Rev & T C §62(d)(2), 18 Cal C Reg §462(i)(2)(B). No reappraisal until trust becomes irrevocable. Rev & T C §61(g), 18 Cal C Reg §462(i)(2)(B).
44. *H* and *W* execute a revocable trust, transfer property into it with *H* and *W* as trustees and life beneficiaries; remainder to *C*.		
a. Creation.	No Reappraisal	No transfer of present interest or beneficial use. Rev & T C §§60, 62(d), 18 Cal C Reg §462(i)(2)(B).
b. Revocation by *H* and *W*.	No Reappraisal	No transfer of present interest or beneficial use (both still held by *H* and *W*). Rev & T C §§60, 62(d), 18 Cal C Reg §462(i)(4)(B).

Type of Transfer	Action Required	Remarks—Rev & TC and 18 Cal C Reg
c. H and W die—C takes property. (Ignore b above.)	Reappraisal	Termination of precedent interest (H and W). Right of possession vests in C. Rev & T C §61(f), 18 Cal C Reg §462(i)(3).
d. H dies, W revokes trust. (Ignore b and c above.)	No Reappraisal	No present interest transferred. Rev & T C §62(d), 18 Cal C Reg §462(i)(4)(B).
e. H dies, C dies, with W as sole heir of both. (Ignore b, c, and d above.)	No Reappraisal	C predeceases W, so present interest stays in W as life beneficiary. Rev & T C §60.

Other Transfers

Type of Transfer	Action Required	Remarks—Rev & TC and 18 Cal C Reg
45. Any transfer to an existing assessee to perfect or clear title by deed. Or to correct or reform a deed.	No Reappraisal	No present interest transferred. Rev & T C §§60, 62(b), 18 Cal C Reg §462(m)(1)(A). Original relationship between grantor and grantee cannot change. Rev & T C §62(l).
46. Creation or termination of a security interest without right of possession (trust deed or mortgage).	No Reappraisal	Rev & T C §62(c)(1), 18 Cal C Reg §462(m)(1)(B).
47. Substitution of trustee under security or trust instrument.	No Reappraisal	Rev & T C §62(c)(2), 18 Cal C Reg §462(m)(2).
48. A and B are co-owners of a piece of property. The property is then partitioned and A and B then each have equal-value parcels owned in severalty.	No Reappraisal	This is a change in the method of holding title with no change in proportional interests (based on value). Rev & T C §62(a), 18 Cal C Reg §462(b)(2)(A).

49. A and B are co-owners; property is partitioned unequally. (Value of B's portion differs from value of A's portion.)	Reappraise the interest transferred	A receives B's 50 percent interest in one parcel, and B receives A's 50 percent interest in the other parcel. Rev & T C §61(c). Rev & T C §62(a), 18 Cal C Reg §462(b)(2)(A) do not apply to unequal partitions.
50. Title to a property transfers by foreclosure sale with no further right of redemption.	Reappraisal	Fee transfer. Rev & T C §§60, 67, 18 Cal C Reg §§462(g)(1), 462(g)(2).
51. Sale at auction of tax-deeded property.	Reappraisal	Fee transfer. Rev & T C §§60, 67, 18 Cal C Reg §462(h).
52. Change of name.	No Reappraisal	No interest transferred. 18 Cal C Reg §462(a)(2).
53. Transfer of bare legal title to person, corporation, or other legal entity.	No Reappraisal	No transfer of equitable title. 18 Cal C Reg §462(m)(1).
54. R purchases freehold estate from Y.	Reappraisal	A purchase is an ownership change. Rev & T C §§60, 65.1, 67, 18 Cal C Reg §462(a)(2).
55. Transfers to minor child or among minor siblings at death of parent.	No Reappraisal	No reappraisal only if property transferred was minor's principal residence. Rev & T C §62(m).
56. Transfers between parents and children of the principal residence of either.	No Reappraisal	Rev & T C §63.1(a)(1)
57. Transfers between parents and children of real property other than personal residence.	No Reappraisal	No reappraisal only of first $1,000,000 of full cash value per transferor. Rev & T C §63.1(a)(2), (b)(2).
58. Reorganization of farm credit institutions under federal Farm Credit Act of 1971	No Reappraisal	Rev & T C §64(b)

Table of References

The following titles are additions or replacements to the Book Table of References. Section numbers refer to Update sections.

Advising California Partnerships (2d ed Cal CEB 1988): §§3.22–3.23.

Bowman, Arthur G. & W. Denny Milligan. Real Estate Law in California. 8th ed. Englewood Cliffs, N.J.: Prentice-Hall, 1992: §8.18

Brown, Curtis M. & Winfield H. Eldridge. Evidence and Procedures for Boundary Location. 2d ed. New York: John Wiley & Sons, 1981.

Business Buy-Sell Agreements (Cal CEB 1991) replaces Business Buy-Out Agreements (Cal CEB 1976)).

Bureau of Land Management. Manual of Instructions for the Survey of the Public Lands of the United States. Rev ed. Washington, D.C.: U.S. Goverment Printing Office, 1983.

California Administrative Mandamus (2d ed Cal CEB 1989).

California Civil Procedure Before Trial (3d ed Cal CEB 1990) replaces the 1st edition published in 1977: §12.86.

1, 2 California Conservatorships and Guardianships (Cal CEB 1990): §3.13.

1, 2 California Decedent Estate Practice (Cal CEB 1986) replaces 1 California Decedent Estate Administration (Cal CEB 1971): §§3.9, 7.21, 7.55.

California Marital Termination Agreements (Cal CEB 1988) replaces California Marital Termination Settlements (Cal CEB 1971).

California Mechanics' Liens and Other Remedies (2d ed Cal CEB 1988) replaces the 1st edition published in 1972: §§3.103, 5.50.

California Mortgage and Deed of Trust Practice (2d ed Cal CEB 1990) replaces the 1st edition published in 1979: §§3.9, 3.50, 3.100, 5.5, 5.9, 5.13, 5.19–5.21, 5.24, 5.27, 5.30, 5.39, 6.27, 6.42, 6.55, 7.37, 10.17, 11.42, 11.66, 11.69, 12.1–12.2.

California Taxes. 2 vols (2d ed Cal CEB 1988).

California Will Drafting (3d ed Cal CEB 1992) replaces California Will Drafting (Cal CEB 1965): §§3.27, 7.26.

Drafting Agreements for the Sale of Businesses (2d ed Cal CEB 1988).

Friedman, Milton R. Contracts and Conveyances of Real Property. 4th ed. New York: Practising Law Institute, 1984 (replaces the 3d edition published in 1975): §3.69

Grossman, Harvey M. & Arvo Van Alstyne. California Pleading. vol. 7 St. Paul, Minn.: West Publishing, 1981.

Manolakas, Thomas G., Tax Factors in Real Estate Operations. 7th ed. Englewood Cliffs, N.J., Prentice Hall, 1990 (replaces the 6th edition, by Paul E. Anderson, published in 1980): §§5.7, 5.14, 5.31–5.32.

1 Miller, Harry D. & Marvin B. Starr. Current Law of California Real Estate. 2d ed. San Francisco: Bancroft-Whitney, 1989: §§2.10, 2.12, 2.27, 2.37, 2.40, 2.71, 2.120, 3.47, 3.78, 4.7, 5.29–5.30, 12.1, 12.46, 12.53, 12.72, 12.103.

2 _____. 1989: §§3.83, 3.203, 5.39–5.41, 5.43, 5.53, 7.5, 11.10, 11.91, 12.87.

Powell, Richard R. The Law of Real Property. Rev. ed. Albany, N.Y.: Matthew Bender, 1977: §3.95.

203

Secured Transactions in California Commercial Law Practice (Cal CEB 1986) replaces 3 California Commercial Law (Cal CEB 1966): §8.64.

Title Insurance & Trust Company. Title Handbook for Title Men. 32d ed. Los Angeles: Title Insurance & Trust Co., 1990 (replaces the 22d edition published in 1980): §§1.18, 8.40.

Wattles, William C. Writing Legal Descriptions in Conjunction With Survey Boundary Control. Los Angeles: Title Insurance & Trust Co., 1979.

Williston, Samuel A. A Treatise on the Law of Contracts. Richard A. Lord, editor. 4th ed. Rochester, N.Y.: Lawyers Cooperative Publishing, 1990 (replaces the 3d edition, published Mount Kisco, N.Y., Baker, Voorhis, 1963).

Witkin, B.E. California Evidence. 3d ed. San Francisco: Bancroft-Whitney, 1986. 3 vols: §3.186.

_____. California Procedure. 3d ed. San Francisco: Bancroft-Whitney, 1985. 10 vols: §§3.8, 8.45.

_____ . Summary of California Law. 9th ed. San Francisco: Bancroft-Whitney, 1987. 13 vols: §§2.88, 3.20, 3.22–3.23, 3.36, 3.65, 3.188.

Wydick, Richard C. Plain English for Lawyers. Durham, N.C.: Carolina Academic Press, 1979 (replaces the 2d edition published in 1985): §3.5.

Table of Statutes, Regulations, and Rules

2379: §2.20
2400–2423: §3.18
2920(b): §§5.5, 12.2
2924: §§5.5, 12.2
2924–2924h: §§5.5, 12.2
2924c: §5.21
2924e: §5.1B
2924.7: §§6.45–6.46
2943: §11.49
2945–2945.8: §3.8
2945–2945.9: §3.8
2945.2: §3.8
2954.8: §6.5
2954.9: §§5.13, 5.20
2954.10: §5.24
2956: §5.1A
2956–2967: §§2.89, 5.1A
2957(a): §5.1A
2958: §5.1A
2963: §5.1B
2963(a)–(p): §5.1A
2985: §§3.40, 12.43A
2995: §11.32
3154: §3.103
3294: §12.34
3306: §§4.22, 12.13–12.14, 12.19
3307: §12.19
3386: §12.46
3387: §12.39
3395: §3.181
3439–3439.11: §7.13
3439–3439.12: §7.13
3439–3439.12 (former): §7.13
3440: §3.160
3440–3440.1: §3.160
4452: §3.30
4800.1: §3.30
4800.2: §3.30
5100: §3.30
5100–5119: §3.30
5102: §3.9
5103: §7.35
5110: §3.30
5127–5128: §3.9

CODE OF CIVIL PROCEDURE
337(3): §12.104
339(3): §12.104
409 (former): §12.87
409(a): §12.87

409(b): §12.87
409(b)–(c): §12.87
409(c): §§12.87, 12.91
409.1: §§12.87, 12.91
409.2: §§12.87, 12.89
409.9: §12.87
409.55: §12.91A
580b: §5.39
638–645.1: §3.18A
688.1 (former): §12.45
695.030(b)(2): §12.45
699.720(a)(3): §12.45
701: §12.53
701.545: §12.53
701.680(a): §12.53
702 (former): §12.53
704.710–704.850: §3.9
704.910–704.990: §3.9
704.920: §§11.91–11.97
704.940: §§3.9, 3.15
704.960(a): §3.9
704.980(b): §3.15
708.210–708.290: §11.23
708.250: §11.23
708.410–708.480: §12.45
729.010–729.090: §12.53
916: §12.87
917.4: §12.87
1005: §12.91
1005(a): §12.91
1005(a)(11): §12.91
1005(b): §12.91
1062.10: §12.43A
1283.05: §3.40
1287.4: §2.109
1298: §3.183
1298(a): §3.183
1298(b): §3.183
1298(c): §3.183
1298.5: §3.183
1298.7: §3.183
1298.8: §3.183

CORPORATIONS CODE
15009(1): §3.22
15010.5: §3.31
15010.7: §3.22
15019–15022: §§4.11, 7.35
15502: §§3.23, 3.31
15502(4): §3.23

462(b)(1): App
462(b)(2): App
462(b)(2)(A): App
462(b)(2)(C): App
462(b)(2)(C)–(D): App
462(c): App
462(c)(1): App
462(c)(1)(A)(ii): App
462(c)(2): App
462(c)(2)(A): App
462(c)(2)(B): App
462(c)(2)(C)(i): App
462(c)(2)(D)(ii): App
462(c)(2)(F): App
462(c)(2)(H): App
462(d)(1): App
462(e): App
462(f)(1): App
462(f)(1)(A)(ii): App
462(f)(1)(B)(i): App
462(f)(2)(A)(ii): App
462(f)(2)(B): App
462(f)(4): App
462(g)(1)–(2): App
462(h): App
462(i)(1): App
462(i)(2)(A): App
462(i)(2)(B): App
462(i)(2)(C): App
462(i)(2)(D): App
462(i)(3): App
462(i)(3)–(4): App
462(i)(4)(B): App
462(i)(4)(C): App
462(i)(4)(D): App
462(j)(1): App
462(j)(2): App
462(j)(2)(B): App
462(j)(3): App
462(j)(4): App
462(j)(5)(A): App
462(j)(5)(B): App
462(*l*): *See* Supp §3.20; App
462(*l*)(1): App
462(*l*)(2): App
462(*l*)(3): App
462(m)(1): §3.20, App
462(m)(1)(A): App
462(m)(1)(B): App
462(m)(2): App

468–469: App
Title 21
7100–7117 (former): §6.37
7101–7117: §6.37
7101–7122 (former): §6.37
Title 55
34532: §1.35

Rules

CALIFORNIA RULES OF COURT
244: §3.183A

STATE BAR OF CALIFORNIA RULES OF PROFESSIONAL CONDUCT
2–107 (former): §§1.23–1.25
3–110: §§1.12–1.13
3–300: §§1.12–1.13
3–310: §§1.12–1.15, 1.25
4–101 (former): §§1.14–1.15, 1.25
4–200: §§1.23–1.25
5–101 (former): §§1.12–1.13
5–102 (former): §§1.12–1.13
6–101 (former): §§1.12–1.13

UNITED STATES

Statutes

INTERNAL REVENUE CODE
167: §3.31
168: §3.31
168(b)(3): §3.31
168(c): §3.31
168(e)(2): §3.31
368: App
453–453B: §§5.7, 5.10–5.14
453B(g): §§5.10–5.14
501(c)(3): §6.17
1031(a): §1.59
1445: §3.40
1445(b)(2): §1.79
3306(i)(1): *See* §2.12
3401(d): §2.12
6166: §3.85
6166A (former): §3.85

Table of Cases

Bruckman v Parliament Escrow Corp. (1987) 190 CA3d 1051, 235 CR 813: §11.23

Brumbaugh v County of Imperial (1982) 134 CA3d 556, 184 CR 11: §8.38

Buol, Marriage of (1985) 39 C3d 751, 218 CR 31: §3.30

Burger v Superior Court (1984) 151 CA3d 1013, 199 CR 227: §12.87

C

Cairo, Marriage of (1988) 204 CA3d 1255, 251 CR 731: §3.30

California Coastal Comm'n v Quanta Inv. Corp. (1980) 113 CA3d 579, 170 CR 263: §3.149

Carpenter, Estate of (1983) 140 CA3d 709, 189 CR 651: §§3.28, 7.50

Carpenters Health & Welfare Trust Fund v Shafer (1983) 146 CA3d 504, 194 CR 266: §11.96

Chapman v Farr (1982) 132 CA3d 1021, 183 CR 606: §2.3

Chodur v Edmonds (1985) 174 CA3d 565, 220 CR 80: §2.110

Christiansen v Roddy (1986) 186 CA3d 780, 231 CR 72: §1.35

City of Turlock v Paul M. Zagaris, Inc. (1989) 209 CA3d 189, 256 CR 902: §2.35

Claremont Terrace Homeowners' Ass'n v U.S. (1983) 146 CA3d 398, 194 CR 216: §11.97

Classen v Weller (1983) 145 CA3d 27, 192 CR 914: §2.59

Cohen v Citizens Nat'l Trust & Sav. Bank (1956) 143 CA2d 480, 300 P2d 14: §2.121

Collins v Vickter Manor, Inc. (1957) 47 C2d 875, 306 P2d 783: §2.35

Contemporary Inv. v Safeco Title Ins. (1983) 145 CA3d 999, 193 CR 822: §11.22

Converse v Fong (1984) 159 CA3d 86, 205 CR 242: §12.46

Coppinger v Superior Court (1982) 134 CA3d 883, 185 CR 24: §12.87

D

Daum Dev. Corp. v Yuba Plaza Inc. (1970) 11 CA3d 65, 89 CR 458: §12.11

Deane v Superior Court (1985) 164 CA3d 292, 210 CR 406: §12.87

Deas v Knapp (1981) 29 C3d 69, 171 CR 823: §2.109

Deas v Knapp (1982) 129 CA3d 443, 181 CR 76: §2.109

Deeter v Angus (1986) 179 CA3d 241, 224 CR 801: §2.44

Delanoy v Delanoy (1932) 216 C 23, 13 P2d 513: §3.28

Department of Veterans Affairs v Duerksen (1982) 138 CA3d 149, 187 CR 832: §5.24

Derish v San Mateo-Burlingame Bd. of Realtors (1982) 136 CA3d 534, 186 CR 390: §2.26

Dierenfield v Stabile (1988) 198 CA3d 126, 243 CR 598: §2.109

E

Easton v Strassburger (1984) 152 CA3d 90, 199 CR 383: §§2.89, 12.104

Edmonds v Augustyn (1987) 193 CA3d 1056, 238 CR 704: §2.109

Ektelon v City of San Diego (1988) 200 CA3d 804, 246 CR 483: §3.117

Eldridge v Burns (1982) 136 CA3d 907, 186 CR 784: §5.59

Eldridge v Burns (1978) 76 CA3d 396, 142 CR 845: §5.59

Erb v Superior Court (1988) 205 CA3d 1156, 252 CR 881: §12.89

Erich v Granoff (1980) 109 CA3d 920, 167 CR 538: §4.22

Estate of Carpenter (1983) 140 CA3d 709, 189 CR 651: §§3.28, 7.50

Estate of Grigsby (1982) 134 CA3d 611, 184 CR 886: §§3.15, 7.50

F

Fabian, Marriage of (1986) 41 C3d 440, 224 CR 333: §3.30

Table of Forms: Book

Table of Forms: Update

Index

233

Make sure you are using the latest update

For your convenience, the following list identifies the most recent publication date of each CEB update (as of May, 1992).

Update Title	Product Number	Publication Date
Advising California Employers	BU-35516	12/91
Advising California Nonprofit Corporations	BU-36626	6/91
Advising California Partnerships, 2d Edition	BU-35634	4/92
Appeals and Writs in Criminal Cases	CR-33485	3/92
Attorney's Guide to California Construction Contracts and Disputes, 2d Edition	RE-31441	9/91
Attorney's Guide to California Professional Corporations, 4th Edition	TX-30933	4/91
Attorney's Guide to Pension and Profit-Sharing Plans, 3d Edition	TX-30732	2/89
Attorney's Guide to Trade Secrets	BU-30039	6/91
California Administrative Hearing Practice	CP-35656	9/91
California Administrative Mandamus, 2d Edition	CP-38812	6/91
California Attorney's Damages Guide	CP-31438	6/91
California Attorney's Fees Award Practice	CP-30396	6/91
California Automobile Insurance Law Guide	TO-30753	1/92
California Breach of Contract Remedies	CP-34462	10/91
California Civil Appellate Practice, 2d Edition	CP-32329	5/92
California Civil Litigation Forms Manual	CP-34472	9/91
California Civil Procedure Before Trial, 3d Edition	CP-31541	1/92
California Civil Procedure During Trial, Volume 1	CP-36657	5/91

Update Title	Product Number	Publication Date
California Civil Procedure During Trial, Volume 2	CP-38827	3/92
California Civil Writ Practice, 2d Edition	CP-30644	3/92
California Commercial Law (I, II)	BU-30043	6/91
California Condominium and Planned Development Practice	RE-38876	5/91
California Conservatorships and Guardianships	ES-31502	12/91
California Criminal Law Procedure and Practice	CR-30783	12/90
California Decedent Estate Practice 1, 2	ES-35664	3/92
California Decedent Estate Practice 3	ES-30864	3/92
California Durable Power of Attorney Handbook	ES–31293	3/92
California Eviction Defense Manual	RE-30459	5/92
California Evidence Benchbook, 2d Edition	CP-32371	6/90
California Juvenile Court Practice, Volume 1	CR-35528	5/91
California Juvenile Court Practice, Volume 2	CR-35537	9/91
California Liability Insurance Practice 1, 2	CP-39261	5/92
California Lis Pendens Practice	RE-30597	12/91
California Local Probate Rules, 13th Edition	ES-39663	2/92
California Marital Termination Agreements	FA-30873	6/91
California Mechanics' Liens and Other Remedies, 2d Edition	RE-30993	12/91
California Mortgage and Deed of Trust Practice, 2d Edition	RE-31342	5/92
California Personal Injury Proof	TO-30565	5/92
California Probate Code Annotated to CEB Publications	ES-31193	3/92
California Probate Workflow Manual	ES-31562	10/91
California Real Property Financing, Volume 1	RE-30972	6/91
California Real Property Financing, Volume 2	RE-30891	5/91
California Real Property Practice Forms Manual	RE-30923	1/92
California Real Property Remedies Practice	RE-38869	5/91
California Real Property Sales Transactions	RE-36612	5/92

Update Title	Product Number	Publication Date
California Residential Landlord-Tenant Practice	RE-37735	8/91
California Search and Seizure Practice, 2d Edition	CR-31329	9/91
California Subdivision Map Act Practice	RE-32354	6/91
California Surety and Fidelity Bond Practice	BU-30137	6/91
California Taxes, 2d Edition, Volume 1	TX-30943	5/92
California Taxes, 2d Edition, Volume 2	TX-30953	5/92
California Title Insurance Practice	RE-33367	6/90
California Tort Damages	TO-30883	5/92
California Tort Guide, 2d Edition	TO-32288	11/91
California Trial Objections, 2d Edition	CP-34576	12/91
California Trust Administration	ES-30091	3/90
California Trust Drafting—Trustmaster System	ES-24003	6/90
California Uninsured Motorist Practice	TO-30585	3/92
California Workers' Compensation Practice, 3d Edition	WC-35626	2/92
California Workers' Damages Practice	WC-30776	1/92
California Zoning Practice	RE-30513	5/91
Civil Discovery Practice in California	CP-30763	6/91
Civil Trials Benchbook	CP-34554	11/91
Commercial Real Property Lease Practice	RE-30334	1/92
Condemnation Practice in California	RE-30684	1/92
Counseling California Corporations	BU-39231	3/92
Debt Collection Practice in California	BU-30813	6/91
Debt Collection Tort Practice	TO-30109	6/91
Drafting Agreements for the Sale of Businesses, 2d Edition	BU-39673	3/92
Drafting California Irrevocable Living Trusts, 2d Edition	ES-32343	2/92
Drafting California Revocable Living Trusts	ES-38836	2/92
Effective Direct & Cross Examination	CP-32336	4/92
Effective Introduction of Evidence	CP-31351	12/91
Estate Planning Practice 1, 2	ES-30853	8/91
Fee Agreement Forms Manual	MI-30441	12/91
Financing California Businesses	BU-37801	6/91
Ground Lease Practice	RE-30529	12/91
Guide to California Subdivision Sales Law	RE-31323	8/91
Landslide and Subsidence Liability	RE-31038	4/91
Managing an Estate Planning Practice, 3d Edition	ES-30191	5/83

Update Title	Product Number	Publication Date
Organizing Corporations in California, 2d Edition	BU-37767	5/92
Personal Tax Planning for Professionals and Owners of Small Businesses	TX-36636	3/92
Persuasive Opening Statements and Closing Arguments	CP-39652	3/91
Practicing California Judicial Arbitration	CP-30667	6/91
Real Property Exchanges	RE-34536	4/91
Secured Transactions in California Commercial Law Practice	BU-32314	5/92
Tax Aspects of California Partnerships	TX-37746	2/92
Tax Aspects of Marital Dissolutions, 2d Edition	TX-31331	5/90
Tax Practice in California	TX-30494	9/90
Taxation of Real Property Transfers	RE-37757	3/92
Trial Attorney's Evidence Code Notebook, 3d Edition	CP-30298	3/92
Wrongful Employment Termination Practice	CP-30903	11/91

Not Yet Updated	Product Number
Advising California Condominium and Homeowners Associations	RE-3163*
Business Buy-Sell Agreements	BU-3149*
California Expert Witness Guide, 2d Edition	CP-3168*
California Government Tort Liability Practice, 2d Edition	TO–3169*
California Practice Under the Family Law Act	FA–3195*
California Will Drafting	ES–3032*
Competitive Business Practices, 2d Edition	BU-3165*
Jefferson's Synopsis of California Evidence Law	CP-3079*